The
MAKING OF
MODERN
BRISTOL

EDITED BY MADGE DRESSER
AND PHILIP OLLERENSHAW

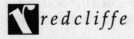

First published in 1996
by Redcliffe Press

Copyright © 1996 Madge Dresser, Philip Ollerenshaw and
the several authors each in respect of the material contributed.

A CIP Record for this book is available from the British Library

ISBN 1 900178 25 7

REDCLIFFE PRESS

Halsgrove House
Lower Moor Way
Tiverton EX16 6SS
Telephone: 01884 243242
Facsimile: 01884 243325

First printed in Great Britain
by Bookcraft, Midsomer Norton

CONTENTS

LIST OF TABLES

LIST OF FIGURES

PREFACE

There have been a number of histories written about Bristol, some academic, some popular. The aim of this volume is to synthesise the results of previous specialist work with original new research on a wide range of historical themes. Whilst this collection makes no claims to be comprehensive, it does ask new questions of Bristol's past.

The project began as a result of a group of historians teaching a postgraduate course on local history at the University of the West of England. Our experience there convinced us of the need for an up-dated historical study of Bristol. To assist us in this venture, we invited two contributors from Exeter and Brunel universities, both of whom have long-standing interests in Bristol's history. It became clear from our discussions that the city's economic development was central to an understanding of its social and political life. Peter Fleming's wide-ranging introductory chapter devotes considerable space to sixteenth- and seventeenth-century economic development. Two other chapters focus specifically on this, the first by Kenneth Morgan, deals with the period to the mid-nineteenth century and a later chapter by Philip Ollerenshaw and Peter Wardley addresses the period from then to the later twentieth century.

An important theme which emerges in a number of chapters is that of civic identity. The title of Jonathan Barry's essay 'Bristol Pride' analyses the various factors involved in the construction of a local identity in the period up to 1775. Steve Poole's 'To be a Bristolian' reminds us in its discussion of civic disorder and riot in the late eighteenth and early nineteenth centuries that the poor and politically excluded resisted their relegation to the margins of civic life. Religion was a central element in civic identity and Madge Dresser's 'Protestants, Catholics and Jews' considers how religious and ethnic difference affected the political status of Bristol residents before 1850.

With few exceptions, the treatment of poverty, the experience of labour and the role of women have been neglected in historical surveys of Bristol. Moira Martin's study of the administration of the poor law examines the policies towards old people, children and single parents as well as the assumptions of the administrators, who included an increasing number of women. June Hannam's work retraces the networks of social and political support which connected various aspects of the women's movement in Bristol, a movement whose concerns went far beyond the achievement of female suffrage. Kieran Kelly and Mike Richardson bring together studies of Bristol's labour movement to consider how well this movement has defended its own interests since the mid-nineteenth century.

These studies utilize new primary material and interrogate more familiar sources in different ways, but there are many important historical issues which are not addressed in this volume. These include the experience of the city's New Commonwealth immigrants and that of their Bristol-born children; the social history of artistic and scientific life; the role of organized religion since 1914; and the impact of the welfare state. Despite these gaps, we hope that this volume will inform the general as well as the specialist reader and stimulate further research into the development of this historic city.

No venture of this type can succeed without the co-operation and generosity of many people. We should particularly like to thank Matthew Woollard, Research Associate of the Bristol Historical Databases Project whose energy, expertise and support was crucial to its realization. Thanks are also due to Mark Barton of UWE's Faculty's audio-visual unit, Amanda Salter, Humanities subject librarian and to Professor Geoffrey Channon. We are also particularly grateful to Francis Greenacre of the Bristol City Museum and Art Gallery, and to Robert Harrison, Jane Bradley and Dawn Dyer of the Bristol Reference Library, Richard Burley and John Williams of the Bristol Record Office, Nick Lee and Mike Richardson of the Special Collections section of Bristol University Library and members of staff at the Bristol Industrial Museum. Thanks are also due to Dr Martin Crossley Evans, Sandra Holton, Spencer Jordan and Judith Samuel. The editors would finally like to thank their families for their patience during the production of this book, and all the contributors for meeting a tight schedule with such professionalism and good grace.

Madge Dresser
Philip Ollerenshaw

CONTRIBUTORS

Jonathan Barry

Jonathan Barry is Senior Lecturer and Head of History and Archaeology at the University of Exeter. He has published widely on urban, cultural and social history and is editor of *The Tudor and Stuart Town* (1990) and (with Chris Brooks) *The Middling Sort of People* (1994). His study of the cultural life of early modern Bristol will shortly be published by Oxford University Press.

Madge Dresser

Madge Dresser is Principal Lecturer in Social History at the University of the West of England. Her main interests are religion, national identity and race in the early industrial period. Her published work on Bristol includes 'The People's Housing', in Ian Bild, ed., *Bristol's Other History* (1984) and *Black and White on the Buses* (1986). More recent publications included a study of the national symbol Britannia and an examination of the Bristol Moravians.

Peter Fleming

Peter Fleming is Senior Lecturer in Early Modern History at the University of the West of England. His research interests include fifteenth- and sixteenth-century social, political and gender history, on which he has published a number of articles. He is currently working on a study of the family and household in medieval England.

June Hannam

June Hannam is Principal Lecturer and Head of History at the University of the West of England. She has published articles and essays on feminist and socialist politics of the late-nineteenth and early twentieth centuries. Among her books are *Isabella Ford: 1855-1924* (1989) and (with Ann Hughes and Pauline Stafford) *A Bibliography of Women's History* (1996).

Kieran Kelly

Kieran Kelly is a Tutor in History at the University of the West of England where he is completing a PhD thesis on the Port of Bristol in the inter-war period. He has been an active white collar trade unionist and involved with a number of labour movement campaigns in Bristol.

Moira Martin

Moira Martin is Lecturer in British Social History at the University of the West of England. Her main teaching interests are the history of welfare and health policies. Her PhD thesis, completed at the School of Advanced Urban Studies, Bristol, examined Poor Law policy with regard to elderly people and she has recently written an article on the development of geriatric medicine in the 1950s which was published in *Social History of Medicine* (1996).

Kenneth Morgan

Kenneth Morgan is Principal Lecturer in History at Brunel University College. His many articles have appeared in journals such as *English Historical Review, Transactions of the Royal Historical Society* and *William and Mary Quarterly*. Among his books is *Bristol and the Atlantic Trade in the Eighteenth Century* (1993).

Philip Ollerenshaw

Philip Ollerenshaw is Principal Lecturer in Economic and Business History at the University of the West of England. He is editor (with Liam Kennedy) of *An Economic History of Ulster 1820-1939* (1985) and author of *Banking in the Nineteenth Century Ireland* (1987). He is currently working on a study of businessmen and the development of Ulster Unionism, 1886-1921.

Steve Poole

Steve Poole is a British Academy Postdoctoral Research Fellow at the University of the West of England. His PhD thesis on 'Popular Politics in Bristol, Somerset and Wiltshire, 1791-1805' was completed at the University of Bristol in 1993. Among his publications is 'Scarcity and Civic Tradition in Bristol, 1709-1815', in A. Charlesworth and A.J.Randall, eds, *Markets, Market Culture and Popular Protest in Eighteenth Century Britain* (forthcoming).

Mike Richardson

Mike Richardson is a Tutor in History at the University of the West of England where, in 1995, he completed a PhD thesis on 'Industrial Relations in the British Printing Industry between the Wars'. In the 1970s and 1980s he was employed in the printing industry and was actively involved in trade unionism and the Bristol labour movement.

Peter Wardley

Peter Wardley is Senior Lecturer in Economic and Business History at the University of the West of England. He has published widely on modern economic history and the development of historical computing, in journals such as *Business History, Explorations in Economic History, Economic History Review* and *History and Computing*. He is editor (with Jennifer Green and Philip Ollerenshaw) of *Business in Avon and Somerset: A Survey of Archives* (1991).

ACKNOWLEDGEMENTS

The publishers and editors are grateful to the following for permission to reproduce illustrations:

Plates IV, VI, VII, VIII, IX, X, XI, XII, XIII, XIV, XV, XVI, XVIII, XX, XXI, XXII, XXIIIc
        City of Bristol Museum and Art Gallery

Plates I, II, III, V, XIXa and c,
        Bristol Reference Library

Plates XXIIIa and b, XXIVa and b,
        Bristol Record Office

Plate XVI,   Main picture, *The Architect*, 21 August 1875; insets, M.J.Shaen (ed.), *Memorials of Two Sisters: Susanna and Catherine Winkworth*, 1908.

Plate XVII a,   *Girls' Realm*, V (September 1903);
        b,   E.Sturge, *Reminiscences of My Life* (1928).

Plate XIXb,   *Western Daily Press*, 13 September 1900.

TABLE OF AUTHORITIES

THE EMERGENCE OF
MODERN BRISTOL

Peter Fleming

Introduction

This chapter provides an account of Bristol's history from the early sixteenth to the middle of the seventeenth centuries: broadly speaking, from the Reformation to the Restoration. Many of the developments discussed in subsequent chapters may be traced back to this period, when Bristol was transformed from a medieval town in to a recognizably modern city. Consequently, one of the aims of this chapter is to provide a point of departure, particularly for those readers who may be unfamiliar with Tudor and Stuart Bristol.

A second aim is to provide a guide to further reading in Bristol's sixteenth- and early seventeenth-century history. Emphasis is placed on secondary works, and editions of primary sources are mentioned only if they contain relevant introductions. Further, most of the works cited here are relatively recent – that is, no more than thirty years old. Space has not permitted an extensive review of older literature, but inevitably any exercise of this sort must owe a considerable debt to past generations of Bristol historians.[1]

Trade and Industry

Bristol's eighteenth-century 'Golden Age' was built on the trans-Atlantic trade. Because of the voyages of the Cabots three centuries earlier, Bristol occupies a prominent place in the history of Atlantic exploration, but after the discovery of Newfoundland Bristolians were for the most part content to allow others – usually Londoners or those with London backing – to take the lead. For most sixteenth-century Bristolians, the main attractions of the New World, if any, lay with its fishing grounds. Short-term commercial advantage, rather than the challenge of the unknown, seems to have been the motivation behind most of Bristol's trans-Atlantic interests after the initial 'heroic age' of the 1480s and 1490s. In fact, the Americas were not to loom large in Bristol's affairs until the second half of the seventeenth century.[2]

Throughout the early modern period Bristol's overseas trade was heavily dependent on the import of luxury goods. Until the middle of

1

the seventeenth century these came mainly from – or were supplied through – southern Europe; the other trades, with northern Europe and the American fisheries, served mainly to provide commodities to trade in the south for luxury goods. Thereafter, the Americas became a major supplier of luxuries such as sugar and tobacco. There were significant variations within this general pattern, however, resulting from a range of economic, political and social factors.[3]

In the two hundred years after the loss of the Hundred Years' War in 1453 and the subsequent collapse of the French wine-cloth trade, Bristol merchants were gradually forced to find new markets and new commodities in northern Europe, the Iberian Peninsula, the Mediterranean and the Atlantic. This diversification of trading patterns encouraged the development in Bristol of sophisticated commercial and credit structures and practices before many other English towns. The processing of imported raw materials or semi-finished goods, and the demand for manufactured items for export to these new markets, stimulated the development of an enormous range of industries and an increasingly sophisticated distribution network. Growing diversification and complexity encouraged increasing specialization of economic activity, separating production and whole-sale and retail distribution in different hands.

By the 1490s the supplies of French wine had been strongly reinforced by those of Spain and the Portuguese Atlantic possessions, and economic prospects seemed bright.[4] But the first quarter of the sixteenth century saw a serious depression in cloth, still the core of Bristol's economy, partly as a result of increasing competition from London merchants and rural clothiers and partly through changing demands in foreign markets. A promising recovery in the 1530s and 1540s was then brought to an end by a combination of mid-century crises: abroad, the French Wars of Religion, piracy, international protectionism and an economic crisis in Spain; at home, political uncertainty, increased competition from London monopoly compa-nies, currency devaluation, inflation, bad harvests and influenza epidemics.[5]

The Iberian trade assumed particular importance in the sixteenth century. It required experienced agents, a sound knowledge of foreign market conditions, good political connections and sophisticated credit arrangements. These were extremely difficult trading conditions for those without the resources and expertise of the great overseas merchants. For these, the elite of Bristol's trading community, the Iberian trade was of central importance, and from the middle of the

sixteenth century they attempted to protect their enormous investment in this difficult and volatile market by converting their natural
advantage into a practical and legally recognized monopoly.[6] The
means by which they sought to achieve this was a new representative
body, the Society of Merchant Venturers.

The Merchant Venturers have played a central part in Bristol's
history since the mid-sixteenth century, and have aroused strong
opinions among their supporters and detractors.[7] After similar, unsuc-
cessful attempts in the fifteenth century, the Society was established by
Edward VI's letters patent in 1552 as an exclusive organization of
overseas traders. The initial motive behind their foundation seems to
have been defensive: these were hard times for overseas traders, and
the Merchant Venturers attempted to preserve for themselves as large
a slice as possible of a dwindling cake.

In the last quarter of the sixteenth century the city's cloth finishing
industry continued to decline, and while new or resurgent industries
like shipbuilding, metalworking, leather and ropemaking, soap
boiling and sugar refining would emerge to take its place, there was
probably a good deal of hardship caused in the transition.[8] Bristol's
economy also suffered from a combination of war with Spain, high
customs duties and the depredations of London-based monopoly
companies.[9] Bristol's overseas merchants answered the customs
official and monopolist by increasing their smuggling activities; they
reacted to the disruption of peaceful trade by diverting their energies
into privateering, an expedient which brought some spectacular gains,
but which in the long run further disrupted the port's trade.[10]

Peace with Spain in 1604 brought a return to prosperity for Bristol's
traders, punctuated by renewed warfare from 1625 to 1630, but trade
in the 1640s was severely disrupted by the Civil Wars. From the 1650s
onwards Bristol merchants took advantage of new trading opportunities, particularly in the New World. During the second quarter of the
seventeenth century Bristol's trans-Atlantic trade, primarily with the
Chesapeake and the West Indies, grew from small beginnings to
become a major element in its economy, and by the 1680s it may have
accounted for as much as a quarter of Bristol's seaborne trade.[11]

The Merchant Venturers were still mainly orientated towards
Europe, and the Atlantic trade was largely in the hands of men from
outside the commercial elite. Unlike operations in most of the
European markets, the Atlantic trade, based on the exchange of
European manufactured goods and luxuries for a few commodities
such as sugar and tobacco, did not demand great resources of capital

3

and expertise. The market was predictable, did not depend on sophisticated credit networks, and was not beset by political and linguistic complications, since nearly everyone involved was an English subject. Unlike the European trades therefore, it could not be easily monopolized by any one group of traders, no matter how powerful. For the Merchant Venturers, even more aggravating than their inability to enforce a monopoly was the fact that much of Bristol's Atlantic trade was in the hands of non-freemen, either non-Bristolians or members of the city's nonconformist communities, using freemen or shipmen as their agents. Tarred with the brush of radical politics as well as radical religion, these nonconformist independent Atlantic traders neatly combined all of the primarily conservative and Anglican Merchant Venturers' pet hates.[12]

One of Bristol's most important exports to the Americas was labour for the plantations. Before the rise of the slave trade, this consisted of British-born 'servants'. Some acted as merchants' agents, sent to safeguard their masters' interests in the New World; others were offered advantageous terms in return for their specialized skills, but many had little to offer beyond their labour, and for them, conditions of service were often in practice little better than slavery. Over 10,000 servants were shipped between 1654 and 1679 alone.[13] Much of this trade was in the hands of non-Merchant Venturers, and it has been suggested that the city ordinance of 1654 which established a register of servants bound for the New World, with the stated aim of preventing the kidnapping or duping of individuals into service abroad, was actually part of a campaign by the Merchant Venturers to force these 'interlopers' out of business.[14]

Social Provision

The elite of early-modern Bristol have a well-earned reputation for their concern for poor relief. Provision in Bristol seems to have been as generous and imaginative as anywhere else in England: by 1660 the city had ten almshouses, and according to one estimate its various schemes of outdoor relief could possibly have given help to as many as 2300 paupers, or about 12 per cent of the population.[15] These figures represent a considerable achievement, but they may also indicate the scale of a pressing social problem. Trends in the provision of poor relief suggest that poverty was perceived to be a particular problem in the late sixteenth and early seventeenth centuries, with bequests to the poor showing a considerable increase in real value over the last two

4

decades of the sixteenth century, while in the following forty years over half the value of all bequests went to this cause. The decades either side of 1600 saw widespread poverty throughout England, but Bristol had its own particular problems.[16] Exacerbating the problems of bad harvests and epidemics was the presence of large numbers of soldiers billeted on Bristol en route for the Irish wars.[17]

Like other early-modern cities, Bristol acted as a magnet for those seeking employment, and in turn it relied on immigration to sustain its population. Apprenticeship provided the prime mechanism by which outsiders were drawn into the city, and apprentices constituted a large and potentially volatile segment of Bristol society.[18] The great majority of apprentices came from outside the city.[19] Of the apprentices of Bristol origin, almost all were placed outside their own families. Clearly, apprenticeship made an important contribution towards the dynamism of Bristol society, providing a vocational training and socializing young people into their future roles as responsible adults.[20] However, from the middle of the sixteenth century onwards apprenticeship gradually became more exclusive, as guilds charged higher fees and put other barriers in the way of children from humbler backgrounds. Increasing demand for apprenticeships, initially from outside the city, seems to have been one reason for this growing exclusivity, and there was no decline in the total number of Bristol apprentices in the seventeenth century.[21] One effect was to marginalize female apprentices still further: throughout our period the proportion of apprentices who were female remained fairly stable at between two and three per cent, but whereas at the beginning of the sixteenth century about a third of these were apprenticed to relatively high-status 'male' occupations, by the seventeenth century virtually all female apprenticeships were to low-status, exclusively female, occupations such as 'housewifery', spinning and seamstressing. In addition, the small number of girls from gentry or yeoman backgrounds disappeared altogether, there was a concomitant increase in the number of 'parish' apprenticeships, that is orphans and paupers apprenticed out as a form of poor relief, and it appears that there was now no longer any possibility of female apprentices becoming freemen.

The elite of post-Reformation Bristol showed a prodigious interest in education within their city. Jordan found that under Elizabeth almost half of the resources expended by Bristol testators on charity went to education. Much of this is accounted for by the munificence of a few rich men, often former mayors and aldermen. A number of schools were founded in the period 1530 to 1630, some of which have

5

only a shadowy existence in the records, but the three most prestigious foundations were those of the Thornes' Bristol Grammar School (whose complicated birth took place between 1532 and 1546), John Carr's Queen Elizabeth's Hospital (1586-7) and John Whitson's Red Maids (1629-30), a pioneering effort to equip girls to find respectable positions and husbands. The common motivation behind most of these benefactions was the desire to provide cheap or free education and training of a good standard for children who might otherwise descend into poverty. While the vast majority of children from pauper backgrounds received little benefit from these schools, whose definition of 'poor' proved to be somewhat elastic, these efforts do testify both to the sense of civic identity common among the Bristol elite, and to their imagination in providing practical solutions to social problems. In the same spirit, Bristol had the country's second public library, established in 1614.[22]

Religion

Bristol was a notorious centre of later medieval heresy (or Lollardy, in contemporary parlance), and it retained this reputation into the early sixteenth century.[23] Split between the dioceses of Bath and Wells and of distant Worcester (whose bishop was usually an absentee Italian), Bristol was not readily amenable to episcopal supervision. Heresy was closely associated with artisans and craftsmen, particularly textile workers, and Bristol's own cloth industry, concentrated in Redcliffe and Temple, together with its ready communications with the Cotswolds and the Forest of Dean, other notable exporters of cloth and heresy, seems to have made it the regional centre for evangelizing heretics. Heresy and anti-clericalism are not inevitable companions, but relations between laity and clergy in pre-Reformation Bristol were not always amicable: for example, from the 1490s the Corporation was violently at odds with the Abbot of St Augustine's over their conflicting jurisdictions.[24]

While historians are divided over the extent to which England's native heretical tradition formed the stock on to which were grafted the imported doctrines of Luther and Calvin, Bristol's record of heresy and poor town–church relations helps to explain why it experienced unusually early and intense agitation around the question of religious reform. In the 1530s it played host to a 'battle of the pulpits'. Such a series of public disputations between conservative and reformist preachers, while relatively common on the Continent, was otherwise

6

practically unknown in England.[25] In 1533 the mayor of Bristol invited Hugh Latimer, the future Protestant bishop of Worcester, to preach the Easter sermons. By this time Latimer had already acquired a reputation as a controversial reformer, but his support for Henry VIII's divorce from Catherine of Aragon had brought him a measure of royal protection. The Corporation's motives are obscure, and could have ranged from simple curiosity to a calculated desire to challenge clerical legitimacy. Latimer's Easter preaching provoked Bristol conservatives to mount their own series of sermons, and the situation threatened to become uncontrollable, with laity and clergy split into reformist and conservative factions. Thomas Cromwell, the king's chief minister, came to hear of this, and since Latimer's reformist opinions coincided with his own plans for the reform of the church under increased royal control, he intervened on the side of the reformists. Latimer's opponents were silenced, and he moved on to greater things, becoming bishop of Worcester in 1535.

From 1537 to 1539 there were further squabbles between reformists and conservatives. This decade has been portrayed as a crucial stage in a process whereby Bristol's clerical community was fragmented and disempowered in the face of an increasingly aggressive Crown abetted, largely out of self-interest, by powerful members of the local laity. Bristol's clerical community may have been unable to maintain a united opposition to what appeared to be a challenge to its authority often encouraged, if not engineered, by the Corporation. But this was not a victory for the lay elite in a straightforward struggle between church and town. The Corporation appear to have been surprised by the vehemence of the conservative reaction, and it has been suggested that their clumsy efforts to manage these controversies exposed their dependence on the Crown as the guarantor of their authority, presenting Cromwell with an opportunity to extend his influence in the town.[26]

The Dissolution, beginning with the smaller religious houses in 1536 and ending with the chantries in 1548, represented a far greater intervention in Bristol affairs by the Crown, and changed forever the nature of its clerical and lay communities, their relations with each other, and their relations with central government.[27] While lay Bristolians may not have been extravagant in their support for their churches and religious houses at the beginning of the century, apart from the small group of heretics they showed no signs of fundamental disenchantment with medieval Catholicism. Indeed, religious bequests, including chantry foundations to provide prayers for souls in Purgatory, continued to be made up to the very brink of Dissolution.[28] Yet the destruction over a period of only twelve years of structures which down the centuries had provided spiritual and physical comfort in this life and the promise of salvation in the next, as well as arguably the most important focus of local community senti-ment, went virtually unopposed.

Apart from a small Protestant hard core, the laity were generally lukewarm in their reception of the new doctrines, and Bristol's acqui-escence in the Reformation cannot be accounted for by some overnight conversion.[29] Certainly, it was an unusually courageous, or foolhardy, individual who stood up to the powerful and ruthless Tudor regime, while the emergent clerical factionalism in the 1530s may have under-mined clerical morale and could only have added to the laity's awareness of their clergy's shortcomings. However, beyond fear and sullen anti-clericalism there may have been more fundamental reasons for Bristol's quiescence.[30] The religious houses represented the medieval ideal of an organic community founded on Christian princi-ples of solidarity and co-operation. This was unattainable as a model for civic society (and was seldom approached in the houses themselves), but nonetheless this myth of Christian fellowship did provide a standard against which the laity of medieval Bristol could measure their own behaviour. Early Tudor Bristol, however, was home to a precocious breed of aggressive proto-capitalism and in this market-orientated, competitive, mercantile society medieval commu-nalism may have seemed increasingly irrelevant: quite simply, it got in the way of business. Changing social rather than religious attitudes may therefore provide the more promising line of explanation for Bristol's acceptance of the Dissolution. Perhaps the Crown's political agenda gave Bristol's commercial elites the justification for their renunciation of loyalties to a religious ethos that was by then perceived as largely moribund, albeit without offering very much in its place.[31]

The Dissolution has been portrayed as a decisive stage in the disin-tegration of Bristol's sense of itself as a Christian community, giving birth to a new secular vision of civic life. This view is supported by the fate of the former monastic and chantry endowed property. More work needs to be done on the private recipients of the Bristol properties, but it seems that most individual purchasers were either connected with the court or were local gentry and merchants.[32] Bristol Corporation was a major purchaser. Between 1541 and 1548 the Corporation, using parish church plate as collateral for some of the deals, bought the properties formerly owned by the Carmelite and Franciscan friaries and by St Mark's Hospital, and several other former monastic properties.[33] The income from these properties would form the largest single contribution to Corporation funds (allowing them to abolish several tolls), and would thereby accentuate the increasingly marked contrast between the relative affluence of the secular community and the poverty of the church.

Another indication of the new secular order is provided by the decline in the parish clergy. The former monks, friars and chantry priests found themselves flung into a clerical job market that was far from encouraging.[34] The urban parish incomes, increasingly dependent on money rates rather than tithes in kind, were suffering as a result of inflation and increasing clerical taxation. The post-Reformation married clergy faced the additional difficulty of supporting a family on this declining income. In such circumstances a clerical career was a less-than-inviting prospect, and not surprisingly the quality of the clergy – crudely measured in terms of the proportion of university graduates – declined markedly after the 1530s. Many were forced to resort to pluralism (the holding of more than one living) in order to make ends meet, while at the same time there was a significant rise in the number of vacant livings, which would then be filled by temporary curates on stipends. Short-term contracts and uncertain incomes had traditionally been the lot of pre-Reformation chantry and guild priests, but such economic insecurity was now afflicting many parish priests. This erosion of economic position may have been accompanied by a consequent loss of status in the eyes of their parishioners, who increasingly controlled the purse strings. Despite Protestantism's emphasis on preaching and education, Bristol's post-Reformation lay elite seem to have been unmoved by the plight of their clergy and churches: testamentary bequests to religious causes appear to have dried to a trickle after the 1530s. However, these resources were increasingly applied to education, and perhaps this did eventually improve clerical standards.[35] While potential donors may have been discouraged from investing in churches with the memory of the Dissolution still fresh, the prospect of a humble clergy under lay control may not have been totally unwelcome to Bristol's secular elite.[36] The poor quality of the Elizabethan parish clergy may also have encouraged a further lay erosion of ecclesiastical authority, in the form of corporation lecturers. These were established from 1585 when the city provided a stipend for a lecturer or preacher. While the corporation lecturers were regulated by the ecclesiastical authorities, the church's monopoly of preaching had been broken. In times of tension between church and Corporation the mayor and councillors now had an alternative source of spiritual sustenance: one that would not answer back, since it was based on an employer-employee relationship between laity and clergy. Additionally, it may have been the Corporation's intention that the tax levied on Bristol parishes to support the corporation lecturers would also have restricted the parishioners' ability to hire their own preachers, some of whom might have been viewed as subversive by the city's elite.[37]

The creation of the Diocese of Bristol in 1542 probably had only a marginal effect on the balance of power between church and laity.[38] In September 1541 Bristol had been included in the new diocese of Gloucester which had been carved out of the enormous medieval diocese of Worcester, but a mere nine months later Bristol was given its own diocese. For the purposes of administration and pastoral care the new diocese was an unsatisfactory hotchpotch: it included the town and county of Bristol, as constituted in 1373, together with some adjoining and nearby parishes in north Somerset and south Gloucestershire, but this otherwise wholly inadequate provision was supplemented by the inclusion of most of the county of Dorset, whose border was 40 miles away from Bristol. The cathedral was founded in the former Augustinian abbey, whose nave had been demolished before the Reformation and would not be rebuilt until the nineteenth century. With its meagre endowments, bizarre composition and truncated cathedral, Bristol was destined to be one of the least attractive destinations for ambitious prelates: during much of Elizabeth's reign the see was held jointly with that of Gloucester, and from 1593 to 1603 it was vacant altogether.

The reasons for the Crown's uncertainty with regard to the formation of Gloucester and Bristol dioceses are unclear. In all likelihood the king and his advisers realized that in their haste to reform the medieval diocesan system, Gloucester had been given ecclesiastical authority over the far more important town of Bristol. But there is also the possibility that the initiative came from members of the Bristol elite: after centuries of supervision from far-off Worcester, they wanted their own cathedral, particularly if the alternative was control from Gloucester, Bristol's great local rival.

Securing the cathedral in Bristol had one other great advantage for the lay elite of the city. With the seat of local ecclesiastical authority on their doorstep, and with its endowment insufficient to allow it to challenge their own authority, Bristol's leaders had little difficulty in asserting their influence over the church at diocesan level, just as they were in the process of doing in the parishes. While relations between the city and the bishop and dean and chapter were not always cordial, in general the diocesan authorities appear to have been susceptible to the influence of the Corporation through ties of kinship, patronage, or simply self-interest.[39]

Under Mary (1553-1558) members of the Corporation had to be ordered by the Privy Council to attend mass at the cathedral, but it is likely that their reluctance was an expression of chagrin at their temporary loss of influence over the new episcopal regime, rather than the result of Protestant revulsion at Catholic practices.[40] By and large, the city's lay elite put the maintenance of order – and the promotion of their own authority and interests – before doctrinal scruples. They were quite prepared, for example, to collude in the persecution of heretics. Between four and eight people were burned at Bristol for their opposition to Marian religious orthodoxy. These probably all came from artisan or craft backgrounds, mostly related to the textile industry, and rejection of the doctrine of transubstantiation appears to have been the common element in their heresy. In short, there seems little to differentiate these heretics from the later medieval Lollards, which strongly suggests that we should see them as evidence not of the success of Protestant evangelizing, but of the continued survival of native heresy.[41]

There is rather more evidence for the acceptance of Protestantism among the upper ranks of Bristol society in the second half of the sixteenth century. The reformed religion's emphasis on individualism and the importance of the written word is more likely to have appealed to the literate commercial classes than to their social inferiors, and so this could be seen as another factor in the disintegration of the medieval communal ideal.[42] The Reformation had brought Bristol's lay elite unprecedented opportunities; for Bristol's clergy it had brought crisis. The 'complex, competent, and independent clerical community' of the later middle ages had, by the 1570s, been reduced to a small elite core surrounded by 'an impoverished, uneducated, and fragmented clerical periphery, both lay dominated'.[43]

To judge by testamentary bequests, the period from the Reformation to the opening of the 1620s was marked in Bristol by a level of lay indifference to the health of the city's religious institutions that was not to be found anywhere else in England.[44] The one spark of interest appeared in the last of these three generations, when testators began to leave bequests to found lectureships, doubtless following the

Corporation's lead. This practice continued into the second quarter of the seventeenth century, when testators once more provided resources for the repair and redecoration of the city's crumbling church fabric: it is tempting, but probably too simplistic, to see the lectureships as a puritan enthusiasm, while conservatives, encouraged by the example of Archbishop Laud, turned to the adornment of churches.

There seems to have been a limited recovery within Bristol's clerical community by the mid-seventeenth century: lay patrons continued to enjoy considerable influence, but the clergy were generally respected and were able to exercise considerable local authority, at least over the less august members of their congregations.[45] Perhaps the considerable resources poured into education under Elizabeth had finally paid off. By this time too the parish had become an important centre of social and cultural, as well as religious life. The parish also served an important function in the organization of poor relief. By 1640 many Bristol parishes had developed 'select vestries', self-perpetuating oligarchies made up of the leading parishioners, in a perhaps conscious echo of the increasingly exclusive city government. Firm control of the parishes was important to the elites, since the parish was the prime means of maintaining religious and social unity within the city.

However, the generally low-key religious life of the Anglican parish was not entirely fulfilling for those who sought a more intense spirituality. In pre-Reformation Bristol such people had been well served by the rich and diverse religious community, but this diversity of religious provision could not be matched by the Anglican parishes and their uninspiring diocesan leadership. Such unfulfilled aspirations help to explain the interest in sponsored lectureships, but these alone could not satisfy the more committed. Gradually, lay initiatives to supplement official provision grew into virtually alternative parish structures. Radical parishioners exercised their rights as consumers to take their custom elsewhere, and while there is little evidence that they set out to reject the Anglican communion, their position gradually became untenable. During the Civil Wars and Commonwealth the Anglican consensus was shattered, and the shards of often militant sectarianism that resulted were never reincorporated into the Anglican mainstream. Thus, around the middle of the seventeenth century, various protestant sects – Baptists, Congregationalists, Presbyterians, Quakers – established themselves as rivals to the established religion, and since in Restoration Bristol the Anglican church was in effect the Corporation at prayer, this religious rivalry was accompanied by political ostracism of varying degrees of intensity. After the 1660s, Bristol's reputation as a centre of nonconformity matched its medieval notoriety for heresy.[46]

Quakers first appeared in Bristol in 1654, and the city had strong associations with several leading Quakers, including George Fox, Margaret Fell and William Penn.[47] The first generation did not reject provocative and confrontational tactics, which included disrupting Anglican and Baptist services. James Nayler's donkey ride through the streets of Bristol on Palm Sunday 1656 was widely perceived as both blasphemous and as a parody of civic ritual, and he was cruelly punished for his provocation. Nayler was not a Bristolian, and while his demonstration was not typical of the Bristol Quakers' activities, it did nonetheless encourage the often brutal persecution of the local Quaker community.

Since the Quakers objected to swearing oaths, they effectively barred themselves from taking municipal office, becoming freemen (thereby preventing them, technically, from practising a trade in the city) or prosecuting others for debt. In addition, at times of political tension, or at the whim of particularly hostile mayors and sheriffs, they could be subjected to a range of punishments, from imprisonment, fines for non-attendance at church or for refusal to take office, to the closure of their meeting houses and random assaults in the street.

Politics and Administration

The structure of Bristol's local government and administration was determined by royal charter in 1499 and did not change significantly until 1835.[48] The 1499 charter represented a tightening of the already oligarchic form of government established under the original charter of 1373. After 1499 Bristol's Common Council comprised 43 burgesses, but the real power lay with an inner 'cabinet' of five aldermen (12 after 1581) and the recorder, over whom presided the mayor. Vacancies on the board of aldermen were filled by co-option, and members of the Common Council were appointed by the mayor and two aldermen. In the words of R.C. Latham, 'the affairs of a large and growing community of six thousand people were in the hands of about 45 individuals who elected themselves and were, politically speaking, answerable only to themselves.'[49]

The main purpose of the 1499 charter was probably to put in place an effective system of law enforcement. The mayor, recorder and aldermen took over from the sheriffs the administration of criminal jurisdiction, becoming *ex officio* justices of the peace and of gaol delivery. With this move the Crown had relinquished its right to appoint justices within the City and County, and given enormous power to these self-appointing local officials. Henceforth, the Crown would have to trust to its – not inconsiderable – informal levers of influence and the Bristol elite's perception of a shared community of interest with central government. As justices, the mayor and aldermen became intimately involved in many areas of the city's life, including the administration of poor relief and the suppression of religious dissent.

The Corporation's practice of appointing prominent courtiers to the Recordership and to the office of Lord High Steward to cultivate court patrons indicates that from the 1530s the Bristol elite felt the need to seek protection in high places.[50] They may well have felt threatened by two competing jurisdictions, the Council of the Marches of Wales and the High Court of Admiralty. Both of these bodies claimed that their writs ran within the City and County.[51]

Increasing financial burdens and time-consuming duties meant that in practice only the richest could afford to participate in the highest reaches of municipal government.[52] The mayors and aldermen were increasingly drawn from the ranks of the overseas merchants and the few leading retailers and manufacturers. This meant that the Corporation came to be dominated by – and increasingly identified with – the Society of Merchant Venturers.[53] After 1566, when a royal statute established the Society's right to enforce its monopoly of overseas trade on non-members, Bristol's commercial community was split by a struggle between Merchant Venturers and their opponents from the retail and manufacturing sectors. Both sides used local elections, parliamentary lobbying and their respective court connections in their battles over the Society's monopoly. In 1605, after the Society had almost been forced into extinction by the London-based Spanish Company, it was re-founded under the sponsorship of the Corporation, who informally allowed the Society to collect wharfage dues to finance itself. In 1639 letters patent re-established the Society's right to enforce its ordinances on non-members. After its eclipse during the Civil Wars and Commonwealth, in 1661 the Society again found favour under the Stuarts and its relations with the Corporation were formalized, and its right to collect wharfage and other duties was legally recognized.[54]

While the evidence is unclear, Bristol's early seventeenth-century political elite were probably largely Laudian, or conservative, in their religious positions, and those outside this elite probably tended towards more radical shades of religious opinion, with a significant proportion of sectaries or dissenters among them. Inevitably, religious positions had their political analogues, and Bristol's commercial and political elite tended to be Royalist, while its 'middling sort' – most retailers, manufacturers and craftsmen – tended to be sympathetic to Parliament.[55] In the 1620s the government's ineffectual war policy disrupted Bristol's overseas trade, while in the following decade aggressive royal officials seeking concealed prizes and unpaid customs further antagonized Bristol merchants. However, the mercantile elite did not consider these provocations sufficient cause for disloyalty to King Charles.[56] Indeed, this elite was most unlikely to abandon the king's cause, whatever the provocation, since it looked to the Crown to guarantee the Merchant Venturers' monopoly of Bristol's overseas trade. Thus, the question of monopoly can be seen as central to political allegiance in Bristol in the 1640s: while Bristolians of all persuasions resented the London-based monopolists, whose position was guaranteed by their royal charters, only those excluded from the Merchant Venturers' charmed circle could object to monopoly in principle, and for many this particular iniquity became an important symbol of royal despotism.[57]

Bristol Corporation's allegiance at the outbreak of civil war is now difficult to fathom.[58] The city was entered by Colonel Essex's Parliamentary troops in December 1642. The Bristol elite's pragmatism at this juncture may be judged by the fact that no member of the Common Council was removed by the occupying forces. However, the following March two Merchant Venturers, Robert Yeamans and George Butcher, were executed for plotting with some other merchants and a few less exalted individuals to betray the city to the Royalists.

In July 1643 Bristol fell to the King. Some citizens seem to have fought alongside the Parliamentary garrison during the siege, but the Royalists removed only two members of the Common Council and, while the city had to wait seven tense months before it received a general pardon from the King, the only Bristolians excluded from the pardon were those responsible for the executions of Yeamans and Butcher.[59] However, Bristol suffered greatly under Royalist occupation. In addition to a series of exactions and sequestrations, the city fell prey to famine, plague, and the other consequences of playing host to an army of occupation.[60]

After a second, month-long, siege Bristol was recaptured by Parliament in September 1645. This time there was a thorough purge of the Common Council – the mayor, five aldermen and seven councillors were removed – indicating that there had been a high level of co-operation between the Corporation and the Royalist garrison. As a result of this purge Merchant Venturer representation on the Council dropped sharply, while that of the 'middling sort' – manufacturers and retailers – increased. In addition, the new regime attempted to put the other trade and craft guilds on an equal footing with the Society of Merchant Venturers in an attempt to counterbalance the latter's overweening power.[61]

The Restoration government did not immediately feel ready to remove the radical members of the Corporation left over from the Commonwealth regime, and it was only in September 1660, after prompting from Bristol Royalists, that the King ordered the Corporation to purge itself.[62] Threats of suspension of the charters were required before the Corporation complied in the following autumn. A further, limited, purge was carried out by royal commissioners early in 1662. Two years later Bristol at last received the royal confirmation of its charters: the final indication of the new regime's approval.

Conclusions

Bristol's emergence into 'modernity' can be followed along many streams of economic, political, social and religious development. Their source, for the most part, lay at the conjunction between two great processes of transformation: on the one hand, the transformation of relationships within the community, and on the other, the transformation of that community's relations with the outside world.

Within the city, social, commercial and industrial activity became more complex and diverse. Later medieval Bristol's prosperity had been founded on a relatively simple trade in cloth and wine, and this was reflected in a social structure that had at its apex a largely undifferentiated elite of clothiers and merchants. While there was a richer religious life in medieval Bristol than would be the case between the Reformation and Restoration, this does not seem to have manifested itself in terms of permanent, ideological divisions, leaving aside the small but troublesome group of Lollards. The medieval ideal of a 'reciprocal community', of which every member shared responsibility for the maintenance of social stability and had a vested interest in the prosperity of the entire commonwealth, could be sustained without too much straining of credibility before the Reformation. The link between ideal and reality was finally broken under pressure from emergent capitalism, both as economic system and as *mentalité*. To understand the reasons for this, we must look far beyond the city walls.[63]

The transformation of Bristol's relations with the wider world was itself the result of three developments on a national or international scale: new patterns of trade and industry, the Reformation, and the growing influence of London, particularly in the economic and political spheres. By 1660 Bristol's international trade had expanded into areas that had only been dreamed of by Europeans two centuries earlier. Growth had been accompanied by growing diversity and specialization, as Bristol's merchants fought for survival in increasingly competitive markets. Bristol's role in the domestic economy changed as its textile industry was eclipsed by rural producers and metropolitan finance and distribution networks.

These economic developments had important social and political consequences. The guilds, symbols and guardians of the medieval ideal of community, struggled to accommodate themselves to the increasingly complex world of early capitalism: the textile guilds, once at the pinnacle of Bristol's manufacturing community, were now undermined by competition from rural clothiers. The emergence of a mercantile elite, represented by the Merchant Venturers with their strong monopolistic tendencies, challenged the solidarity of the old trading community. The identification of this mercantile elite with the increasingly oligarchic Corporation replicated this split in the political sphere. The growth of religious dissent and nonconformity, perhaps in part a reaction against the Anglican political-economic elite, deepened the faultlines.

Bristol's commercial community fought hard to resist being absorbed into London's ever-widening economic sphere; in this they had considerable success, but the political influence of London proved impossible to resist. As the government and administration of England became increasingly centred on London, and as the power of the Tudor and Stuart state grew ever more intrusive in local affairs, Bristol's medieval autonomy was drastically eroded. But this was not simply a case of metropolitan imperialism and ineffective local resistance. As Bristol's elite drew farther apart from those beneath them in the city's hierarchy, they increasingly relied on central government for support. Restoration Bristol was Janus-faced: it looked westward towards the unbounded promise of the Atlantic; but to the east loomed the burgeoning metropolis, whose presence Bristolians could never ignore.

17

Notes

1   Foremost among these is John Latimer, whose narratives of Bristol history are still of great value: *Sixteenth-Century Bristol* (Bristol, 1908); *The Annals of Bristol in the Seventeenth Century* (Bristol, 1900). More recent surveys include B. S. Smith and E. Ralph, *History of Bristol and Gloucestershire* (Beaconsfield, 1972); C. M. MacInnes and W. F. Whittard, *Bristol and its Adjoining Counties* (Bristol, 1955); B. Little, *The City and County of Bristol* (Bristol, 1954). An excellent brief description of seventeenth-century Bristol is provided by P. McGrath, *The Merchant Venturers of Bristol: A History of the Society of Merchant Venturers of the City of Bristol from its Origin to the Present Day* (Bristol, 1975), chap. 3. For the physical development of the city, see M. D. Lobel and E. Carus-Wilson, *Historic Towns: Bristol* (1975).

2   There is not space in this essay to give proper consideration to work on Bristol and exploration. The following should provide an adequate introduction to a subject that is fascinating in its own right, but which with a few exceptions stands outside the main interests of this volume. For a useful short overview, see P. McGrath, 'Bristol and America, 1480-1631', in K. R. Andrews, N. P. Canny and P. E. H. Hair, eds, *The Westward Enterprise* (Liverpool, 1978), 81-102. The standard work on Bristol's overseas links, C. M. MacInnes, *Bristol: A Gateway of Empire* (1st ed., Bristol, 1939, 2nd ed., Newton Abbot, 1968) while at points outdated, is still essential reading on this topic. The difficulties of piecing together the Cabots' story have spawned a wealth of literature: a convenient introduction to the Cabots and the historical debates that have surrounded them is provided by D. B. Quinn, *Sebastian Cabot and Bristol Exploration* (BHA, 21, 2nd ed., 1993); in particular, this neatly summarizes new findings on the second voyage as reported in L. Vigneras, 'New Light on the 1497 Cabot Voyage to America', *Hispanic American Historical Review*, 36 (1956), 506-9; standard older works include J. A. Williamson, *The Voyages of the Cabots and the English Discovery of North America under Henry VII and Henry VIII* (1929), and id., *The Cabot Voyages and Bristol Discovery under Henry VII* (Hakluyt Society, 2nd series, 120, 1962). Two later figures are dealt with by Professor MacInnes in separate monographs, *Ferdinando Gorges and New England* (BHA, 12, 1965), and *Captain Thomas James and the North West Passage* (BHA, 19, 1967); for more on Captain James and his rival, see M. Christy, *The Voyages of Captain Luke Fox of Hull and Captain James of Bristol in Search of the North-West Passage* (Hakluyt Society, 2 vols., 1894).

3   This and the following paragraph are drawn largely from D. H. Sacks, *The Widening Gate: Bristol and the Atlantic Economy, 1450-1700* (Berkeley, CA., 1991), chaps 1-3.

4   For Bristol's wine trade, see A. Crawford, *Bristol and the Wine Trade* (BHA, 57, 1984).

5   Sacks, *Widening Gate*, chap. 1; J. Vanes, ed., *Documents Illustrating the Overseas Trade of Bristol in the Sixteenth Century* (BRS, 31, 1979), introduction. For a discussion of the navigational problems associated with the port of Bristol, the port's management, Bristol's coastal trade, shipping industry, and general patterns of trade, see her *The Port of Bristol in the Sixteenth Century* (BHA, 39, 1977), which is drawn from her unpublished University of London PhD thesis, 'The Overseas Trade of Bristol in the Sixteenth Century' (1975). For the activities of one early-sixteenth-century Bristol merchant, see J. Angus and J. Vanes, *The Ledger of John Smythe, 1538-1550* (BRS, 28, 1974), introduction, 1-29 (and for more on the Smythes, J. H. Bettey, ed., *Calendar of the Correspondence of the Smyth Family of Ashton Court, 1548-1642* (BRS, 35, 1982), introduction, ix-xxiv).

6   Sacks, *Widening Gate*, chaps 1 and 2.

7   The standard modern work on the Merchant Venturers is McGrath, *Merchant Venturers*, supplemented by his edition of the *Records Relating to the Society of Merchant Venturers of the City of Bristol in the Seventeenth Century* (BRS, 17, 1951) and his articles,

'Merchant Venturers and Bristol Shipping in the Early Seventeenth Century', *Mariners' Mirror*, 36 (1950), 69-80 and 'The Society of Merchant Venturers and the Port of Bristol in the Seventeenth Century', *TBGAS*, 72 (1953), 105-28. However, J. Latimer's *The History of the Society of Merchant Venturers of the City of Bristol* (Bristol, 1903) is still well worth reading, and this Edwardian Liberal's antipathy towards the Merchant Venturers and the Tory, Anglican establishment they stood for in his eyes makes for an interesting comparison with McGrath's altogether more accommodating attitude towards his subject. Sacks's comments on the place of the Merchant Venturers in Bristol and the nation provides a valuable context: *Widening Gate*, chaps 3 and 6.

8   For Bristol's industries, see McGrath, *Merchant Venturers*, 33-5; F. Rogers, 'The Bristol Craft Gilds during the Sixteenth and Seventeenth Centuries' (unpublished MA thesis, University of Bristol, 1949). See also the work of I. V. Hall on the seventeenth-century sugar refineries, 'Whitson Court Sugar House, Bristol, 1665-1824', *TBGAS*, 65 (1946), 'John Knight Junior, Sugar Refiner at the Great House on St Augustine's Back, 1654-1679', *TBGAS*, 75 (1957), and 'Temple St. Sugar House Under the First Partnership of Richard Lane and John Hine, 1662-1678', *TBGAS*, 76 (1958), and his unpublished University of Bristol MA thesis, 'The Sugar Trade in England with Special Attention to the Sugar Trade of Bristol' (1925). For the clay tobacco pipe industry, see I. Walker, *The Bristol Clay Tobacco Pipe Industry* (Bristol, 1971); J. E. Pritchard, 'Tobacco Pipes of Bristol of the Seventeenth Century and their Makers', *TBGAS*, 45 (1923), 165-92; R. Jackson and R. Price, *Bristol Clay Pipes: A Study of Makers and their Marks* (Bristol, 1974); R. Price, R. Jackson and P. Jackson, *Bristol Clay Pipe Makers* (Bristol, 1979). For soap, see the introduction to H. E. Matthews, ed., *Proceedings, Minutes and Enrolments of the Company of Soapmakers, 1562-1642* (BRS, 10, 1940), 1-11, while Judith Milburn, 'The Contribution of Women to Bristol's Economy in the Seventeenth Century' (unpublished MA dissertation, University of the West of England, 1995), discusses women's involvement in Bristol's domestic economy, including their position in the soap industry. For a summary of the debate over Bristol's relative prosperity or poverty, see D. H. Sacks, 'Trade, Society and Politics in Bristol, 1500-1640' (PhD thesis, Harvard University, 1977, published New York, 1985), i, 4-11.

9   For Bristol's involvement in the war with Spain, see J. Vanes, *Bristol at the Time of the Spanish Armada* (BHA, 69, 1988), 14-36.

10   Vanes, *Bristol at the Time of the Spanish Armada*, 6-8; P. McGrath, *John Whitson and the Merchant Community of Bristol* (BHA, 25, 1970). For privateering, see J. W. Damer Powell, *Bristol Privateers and Ships of War* (Bristol, 1930).

11   For Bristol's seventeenth-century overseas trade, see P. McGrath, ed., *Merchants and Merchandise in Seventeenth-Century Bristol* (BRS, 19, 1955), introduction; id., *Merchant Venturers*, 35-8; W. B. Stephens, 'Trade Trends in Bristol, 1600-1700', *TBGAS*, 93 (1974); and Sacks, *Widening Gate*, chap. 8. For shipping, see P. McGrath, 'Merchant Venturers and Bristol Shipping in the Early Seventeenth Century', *Mariners' Mirror*, 36 (1950), 69-80, and his 'Merchant Shipping in the Seventeenth Century: the Evidence of the Bristol Deposition Books', *Mariners' Mirror*, 40 (1954), 282-93 & 41 (1955), 23-7. For inland trade, see T. S. Willan, 'The River Navigation and Trade of the Severn Valley, 1600-1750' *EcHR*, 8 (1937), 68-79 and M. D. G. Wanklyn, 'The Severn Navigation in the Seventeenth Century: The Long-Distance Trade of Shrewsbury Boats', *Midland History*, 13 (1988), 34-58.

12   Sacks, *Widening Gate*, chap. 8.

13   P. W. Coldham, *The Bristol Register of Servants Sent to Foreign Plantations, 1654-1686* (Baltimore, 1988); D. Souden, '"Rogues, Whores and Vagabonds"?: Indentured Servant

Emigrants to North America, and the Case of Mid-Seventeenth-Century Bristol', *Social History*, 3 (1978), 23-41.

14 Sacks, *Widening Gate*, chaps 8-9.

15 W. K. Jordan, *The Forming of the Charitable Institutions of the West of England: A Study of the Changing Patterns of Social Aspirations in Bristol and Somerset, 1480-1660* (Transactions of the American Philosophical Society, New Series, 50, pt. 8 (1960), 21. See also T. J. Manchee, *Bristol Charities*, 2 vols. (Bristol, 1831). For the Merchant Venturers' charitable provision, see McGrath, *Merchant Venturers*, 17-8, 81-4. Charity took many forms: for bequests towards the improvement and maintenance of roads, see R. C. Latham, ed., *Bristol Charters, 1509-1899* (BRS, 12, 1947), 72-4 and E. Ralph, *The Streets of Bristol* (BHA, 49, 1981).

16 For Bristol's particular economic problems in the period c.1580-1620, see above pp.3-4.

17 Vanes, *Bristol at the Time of the Spanish Armada*, 11-12, 33-5. For Bristol's particular sensitivity to the problems of poverty and Irish immigrants, see Sacks, 'Trade, Society and Politics', ii, 231-2.

18 J. Barry, 'Popular Culture in Seventeenth-Century Bristol', in B. Reay, ed., *Popular Culture in Seventeenth-Century England* (1985), suggests that in 1630 there were about 2000 apprentices in the city.

19 A. Yarborough, 'Apprentices as Adolescents in Sixteenth-Century Bristol', *Journal of Social History*, 13 (1979), 67-82, and 'Bristol Apprentices in the Sixteenth Century', *TBGAS*, 98 (1981); for much more on this subject, see Dr Yarborough's unpublished Catholic University of America PhD thesis, 'Bristol Apprentices in the Sixteenth Century: The Cultural and Regional Mobility of an Age Group' (1977). Also, J. Vanes, *Education and Apprenticeship in Sixteenth-Century Bristol* (BHA, 52, 1982) contains a useful description of the institution of apprenticeship. For the apprenticeship records themselves, and an informative introduction, see D. Hollis, ed., *Calendar of the Bristol Apprentice Book, 1532-1565, Part One, 1532-1542* (BRS, 14, 1949), and E. Ralph & N. Hardwick, eds, *Calendar of the Bristol Apprentice Book, Part Two, 1542-1552* (BRS, 33, 1980).

20 For comments on apprenticeship as socialization, see Barry, 'Popular Culture in Seventeenth-Century Bristol', 73-4.

21 Hollis, *Calendar of the Bristol Apprentice Book*, 9-10; and for this and the following, I. K. Ben-Amos, 'Women Apprentices in the Trades and Crafts of Early-Modern Bristol' *Continuity and Change*, 6 (1991), 227-52. See also Dr Ben-Amos's *Adolescence and Youth in Early-Modern England* (Yale University Press, 1994), which draws substantially on Bristol material. A large number of apprentices left before the ends of their terms, many of whom set up businesses in neighbouring villages: I. K. Ben-Amos, 'Failure to Become Freemen: Urban Apprentices in Early Modern England', *Social History*, 16 (1991), 155-72.

22 Norwich had the first. For education, see Jordan, *Forming of the Charitable Institutions*, 10, 36-9; Vanes, *Education and Apprenticeship in Sixteenth-Century Bristol*; D. J. Eames, 'Contributions Made by the Society of Merchant Venturers to the Development of Education in Bristol' (unpublished MA thesis, University of Bristol, 1966); and P. McGrath, 'The Wills of Bristol Merchants in the Great Orphan Books', *TBGAS*, 68 (1949), 91-109, 102 ff., for individual educational bequests. For the Merchant Venturers' school, see McGrath, *Merchant Venturers*, 84. Studies of individual schools include F. R. E. Bowen, *Queen Elizabeth's Hospital, Bristol: The City School* (Clevedon, 1971); C. P. Hill, *The History of Bristol Grammar School* (Bath, 1951); J. Vanes, *Apparelled in Red: The History of the Red Maids' School* (Gloucester, 1984), and McGrath, *John Whitson and the Merchant Community* for Red Maids. For a discussion of literacy in seventeenth-century Bristol, see

Barry, 'Popular Culture in Seventeenth-Century Bristol', 62-9.

23 Lollardy was a term applied by late medieval churchmen to cover a multitude of heretical opinions, many of which were probably no more than misunderstandings of orthodox doctrine, but insofar as it took its origin from the teachings of the fourteenth-century theologian Wycliffe, it consisted of a demand for a vernacular Bible; the rejection, total or partial, of the veneration of images, pilgrimage and papal authority; and belief in the priesthood of all believers and in consubstantiation. M. Skeeters, *Community and Clergy: Bristol and the Reformation, c.1530-c.1570* (Oxford, 1993), is the most comprehensive study of the Reformation in Bristol and its impact on the clergy, and on their relations with the laity. Much of the first part of this section is based on Professor Skeeters's work. See also her unpublished PhD thesis, 'The Clergy of Bristol, c.1530-c1570' (University of Texas, Austin, 1984). A convenient short account of the Reformation in Bristol is in K. G. Powell, *The Marian Martyrs and the Reformation in Bristol* (BHA, 31, 1972).

24 For the local background to the early Reformation, see K. Powell, 'The Beginnings of Protestantism in Gloucestershire', *TBGAS*, 90 (1971), 141-57, and his 'The Social Background to the Reformation in Gloucestershire', *TBGAS*, 92 (1973), 96-120. For friction between laity and clergy, see E. Ralph , ed., *The Great White Book of Bristol* (BRS, 32, 1979), 17-67, and Skeeters, *Community and Clergy*, 67-9.

25 For accounts of Bristol's 'battle of the pulpits', see G. R. Elton, *Policy and Police: The Enforcement of the Reformation in the Age of Thomas Cromwell* (Cambridge, 1972), 112-20; Latham, *Bristol Charters*, 23-4, and Skeeters, *Community and Clergy*, 38-46.

26 Skeeters, *Community and Clergy*, 45-6.

27 J. H. Bettey gives a clear account of the course of the dissolution of the Bristol houses in his *The Suppression of the Monasteries in the West Country* (Gloucester, 1989), and *The Suppression of the Religious Houses in Bristol* (BHA, 74, 1990). These accounts now largely supersede that of C. S. Taylor, 'The Religious Houses of Bristol and their Dissolution', *TBGAS*, 29 (1906), 81-126, although there is additional information on chantries in this article. For the effects of the Reformation on Bristol parish churches, see J. H. Bettey, *Bristol Parish Churches During the Reformation, c.1530-1560* (BHA, 45, 1979). For discussion of the wider implications of the Dissolution for Bristol, see Skeeters, *Community and Clergy*, chap. 5.

28 In addition to Skeeters, see Jordan, *Forming of the Charitable Institutions*, 6-44, particularly 8-9, 40 for discussion of Bristolians' changing attitudes towards the clergy, based on an analysis of wills; Powell, 'Social Background to the Reformation in Gloucestershire', points out that donations for 'catholic' religious purposes continued throughout the 1530s. Dr Clive Burgess has written extensively on popular religion in later medieval Bristol, and his work presents a generally positive picture of the laity's attitude towards the religious community: 'Chantries in Fifteenth-Century Bristol' (unpublished DPhil thesis, University of Oxford, 1981); '"For the Increase of Divine Service": Chantries in the Parish in Late-Medieval Bristol' *Journal of Ecclesiastical History*, 36 (1985), 46-65; 'A Service for the Dead: The Form and Function of the Anniversary in Late-Medieval Bristol', *TBGAS*, 105 (1987), 183-211; '"By Quick and by Dead": Wills and Pious Provision in Late-Medieval Bristol', *EHR*, 102 (1987), 837-58; *The Parish Church and the Laity in Late-Medieval Bristol* (BHA, 80, 1992). For the results of lay church patronage, see M. Q. Smith, *The Medieval Churches of Bristol* (BHA, 24, 1970).

29 This does not conform to Jordan's opinion (*Forming of the Charitable Institutions*, 6-44), but see Skeeters's remarks, *Community and Clergy*, 77-8. For a broader perspective, incorporating Bristol evidence, see R. Hutton, 'The Local Impact of the Tudor

Reformations', in C. Haigh, ed., *The English Reformation Revised* (Cambridge, 1987), 114-38.

30   The sermons of the conservative Bristol preacher Roger Edgeworth suggest that those clergy resisting reform were very much on the defensive in the later 1530s: J. Wilson, *Sermons Very Fruitful, Godly and Learned by Roger Edgeworth: Preaching in the Reformation, c.1535-1553* (Cambridge, 1993), and her, 'The Sermons of Roger Edgeworth: Reformation Preaching in Bristol', in D. Williams ed., *Early Tudor England: Proceedings of the 1987 Harlaxton Symposium* (Woodbridge, 1989), 223-40; J. W. Blench, 'John Longland and Roger Edgeworth: Two Forgotten Preachers of the Early Sixteenth Century', *Review of English Studies*, n.s., 5 (1954), 123-43.

31   Skeeters, *Community and Clergy*, 73-7. This suggested change in social ethos accords with the opinion of Sacks, *Widening Gate*, conclusion.

32   Bettey, *Suppression of the Religious Houses in Bristol*, 29. By comparison, the fate of former monastic and chantry properties in Somerset has been studied in some detail: K. S. H. Wyndham, 'In Pursuit of Crown Land: The Initial Recipients of Somerset Property in the Mid-Tudor Period', *PSANS*, 123 (1979) and G. Woodward, 'The Dispersal of Chantry Lands in Somerset', *Southern History*, 5 (1983), 95-114.

33   A detailed account of the Corporation's purchases is provided by Latham, *Bristol Charters*, 19-35. See also: Skeeters, *Community and Clergy*, 79-82; Bettey, *Suppression of the Religious Houses in Bristol*, 29; id., *Bristol Parish Churches*, 12-13, and Jordan, *Forming of the Charitable Institutions*, 7.

34   The fate of former nuns is for the most part obscure. What follows is largely based on Skeeters, *Community and Clergy*, 82-121, but see also, G. Baskerville, 'The Dispossessed Religious of Gloucestershire', *TBGAS*, 49 (1927), 63-122 and F. W. Weaver, 'The Fate of the Dispossessed Monks and Nuns', PSANS, 38 (1892), 327-46.

35   Jordan, *Forming of the Charitable Institutions*, 40-44.

36   Skeeters, *Community and Clergy*, 117-21.

37   Skeeters, *Community and Clergy*, 145-8.

38   For what follows see Skeeters, *Community and Clergy*, chap. 7, and her, 'The Creation of the Diocese of Bristol', *TBGAS*, 103 (1985), 175-8; J. H. Bettey, 'Paul Bush, the First Bishop of Bristol', *TBGAS*, 106 (1988) and his, 'Paul Bush, First Bishop of Bristol, and the Creation of the Bristol Diocese', in P. Fleming and A. Gross eds, *The Crown and its Provinces* (forthcoming).

39   Skeeters, *Community and Clergy*, 129-38.

40   Powell, *Marian Martyrs*, 16-7.

41   Powell, *Marian Martyrs*, 8-16. For evidence of continued Catholicism in Bristol and Gloucestershire under Elizabeth, see P. McGrath, 'Gloucestershire and the Counter-Reformation in the Reign of Elizabeth I', *TBGAS*, 88 (1969), 5-28.

42   Powell, *Marian Martyrs*, 16-17, and his, 'Social Background to the Reformation'; Skeeters, *Community and Clergy*, 133-8.

43   Skeeters, *Community and Clergy*, 153.

44   Much more work needs to be done on the religious life of Bristol between 1570 and 1640. This paragraph is based upon an interpretation of Jordan, *Forming of the Charitable Institutions*, 39-44.

45   This and the following paragraph are based on J. Barry, 'The Parish in Civic life: Bristol and its Churches, 1640-1750', in S. J. Wright ed., *Parish, Church and People: Local Studies in Lay Religion, 1350-1750* (1988), 152-78. See also his 'The Cultural Life of Bristol, 1640-1775' (unpublished DPhil thesis, University of Oxford, 1985).

46   Nonconformists of various kinds made up at least 25 per cent of Bristol's late seven-

teenth-century population: Barry, 'Popular Culture in Seventeenth-century Bristol', 61.

47 R. Mortimer, *Early Bristol Quakerism: The Society of Friends in the City, 1654-1700* (BHA, 17, 1967) for a concise account, and for further discussion of early Quakerism in the city, see his edition of *Minute Book of the Men's Meeting of the Society of Friends in Bristol, 1667-1686* (BRS, 26, 1971), and *1686-1704* (BRS, 30, 1977) introductions, and his 'Quakerism in seventeenth-century Bristol' (unpublished MA thesis, University of Bristol, 1946). For the Broadmead Baptists, see R. Hayden, ed., *The Records of a Church of Christ in Bristol, 1640-1687* (BRS, 27, 1974), introduction.

48 The fullest treatment of Bristol Corporation's constitution is Latham, *Bristol Charters*, introduction, 1-78. Useful shorter accounts include: E. Ralph, *The Government of Bristol, 1373-1973* (Bristol, 1973), particularly 5-20, and M. Stanford, ed., *The Ordinances of Bristol, 1506-1598* (BRS, 41, 1990), introduction, xvii-xxiv. For accounts of some of the constituents of the city's administrative machinery, see the introductions to the following: Ralph, *Great White Book*; E. E. Rich (ed.), *The Staple Court Books of Bristol* (BRS, 5, 1934).

49 Latham, *Bristol Charters*, 17.

50 The office of Lord High Steward was created in 1548 specifically to win court patronage: Latham, *Bristol Charters*, 18-19; Ralph, *Great White Book*, 8.

51 Latham, *Bristol Charters*, 18-19, 70-1. For more on these competing jurisdictions, see Ralph, *Great White Book*, 5-7.

52 Sacks, *Widening Gate*, chap. 5; Latham, *Bristol Charters*, 3, 14-15.

53 See Jordan, *Forming of the Charitable Institutions*, 13-19 for the merchant elite's dominant share of charitable bequests as another indication of their hegemony.

54 McGrath, *Merchant Venturers*, 10-23, 49-81; Sacks, *Widening Gate*, chap. 6.

55 Sacks, *Widening Gate*, chap. 7. To some extent this interpretation runs counter to that of P. McGrath, *Bristol and the Civil War* (BHA, 50, 1981, 1992), 6.

56 Sacks, *Widening Gate*, chap. 7, and his, 'The Corporate Town and the English State: Bristol's "Little Businesses", 1625-1641', *Past and Present*, 110 (1986), 69-105. For a full discussion of the Merchant Venturers' relations with early-Stuart government, see McGrath, *Merchant Venturers*, 62-70.

57 See also D. H. Sacks, 'Bristol's "Wars of Religion"', in R. C. Richardson, ed., *Town and Countryside in the English Revolution* (Manchester, 1992), 100-129. For the Merchant Venturers' attempts legally to establish their own monopoly and their opposition to London monopolies see McGrath, *Merchant Venturers*, 49-62. Significantly, after Bristol was taken for the King in 1643 the Merchant Venturers' loyalty was rewarded with a new charter that promised to open up the Levant trade to them: McGrath, *Bristol and the Civil War*, 37.

58 McGrath, *Bristol and the Civil War*, 6-20; Sacks, *Widening Gate*, chap. 7. The following account of Bristol in the Civil Wars is mostly taken from McGrath.

59 For the general pardon of 1644, see Latham, *Bristol Charters*, 64-6.

60 Professor McGrath may underplay the effects of the Royalist occupation: compare his account, *Bristol and the Civil War*, 36-7 with the evidence from the Deposition Books (H. E. Nott, ed., *The Deposition Books of Bristol, Vol. I, 1643-1647* (BRS, 6, 1935, references given in introduction, 9-31), and Latham, *Bristol Charters*, 63-4.

61 Sacks, *Widening Gate*, 245-6.

62 This paragraph summarises Latham, *Bristol Charters*, 35-61.

63 These conclusions are heavily influenced by the work of D. H. Sacks: in addition to the works cited above, see his, 'Celebrating Authority in Bristol, 1475-1641', in S. Zimmerman and R. F. E. Weisman, eds, *Urban Life in the Renaissance* (Newark, N.J., 1989),

187-223, and 'The Demise of the Martyrs: The Feasts of St Clement and St Katherine in Bristol, 1400-1600', *Social History*, 11 (1986), 141-69.

BRISTOL PRIDE: CIVIC IDENTITY IN BRISTOL c.1640-1775

Jonathan Barry

In 1640 Bristol already had a long civic tradition. Bristol had survived a difficult period of urban readjustment in the Tudor and early Stuart period, before entering a new phase of growth and prosperity during the later seventeenth century. Having eclipsed in population its main rival as second city of England, namely Norwich, shortly after 1700, for much of the eighteenth century Bristol was accepted as the second city, certainly for commerce, although by 1775 it was already facing a strong challenge from the new towns of Birmingham, Manchester and, most directly in commercial terms, Liverpool. During the period considered here, Bristolians could generally point with pride to their city's achievements. Aristocratic visitors were often disconcerted, not to say piqued, by the independent spirit of the Bristolians, which they associated with their pride both in their town and in themselves. Marmaduke Rawdon of York noted that Bristol freemen were as proud as Roman senators, and sparing with their hats, that is they were reluctant to doff them to their 'superiors'. The aim of this essay is to identify the nature of this 'Bristol pride'. The essay begins by showing how commercial success was placed within a much broader context of civic tradition, incorporating, though not always easily, not just successful entrepreneurs but all elements of Bristol society. It then shows how collective civic values and activities were seen as crucial to social and individual welfare. The conclusion considers the political uses made of this civic tradition.[1]

The Context for Commerce

It was as a trading city that both visitors and Bristolians primarily saw Bristol. Although population and size also counted, Bristol's surest claim to be the second city of England rested on its commercial success, both in overseas trade and as a regional metropolis. William Barrett, who published the first complete history of Bristol in 1789, claimed that commercial success reflected

> greater honour on Bristol than anything we have said
> or can say in its praise for antiquity, the only thing

25

many places more extolled in chronicles or old
histories now have left to boast of whilst this, like a
well-cultivated spot, has been continually flourishing
with renewed vigour.[2]

Visiting dignitaries echoed the emphasis on commerce as Bristol's
distinctive contribution to national greatness. Barrett claimed that this
made urban history more important than county histories to a nation
founded on commerce.[3]

Several features were emphasized that made Bristol 'a well-cultivated spot'. The first was its position, well placed for Irish and colonial
trade and to control the Severn, Wye and Avon valleys. This made
Bristol a natural centre for the trading network that had become
dominant by around 1700, in which Bristol combined long-distance
trading ties with southern Europe and the Americas with its role as a
regional entrepôt for the Bristol channel region and its river connections. Until industrial growth in the midlands and north shifted the
balance, Bristol's hinterland was one of the most densely populated
and economically active areas of England, while Bristol played a
crucial part in the industrial development of South Wales and
Cornwall. No wonder nature seemed, for a while at least, on Bristol's
side.[4]

But nature had to be cultivated, and thus stress was placed on the
character of the inhabitants, in particular their 'virtue and industry'.
Here the role of the merchant, as the central figure activating the
energies and talents of the community, was emphasized. As Sacks
argues, this claim was also less self-evident, more historically limited,
than it seemed. The shift to complex long-distance trade had brought
merchants to the fore at the expense of manufacturers and retailers.
For most of our period they dominated the city economically and
provided the majority of its political leaders, shaping civic policy to
mercantile interests. By the mid-eighteenth century their leadership
was again in question, as Bristol's commercial lead faltered and as new
industries and occupations developed.[5] But even during the golden
age of the merchants, Bristol's economy had always been diverse. All
Bristolians were felt to share the same entrepreneurial qualities;
comments were often made on the bustle of the town and the indus-
triousness of its inhabitants. Lest Bristolians should become
complacent, however, preachers and commentators stressed the frugal
diligence of their ancestors and urged the current generation to live up
to such standards. Popular literature, such as ballads, echoed this in a

more dramatic vein by portraying Bristol as a city of busy merchants and heroic sailors, risking all against pirates and the sea.[6]

There was a dark side, of course, to this obsession with trade, although its most obvious blemish, in our eyes, namely its reliance on slavery, was little discussed until the mid-eighteenth century. Ballads often portrayed a clash between love and money, as the merchant's daughter was ordered to forsake her dashing lover for a rich crony of her father. Chatterton's portrayal of a town of mean philistines is only the most memorable of many such comments.[7] Bristolians themselves were well aware of the dangers attached to money-making, and sought to curb its corrosive effects on society. Preachers and essayists insisted that wealth mattered less than the virtues required to attain it. The rich had to use their wealth properly to earn esteem; the middling were urged to place virtue, contentment and friendship above the struggle for success.[8] Guild insistence that fraternity and security mattered more than entrepreneurship was taken up by the new friendly societies, Freemasons' lodges and other clubs.

I shall return later to the virtues expected of the citizen. But it is also important to stress that commerce itself was believed only to flourish within conditions created by the corporate life of Bristol and the privileges won by its Corporation and guilds. Ceaseless lobbying by Corporation and Merchant Venturers was needed to maintain and extend Bristol trade in an age of mercantilism and warfare. At the very least Bristol had to fight off the monopolizing tendencies of London groups (for example, in 'opening' African trade around 1700) and ensure that its ships were as well protected as possible from piracy or enemy navies. The support of trading interests evolved gradually, as guild and Corporation efforts to woo the court gave way to public meetings and Parliamentary lobbying, but, as Edmund Burke learned to his cost between 1774 and 1780, the MP was judged chiefly on his record in achieving concrete advantages for the city. In short, political activity could not be separated from commercial life.[9] This contemporary reality was reflected in the historical work on Bristol. The key events were seen as new charters and privileges, and the role of town government was stressed. Bristol flourished because of good government. Thomas Ford, in a sketch of what a Bristol history might teach the reader, told the magistrates that

> in the annals of your predecessors you will, with
> pleasure, recognise a magistracy always renowned for
> inviolable loyalty, for wise conduct in government, for

courage tempered with discretion in the administration of justice, for a provident care for the necessities
of the poor in time of scarcity and distress, and
especially for a magnificent economy in entertaining
princes graciously accepted and rewarded by royal
grants of more extended liberties.[10]

The most important of these 'liberties' were the jurisdictional powers
granted to the town, especially its status as a 'county of itself', possess-
ing the full panoply of courts, subject only to the central law courts
and the assize judges. The Corporation were seen by the citizens above
all as magistrates, providing justice and thus allowing the social and
commercial life of the city to continue. Good magistracy would ensure
government favour, as would gifts and addresses of loyalty to London,
together with lavish hospitality to visiting royalty and statesmen. This
view of local government has long been alien to historians, and
Latimer, the great late Victorian historian of Bristol, portrayed expenditure and ceremony of this kind as merely the junketings of an
oligarchy.[11] However, ordinary Bristolians do not seem to have
questioned the need for such activities. Annals or calendars of major
Bristol events (kept in considerable numbers until the advent of
newspapers by shopkeepers and artisans as well as town officials and
members of the professions) show the same obsession with civic privileges and with the Corporation. Indeed the calendars were usually
based on the mayoral year, starting at Michaelmas, and recorded the
mayor and sheriffs for each year.[12]

This emphasis on local government and political privileges in the
history of a commercial city may strike us as parochial and miscon-
ceived. But national government and its behaviour was indeed crucial
for local prosperity, as contemporaries perceived.[13] The town's annalists jumbled together local and national events in their accounts.
Andrew Hooke, who began a history in the 1740s, saw the town's
history in terms of progressive gains in privileges under each ruler,
due to magisterial virtue and wisdom until, under James II, the
freedoms of the whole state, and hence those of Bristol, were in mortal
danger. Although the Whig Hooke had particular reason to anathema-
tize James, the 1680s had seen the most sustained threat to Bristol's
civic autonomy, with a new charter which had ceded to the crown a
veto over the personnel of the city's common council and aldermanic
bench, as well as such key figures as the recorder and town clerk. This
threatened to give *de jure* authority to the interference of central

governments in Bristol affairs which had become commonplace since the Civil War, as successive governments sought to put Bristol, and other key towns, in 'safe hands'. Although such interference did not cease after 1688, the 'Glorious Revolution' did restore the basic autonomy of Bristolians over their own affairs, as confirmed in Queen Anne's charter of 1710.[14]

Until the eighteenth century Englishmen conceived of their history generally as a series of discrete events not a matter of historical processes. The growth in Bristol's privileges reflected the accretion of national liberties within the unchanging framework of an ancient constitution, wisely ruled by kings with obedient subjects, both ideally motivated by a blend of Protestantism and patriotism. This vision of history was reinforced throughout our period by civic ceremony, notably on the two great public holidays of Gunpowder and Restoration Day, when the whole city was expected to join in as the magistrates and guilds paraded through the town to hear a sermon, with bells, music, bonfires and the like. The only Bristolian of this period to turn his back on such a vision of Bristol's past was Josiah Tucker (a long-serving Bristol minister both before and during his period as Dean of Gloucester). He viewed history as a series of progressive stages in which commerce freed itself of political interference and therefore rejected the world of guilds and corporate lobbying as irrelevant to modern society.[15] But it is only in the later eighteenth century that we begin to find extensive evidence of this laissez-faire mentality, hostile to civic traditions, which so influenced the next century.

The traditional emphasis on civic privileges was embodied in stone at the city's heart, in the form of the High Cross (which stood at the meeting place of the four main streets – Broad Street, Wine Street, High Street and Corn Street) with its statues of the monarchs who had granted Bristol privileges. Four statues were added in 1633 and the Cross was repaired and re-gilded in 1697.[16] Seventeenth-century visitors were struck by its splendour, as by the medieval inheritance of walls, gates, crosses, churches, pumps and in particular the underground sewers and waterpipes which kept the hilly city unusually clean. The physical inheritance of the city was of great importance in its image, both to outsiders and inhabitants. Civic government revolved around these medieval structures, literally revolved, as the frequent civic processions moved from the civic buildings by the High Cross in processions to the parish pumps, crosses and churches, to celebrate holidays or to make major announcements. The High Cross was also used by citizens to make private announcements, while the Tolzey nearby in Corn Street was the meeting place for merchants. When the new Exchange was opened a few yards away in 1743, it was marked by lavish ceremony, and the keynote speech emphasized that such public buildings were 'at all times held in esteem and considered as manifestations of the wisdom and grandeur of a state'.[17] The annalists recorded in detail every aspect of municipal betterment of this kind. Barrett singled out the building of the first stone bridge and the new quay in the 1240s as the major event in Bristol's medieval history, chiefly because it symbolized the progressive spirit that had made Bristol great.[18]

This emphasis on buildings as expressions of Bristol's progress created a dilemma in the eighteenth century, when an expanding population created new demands which set heritage against improvement. Until then Bristol could grow by building over its medieval gardens and monastic properties, supplemented from 1654 by the former Castle grounds. But by 1700 it became necessary to move outside the old city boundaries. The Marsh area was drained and developed, notably in the construction of Queen Square, and building began on the hills above the old city and outside the walls, especially along the various roads leading from the city gates. Traditionally these had attracted low quality cottages for the poor, for example in St Philip and St Jacob's parish, but now extensive suburbs grew up, especially in St James's and St Michael's parishes, for the better off. In 1733 the High Cross, and after 1750 the city's gates and walls, and the other pumps and crosses, were removed to allow more space for traffic and broader streets. Much of Bristol was rebuilt in neo-classical style, to meet new expectations about urban life. The Corporation adjusted the venue of civic events to make use of such imposing new sites as Queen Square.[19]

This reflected a more general shift in fashion towards the rural. The cramped medieval city was no longer admired so much, although the new squares and the College Green were praised, as were new suburban developments on the hills around the town, which had fresh air and views. Increasingly, however, Bristol was praised for its hilly situation and the picturesque beauty of the surrounding countryside, notably the Downs and the Gorge. These were simultaneously attracting many visitors to use the Hotwells, which became an important part of Bristol's economy. This in turn hastened the growth of Clifton as a suburb where city and leisured wealth could mingle. As gardens were built over in the city centre and the riverside meadows disappeared, the wealthier citizens began to move out of the centre or to build second homes in the countryside nearby, while the middling flocked out of town on Sundays for fresh air and greenery. Paradoxically, Bristol's 'urban renaissance' was accompanied by a new emphasis on *rus in urbe* and on the city's countryside setting.[20]

But the medieval inheritance was not without its champions. Those who called for the High Cross to be removed in 1733 felt it necessary to argue that any veneration for its antiquity should be outweighed, not just by traffic needs, but by the inappropriateness to civic life of such a 'relic of popish superstition'. The High Cross was originally re-erected on College Green, and there was considerable protest when it was underhandedly sold to Hoare of Stourhead. Meanwhile pieces of the gates and churches, many of which were rebuilt in the eighteenth century, were bought by rich Bristolians to adorn their new villas. This fashionable Gothicism, however, must be distinguished from the attitude of those who valued the old structures as part of the living fabric of the city. When Pope admired the High Cross as a piece of Gothic he deplored the recent gilding which he felt spoiled its 'venerable antiquity', but to antiquarians like Barrett these monuments of the past, and others such as church tombs and inscriptions, were living things, to be repaired and updated as necessary.[21] They recorded in their notes past and present examples of epitaphs, monuments and buildings with equal interest. Visitors commented that Bristolians were zealous in repairing their churches and church furnishings. Because they were torn between approval of civic improvement and love of civic heritage, they could not effectively protect the latter from destruction.

As noted earlier, the most impressive element in the architectural heritage of the city was its churches. Bristol had seventeen parishes, as well as a Cathedral and the civic chapel (St Mark's or the Gaunts), facing each other on College Green and representing the rival claims of episcopal and civic authorities to lead Bristol religious life. Population growth made these parishes increasingly anomalous, some catering for tiny city centre populations, while St James's and St Philip and St Jacob's became far too large for their churches to be able to house all their parishioners. The same suburban parishes were also the location for most of Bristol's nonconformist chapels and it was here that Bristol's growing religious pluralism must have been most evident. Yet the Anglican church was far from moribund in Bristol; many of the parish churches were rebuilt and some of them extended.[22]

The church had a profound effect on civic life and the city's image.

The church calendar was still the basis of holidays, while parishes might have their own special days, including the perambulations, perhaps every three years, which helped to define the city. The Corporation's ritual calendar was based on church festivals, and the councillors attended church services in solemn processions, combining an intricate round of parish attendance with visits to the Cathedral and the civic chapel. The church bells played a central part in making everyone aware of such public events, while the city clergy, through their sermons, were the public interpreters of the meaning of such occasions. Visitors to Bristol often commented on the regularity of church-going, the good order of the churches and the respect paid to the clergy. Guide books and histories were usually organised by parish, devoting most attention to the churches and their monuments, whose examples of past piety and virtue were thought likely to impress the current generation. Interest in the town's history was liveliest among Anglican clerics and their lay supporters, who took every opportunity to highlight the role of the church in Bristol life, past and present.[23]

With the coming of dissent in 1640, however, the status of the Anglican church in the civic community became a controversial matter (which was precisely why the church party stressed its centrality). Churchmen's accounts either ignored the dissenters and their churches, or commented pointedly that their origins lay in Civil War and regicide.[24] The various dissenting groups, meanwhile, adopted a variety of tactics to establish their role in civic life in the face of the Anglican establishment. The largest group, the Presbyterians, with many men of influence, sought to remain active within the existing civic structure. During the 1640s and 1650s, when they dominated the Corporation, they continued its ritual life unabated, supplying the parish churches with suitable ministers. After 1660 they were gradually edged out of civic life, though they tried to remain active in the parishes, but when they returned in numbers to the Corporation after 1688, and especially after 1735, they were quite prepared to join in the Anglican round, though they also brought the main Presbyterian meeting place into the civic circuit.

The more sectarian denominations, such as the Baptists and, in particular, the Quakers, preferred to avoid the civic tradition, with its inbuilt Anglican bias. They refused to honour church festivals or public rejoicings, though they might participate in public fasts which were still held in wartime till the end of this period. But they did not cut themselves off entirely from the city. When they were persecuted they were quick to claim that they were fellow citizens, and accuse their persecutors of violating the ties of neighbourhood and city. There was, moreover, within movements such as the Quakers and Methodists a strong revivalist element which led to extrovert public gestures, challenging the city to repentance. The most notorious of these was James Nayler's ride into Bristol, but Bristol saw many other would-be prophets carry messages of warning or exhortation, urging Bristol to avoid the fate of Babylon and become another Jerusalem. Both Quakers and Methodists held mass meetings in the city which aroused intense interest, as well as hostility, before lapsing into much more introverted sectarian habits. Their civic influence thus extended much beyond their core membership, which was always small.[25]

Both the Anglicans and the dissenters, therefore, might see Bristol as a holy city, but their visions of what this meant were very different and contradictory. In the very long run such tensions encouraged the emergence of secular images of the city which would not raise such divisive feelings. During our period, however, the main effect was to encourage emphasis on two elements in religion which could be non-controversial, namely charity and moral reformation. Bristol was justly famous for its charities even before Colston's massive gifts of the late seventeenth and early eighteenth centuries. It outdid even London in giving per capita and, unlike London, almost all the money was given to causes within the city, itself a potent sign of civic pride. Charity played a growing role in civic ritual, with the establishment of the Gloucestershire and other county societies in 1658, and of Colston societies in the eighteenth century, and Colston's anniversary became almost a public holiday after the 1720s.[26]

Charity was particularly important to a trading city because it offered tangible proof that city wealth was honourably used and that the wealthy were not avaricious or narrow-minded. Both annalists and historians devoted enormous attention to charities. Sermons and essays balanced self-congratulation with exhortations to continued giving. Satirists knew that questioning Bristol charity was particularly painful, and such satire prompted instant replies defending the city's reputation. Those seeking support within the city were careful to establish a reputation for generosity; MPs imitated the mayors in giving ostentatiously to Newgate debtors and other worthies. Guilds and later friendly societies and other clubs offered mutual support and allowed the less well-off to emulate the charity of the wealthy merchants. To supply the needs of others through charity and to provide for one's own future needs through mutual support was to establish one's place as an independent citizen. Though the prudential justification for such charity, namely the maintenance of communal discipline, was prominent, equally prominent was the insistence that such charity cemented the mutual good fellowship of the bourgeoisie and displayed their capacity to overcome the temptations of possessive individualism. This applied both to the individual and to the community as a whole.

We can learn much from the kinds of charity preferred by Bristolians. Although there were still many small gifts of bread or money for the poor, usually administered by the churches, the most prestigious gifts and schemes concerned education and employment, training the poor into the ways of virtue and industry so that they could become proper Bristolians, and the preferred method of doing this was by apprenticeship. Other charities in favour of deserving groups such as widows, orphans or members of specific occupational or religious groups served to strengthen the family unit or existing associational groupings. Some laid down standards of behaviour expected of recipients, while others, by offering patronage and legitimacy to the bodies involved, strengthened their social position.

Charity was to be administered carefully to reinforce the moral standards of the community, and here it coincided with persistent civic efforts for what was then called 'the reformation of manners'. Throughout our period the Corporation and groups of citizens sought to use the law to enforce proper standards of behaviour, attacking immorality, drunkenness, swearing and misuse of the Sabbath. They also sought to strengthen the power of the household, which was seen as the most effective agent of such socialization, or to compensate for the absence of family ties, when parents were dead or themselves unworthy, through schooling, apprenticeship or workhouses. These interests are often associated with the 'Puritan' governments of early Stuart towns, but in Bristol at least such ambitions persisted after 1660. Indeed they reached a climax around 1700 (when warfare caused acute social dislocation), with the efforts of the short-lived Society for the Reformation of Manners (1700-5), alongside the Corporation of the Poor and then the establishment of parochial charity schools. The momentum for reform declined after 1715, but this was largely due to religious and political conflicts about the running and implications of such institutions. Eighteenth-century Bristol retained the image of a Puritan town, unusually sabbatarian and fierce in its punishment of vice.[27] As the town grew larger and more complex, and as the proportion of the poor grew, this became harder to sustain, but the aspirations remained. Such aspirations are normally described as 'social control', aimed at the unruly poor, and so they were, but they were also important as an affirmation of civic, bourgeois identity. Implicitly, and sometimes explicitly, they were employed to contrast Bristol and London, and so rebuke the idle rich and the vicious capital. A late example might be Hannah More, brought up in Bristol, who combined her efforts, through schooling and moral tracts, to teach the poor their proper place, with strenuous denunciations of the vices of the great. With a figure like More we can see the link between the traditions of civic moralism and the evangelical morality of the Victorians.[28]

We have seen, therefore, that Bristol's commercial image was immeasurably enriched by a series of associated and additional identities, relating to civic government, the physical fabric, its religious traditions and the moral character of the city. Here we need to return to Barrett's original observation that commercial success reflected 'greater honour on Bristol than anything we have said or can say in its praise for antiquity'. Two comments can be made on this. First it is worth noting that Barrett was concerned with the 'honour' of the city, and secondly, despite his claim, both he and many other Bristolians were very concerned with the 'antiquity' of the city, and obviously felt it was important to its honour. Those keeping annals usually began their accounts back in the Middle Ages, most often from 1216 when the main offices were settled. Historians of the city sought to trace Bristol's origins back into the mists of time, preferably to the race or group that were believed to have founded Britain itself or established its ancient constitution. Tradition held that two kings, Brennus and Belinus, descendants of Brutus from Troy, had founded the city. Despite critical attacks, Bristolians were loath to abandon a myth which tied Bristol so closely into the national story. Repeated efforts were made to use various kinds of evidence, historical, archaeological and otherwise, to disprove Camden's assertion that Bristol was not important until the tenth century. Evidence of earlier settlement gradually accrued, to be marshalled by Barrett, but unfortunately he also swallowed Thomas Chatterton's helpful provision, through forgeries, of documentary proof of Bristol's early history. At the same time Barrett and others were very tempted by Andrew Hooke's elegant solution to the problem in 1748, when he proposed that a town so favourably placed as Bristol had clearly been a leading commercial city from earliest days, and was noted by geographers, but that the monkish chroniclers Camden had used had ignored it until it had castles and churches.[29]

Hooke's theory all too neatly combined antiquity with commerce, at the expense of the feudal values of warfare and monasticism which Hooke, like Dean Tucker, despised. But most Bristolians probably associated the honour of their city with its important role in the country's war effort. The popular image of Bristol associated it closely with privateering and naval prowess. Just as Bristol's traders alternated between merchant trading in peace and privateering in war, so there was a division in the image of the merchant. Sometimes he was the bold warrior, risking his all for the nation's increase; at other times he was the man of peace, engaged in trade abroad which brought mutual benefit and understanding between nations. Whichever was stressed, however, the 'antiquity and honourableness' of his role could be maintained, to quote the title of a sermon preached to the Society of Merchant Venturers in 1744. It could easily be argued that the merchant's life depended on the taking of risk and the cultivation of credit, and that he therefore had every cause and opportunity to cultivate the virtues of a traditional gentleman.[30]

Unlike the landed gentleman, however, the merchant usually lacked a landed estate or a family tradition. As a result, his claim to honour came to rest to a large extent on his role in civic affairs, particularly in civic government, but also in guilds and other societies. These could provide an element of continuity in a fluid social world, and make up in communal prestige for the relative insignificance of the individual. During the seventeenth century there were many Bristolians who used heraldic devices in their houses or at their funerals, often adopting the arms of their trade or of the city.[31] During the eighteenth century heraldry gradually declined in significance, as did the guilds, but they were replaced by other modes of expressing urban honour. The wealthy could join in polite society, while the middling crowded into the clubs and societies. It is striking how many of these groups, though new, not only appealed to civic values such as charity, virtue and industry, but also sought an honourable past. The various branches of 'the ancient and honourable society' of Freemasons met on traditional guild festival days, while the Gloucestershire and other county societies, together with the Welsh and Scottish societies, appealed back to county myths or to the legends of St David or St Andrew.[32]

The Boundaries of Civic Identity

Mention of these societies, composed of Bristolians born outside the city, who met together annually and raised funds to support their less favoured county brethren, raises an important issue. Like other towns, Bristol's population growth depended on a constant flow of immigrants. The 1778 edition of Defoe's *Tour* claimed that Bristol contained such a 'heterogeneous mixture' of people from Wales, Scotland, Ireland, America and the neighbouring counties, with their different languages and religions, that 'any general characteristics of its inhabitants cannot be given'.[33] Surely this must have weakened any sense of civic identity? Perhaps not so much as one might expect. Traditionally immigrants were introduced to the values of Bristol society by apprenticeship. During the seventeenth century apprenticeship was at a high level while growth was modest, suggesting that most immigrants entered in this manner, or by marriage into Bristol families. There was a rise in the proportion of Bristol-born apprentices, while those from outside came almost entirely from a few nearby counties. An increasing number of these apprentices became freemen of Bristol, rising from a third to just over a half by 1700, while the county societies offered a means for these immigrants to combine pride in place of origin with civic pride, by supporting other apprentices from their area.[34]

Eighteenth-century population growth jeapordized this arrangement. The proportion of apprentices to the working population steadily declined, and more people became free through other methods. Although apprentice numbers picked up after 1750, most were now charity apprentices. Their numbers indicate the continued faith in apprenticeship as the best way to enter civic life, but apprenticeship lost its honourable character as the wealthy no longer regularly passed through this stage. After 1760 apprenticeship also began to lose appeal as the best way to meet civic problems, and more specific charities to help poor women in pregnancy, debtors or prostitutes began to seem more appropriate. Charitable attention was shifting from the moment of entry into civic life towards more specific threats to the fabric of that life.

Significantly, however, these still centred, like apprenticeship, on the regulation of the household. The household remained the basic unit in civic life, and civic measures were always intended to reinforce this. Only the male head of household, however, participated directly in civic affairs, although in Bristol, unlike many other towns, both husband and wife were officially responsible for taking on an apprenticeship and freemen's widows could continue to run businesses and take on apprentices. By remarrying freemen's widows could also convey citizenship to their new husbands, and the freedom was also open to the husbands of freemen's daughters as well. In all cases, however, it was the man who exercised this privilege, even if it passed through the women of the household. Women and children only came into direct contact with the city if the household head died. The Corporation took legal charge of orphans and offered them education, while widows were supported by the guilds, through pensions and places in almshouses, and both widows and orphans were also supported by charitable and friendly societies.[35]

But if charity towards these groups was an important part of civic values, the women and children were still in a largely passive role. Women could express their interests and preferences through giving to charity themselves, and Bristol's women seem to have been particularly prominent in parish charities. But men were almost always appointed to administer such gifts, and men controlled the larger charities which increasingly overshadowed parish charity. Women were officially excluded from politics, although they might play a limited part in civic ceremony. But women who took an active partisan role in public affairs were liable to be criticized for their presumption and unfemininity, whether they were the Parliamentary supporters of 1642, the sectarian prophetesses of the Interregnum, or the Jacobite ladies who flaunted white roses in 1750.[36]

Apprentices were in a similarly equivocal position. Their importance was stressed, as symbols of the city's future, and they were welcomed as passive members of the body politic, but they were distrusted if they used their representative quality to express attitudes distasteful to the authorities. During the troubled seventeenth century they did this in attacks on Quakers, Catholics and brothels, and to protest for a free Parliament in 1660. In most cases the apprentices' supporters could claim that the apprentices were expressing community norms, attacking the traditional enemies of Bristol's order and prosperity when the authorities were not doing their duty. However, the sporadic violence and independence of such occasions always alarmed the city rulers. They suspected that troublesome apprentices were being encouraged by factions within the city.[37]

In many respects the same ambiguity surrounded the participation of the general population in civic affairs. A majority of male heads of household were freemen until the mid-eighteenth century, and the guilds were always expected to participate in public life. But the conditions of their involvement were uncertain, and so was the involvement of the minority of labourers and other poor who had no recognised stake in civic institutions. Sometimes their support was deliberately courted through the encouragement of large crowds, and it is evident from popular demonstrations that everybody knew the characteristic forms and rhetoric of civic culture sufficiently well to be able to evoke them when required.[38] But it is hard to know if those involved felt they were genuine participants in civic culture, or merely knew how to manipulate its forms to their own advantage when appropriate. Often such popular action was orderly, but it was still seen as a potential threat to civic order by 'respectable' citizens. If necessary, those involved could usually be stigmatized as somehow 'other' to Bristol life – as a hired, drunken, disorderly mob, or perhaps as consisting of non-Bristolians such as the Kingswood colliers.[39]

It is hard, then, to be sure whether Bristolian pride extended beyond the middling and upper classes who participated regularly in city events. One might also question the commitment to the city of the merchant elite who formed its rulers. This may sound ridiculous. The merchants dominated the city, and the Society of Merchant Venturers was the major guild. Merchants, particularly Society members, predominated in the Corporation, and the Merchants' Hall was often used to house civic events. On the other hand, the Society did not participate in civic ceremony as a body, its members attending processions as individuals not as a guild. The Society's efforts were chiefly aimed at influencing national government, which it approached independently, not at internal city affairs. A growing number of merchants remained outside the Society, while only an ever-decreasing minority of merchants could expect to see their wealth and importance translated into civic office. Moreover, merchants had broader horizons than other citizens, and the resources and prestige to lead the life of gentlemen in their own right. As the image of the gentleman changed, so did their tastes. In the seventeenth century they might, like John Whitson, hunt and hawk, purchase land and establish their right to bear arms. They also led the city's militia forces. In the eighteenth century it was in some ways easier to be a gentleman in the city, by building new houses, purchasing a carriage and joining polite society and such prestigious institutions as the Library Society or the Infirmary committee. But they also, as we have seen, moved out to the suburbs or retired to the country, so escaping the demands of city life. As their tastes changed, civic culture also changed, but perhaps more slowly.[40]

Bourgeois Collectivism?

The quintessential Bristol citizen, therefore, and the people for whom identity as a Bristolian was probably most important, was a male member of the middling sort (or bourgeoisie). It was from the ranks of these groups, extending from professionals and rich traders down to the humbler artisans, that Bristol's freeman population was drawn and it was such people who dominated Bristol's rich associational life. As I have argued elsewhere, it was for these groups that membership, both of a civic culture and of its many constituent societies, offered an expression and a reinforcement of that independence which gave them the right to claim to be 'freemen', while at the same time recognizing and managing their inevitable dependence on others.[41] The household economy was fundamental and the bourgeoisie at all levels built their lives around the protection and development of the family and household through a series of stages in the life cycle and in response to the challenges posed to it. Whereas the poor had to depend on others for charity or poor relief, a fundamental characteristic of the bourgeoisie was the aspiration (not always achieved) to use mutual support to secure their futures. Unlike today, however, such insurance was based not on impersonal commercial arrangements but on building up a network of social and institutional relationships within Bristol, as well as managing those that catered for the poor. Just as the city invested in the household as the fundamental source of urban stability, so the householder found urban association the necessary prerequisite for household maintenance, thereby strengthening the connection between civic and bourgeois identity.

Civic identity had always been forged out of measures taken by townspeople to counter the effects of flux and mobility. The notion of a corporation and of corporate bodies, which lay at the heart of Bristol's self-definition, rested on the assumption that such institutions created the permanence and immortality which were otherwise unattainable in urban conditions. Equally, Bristol's identity rested as much on the permanence of buildings (walls, gates, castles, churches, market halls, schools, almshouses) and economic privileges (fairs, markets, commercial courts) as on people: yet all these buildings and privileges required upkeep and management organized through association. The 'urban renaissance' in Bristol, as elsewhere, added to these traditional groupings a whole new set of institutions, such as the Infirmary, Exchange, theatre and Library Society, each requiring a supporting association to handle their finances and management.

Bristolians regarded themselves as living in a dangerous world where disorder and disaster constantly threatened. Continuity, as expressed by antiquity and ensured by corporate organization and voluntary association, was thus a great value in itself. Amongst the dangers faced were those of war, civil strife and social discontent, not to mention the constant concern about crime. Frequent wars added to the already fragile conditions of credit in Bristol, where bankruptcy was a constant threat and every trader was part of a complex web of creditors and debtors. In this risky world, an obsession with one's own reputation and that of others, with honour and honesty and with demonstrating that one had friends and associations (which increased one's reliability) was a necessity of business, rather than a costly diversion from business.[42] Associations performed multiple roles in this respect: training the bourgeoisie in self-management, displaying to others their mastery of this art and strengthening social ties with those on whom they relied.

For the reinforcement of both the family and the wider community in the face of the forces of instability was not just a matter of material provision, but also of the promotion of a series of values seen as fundamental to the survival of urban society. Bristol's corporate motto *virtute et industria* (by virtue and industry), epitomizes the various qualities such as thrift, respectability and industry, often labelled the Protestant work-ethic and seen as the foundation of individualism. We may observe not only that their success was assumed to depend on collective rather than individual action, but also that they were matched by a set of overtly collective virtues, of sociability and good fellowship. The expression of these in communal gatherings, eating and drinking, and often in listening together to sermons and marching through the streets on holidays or anniversaries, was common to Bristol associations, old and new. Other sets of values were also embedded in associational life, once again in the form of dialectic tensions. These include those between self-control and obedience to others, between competition and co-operation, between restraint and liberality. We may see the practice of associational life as providing Bristol's bourgeoisie with a constantly renewed experience and representation of how to manage their lives in accord with these values, and in particular how to balance their apparently contradictory requirements. The central notion here, one often evoked by contemporaries as they extolled the virtues of life in the 'middle station', was of the 'golden mean'. To be a member of the middling sort one had to learn how to practise moderation, but the middling sort were seen as uniquely placed to achieve this ideal state, if properly trained. The role of associations in this process of training was twofold. On the one hand the values preached by the sermons, toasts, insignia, recitation of rules and the like at associational events provided a prudential code for Bristolians. Its messages were, however, also embodied in the actual practices needed to carry off such occasions successfully. Association thus succeeded apprenticeship as the proving ground for the independent head of household.

Conclusion – Pride in Politics

Clearly many inequalities were involved in civic tradition, of wealth, occupation and, above all, gender. Yet, if socio-economic trends were weakening features of a common civic culture, ideological divisions were, in some respects at least, reinforcing the importance to all groups, including the (divided) mercantile elite, of participation in civic culture. This can be seen by a brief consideration of some of the ways in which Bristol pride was appealed to, indeed manipulated, by rival political groups in the period after 1640. During these years the city was divided from the top on religious and political issues, into what can in shorthand be called Whig and Tory sides, and these sought to win popular support and approval in their struggles for power. In doing so they exploited to the full the ingredients and ambiguities of Bristol's civic identity, which suggests that the values I have been describing were believed then to have an important hold over Bristolians. Given the very broad extent of the freeman franchise, widened still further by the participatory aspects of local government and street politics, it is clear that these values meant something, if not necessarily the same things, to more than a mere oligarchy.[43]

In the first place, the different sides struggled very hard to maintain the fiction that they represented the common will of Bristolians. From the start of the Civil War, when the wearing of party colours was banned, there was a deep hostility to the breaking of unity. Each group protested that only they could restore civic unity, and sought to appropriate the institutions and symbols which expressed such unity. The Tories played up church and king elements in Bristol's civic life, while their opponents played up anti-Catholic traditions and freemen's rights. Many of these themes retained their vitality until the 1760s, as popular politics, at least, continued to be conducted on the lines of Cavaliers versus Roundheads or Williamites versus Jacobites. For most of the eighteenth century the Whigs had the advantage of controlling the Corporation, and so the official expression of civic feeling. But this was balanced by the Tories' power in the parishes. They used the parishes to organize ever more sophisticated election-eering, based on the parishes but with a city-wide steering committee, the Steadfast Society. The Whigs were forced to respond with their Union Club, and both sides tried to influence the public by civic events, developing ties with guilds and others, and modelling their own public events as closely as they could on the pattern of civic processions. The Tories also exploited to the full the fact that Colston, the great benefactor, was an ardent Tory.

Gradually, during the eighteenth century, these issues of election-eering and charity began to oust the more traditional elements of civic ceremony as the key means of appealing to the Bristol public. By the 1690s, as I have mentioned, Tories and Whigs were vying for favour by establishing new institutions for social reform, such as the Corporation of the Poor, charity schools and the like.[44] From the mid-eighteenth century public meetings became increasingly important, together with associated addresses, petitions and instructions to MPs, as a means of marshalling Bristolian feeling, and the newspapers began to carry an important role. As Bristol grew larger and the range of interest groups within it more complex, so the older forms of civic expression, centred on the Corporation and civic ritual, grew less capable of expressing the desired range of meanings, and societies and pressure groups emerged to address Bristolians directly on particular issues. These new forms of community politics have a modern ring, and their emergence in towns is often hailed as the first stirring of a genuine urban, middle-class consciousness. In Bristol one might date this to the time of the American Revolution, and to those associated with Edmund Burke's campaign in 1774. Many of the leaders of both political sides were themselves increasingly unsympathetic to the rowdy and public forms of politics needed to maintain popular support, and were keen to avoid elections.[45] As Steve Poole argues in his essay, a vision of civic culture emphasizing its ordered nature was being developed in this period.

But it would be a mistake to underestimate the capacity of the older civic traditions I have been describing. They continued to appeal to both radicals and conservatives. During the 1770s the Wilkites and supporters of Burke's colleague Cruger, himself a former Tory, exploited all the earlier Tory tactics to win public support, including ringing the bells, civic processions and the like. Cruger might have found an excellent campaign manager in Thomas Chatterton, had he not committed suicide in 1770. Chatterton used his myths about medieval Bristol, run by charitable merchants and pious priests, as a means to satirize and undermine the complacency of the Bristol he saw around him. But by one of the ironies of history, after his death his forgeries were taken up by William Barrett, who used them in his *History*, published in the portentous year 1789, to create an intensely conservative view of Bristol, which suited an establishment eager to associate Bristol with loyalty to church and crown.[46] Perhaps this can stand as a final tribute to the protean power of Bristol pride.

Notes

1   R. Davies, ed., *Life of Marmaduke Rawdon* (Camden Society, o.s. 85, 1863), 173. Two useful accounts are: P. T. Marcy, *Eighteenth-Century Views of Bristol and Bristolians*, (BHA, 16, 1966) based on his 'A Chapter in the History of the "Bristol Hogs": A Social and Economic History of Bristol, 1740-1780' (unpublished PhD thesis, Claremont Graduate School, 1964); J. H. Bettey, *Bristol Observed* (Bristol, 1986). It is not possible to document all the sources for the arguments made here: for fuller details see J. Barry, 'Cultural Life of Bristol 1640-1775' (unpublished DPhil thesis, University of Oxford, 1985), chap. 7 and, in particular id., 'Provincial Town Culture: Urbane or Civic?', in J. Pittock and A. Wear, ed., *Interpretation and Cultural History* (Basingstoke, 1991), 198-234 and id., 'The History and Antiquities of the City of Bristol: Chatterton in Bristol', *Angelaki*, 1, (1993/4), 55-81.

2   W. Barrett, *History and Antiquities of the City of Bristol* (Bristol, 1789), 66-7.

3   *Gentleman's Magazine*, 8 (1738), 603-4; H.M.C. 64 Verulam, 249; W. Barrett, *Proposals for Publishing a History of Bristol* (Bristol, 1788).

4   D. H. Sacks, 'Trade, Society and Politics in Bristol 1500-1640' (unpublished PhD thesis, Harvard University, 1977; published New York, 1985); D. H. Sacks, *The Widening Gate: Bristol and the Atlantic Economy, 1450-1700* (Berkeley, 1991); K. Morgan, *Bristol and the Atlantic Trade in the Eighteenth Century* (Cambridge, 1993).

5   P. McGrath, ed., *Records relating to the Society of Merchant Venturers of Bristol in the Seventeenth Century* (BRS, 17, 1952); id., ed., *Merchants and Merchandise in Seventeenth-Century Bristol* (BRS, 19, 1955).

6   E. Martin and B. Pickard, eds, *Six Hundred Years of Bristol Poetry* (Bristol, 1973); J. W. D. Powell, *Bristol Privateers and Ships of War* (Bristol, 1930), 140-1. For literature see G. Lamoine, *La Vie Litteraire de Bath et de Bristol*, 2 vols (Lille, 1978); J. Barry, 'The Press and the Politics of Culture in Bristol, 1660-1775', in J. Black and J. Gregory, eds, *Culture, Politics and Society in Britain, 1660-1800* (Manchester, 1991), 49-81.

7   D. S. Taylor with B. S. Hoover, eds, *The Complete Works of Thomas Chatterton*, 2 vols (Oxford, 1971); D. S. Taylor, *Thomas Chatterton's Art* (Princeton, 1978); Marcy, *Eighteenth-Century Views*.

8   For one example among countless sermons on this theme see, H. Waterman, *Sermon Preached before Guardians of Poor* (Bristol, 1699).

9   W. Minchinton, ed., *Politics and the Port of Bristol in the Eighteenth Century* (BRS, 23, 1963); D. H. Sacks, 'The Corporate Town and the British State: Bristol's Little Businesses, 1625-41', *Past and Present*, 110 (1986), 69-105, reprinted in J. Barry, ed., *The Tudor and Stuart Town* (1990), 297-333; P. McGrath, *The Merchant Venturers of Bristol* (Bristol, 1975); P. T. Underdown, 'Edmund Burke Commissary of his Bristol Constituents', *EHR*, 73 (1958), 252-69.

10   J. Whitson, *Farewell to the World and Its Vanities* (ed. Thomas Ford) (1729), v-vi; R. C. Latham, ed., *Bristol Charters, 1500-1899* (BRS, 12, 1947).

11   J. Latimer, *Annals of Bristol in the Seventeenth Century* (n.p., 1900); J. Latimer, *Annals of Bristol in the Eighteenth Century* (n.p., 1893). See D. H. Sacks, 'Celebrating Authority in Bristol 1475-1640', in S. Zimmermann and R. Weissman, eds, *Urban Life in the Renaissance* (Newark, Del., 1989), 187-223; J. Barry, 'Popular Culture in Seventeenth-Century Bristol', in B. Reay, ed., *Popular Culture in Seventeenth-Century England* (Beckenham, 1985), 59-90.

12   Barry, 'Provincial Town Culture', 212-13.

13   Sacks, 'Corporate Town'.

14   A. Hooke, *A Dissertation on the Antiquity of Bristol* (1748), iii-iv; J. Barry, 'The Politics of Religion in Restoration Bristol', in T. Harris, P. Seaward and M. Goldie, eds, *The Politics of Religion in Restoration England* (Oxford, 1990), 163-90; id., 'Provincial Town Culture', 217, 221-2.

15   G. Shelton, *Dean Tucker and Eighteenth-Century Economic and Political Thought* (1981); J. G. A. Pocock, *Virtue, Commerce and History* (Cambridge, 1985), chap. 9; Barry, 'Provincial Town Culture', 220-1; Barry, 'History and Antiquities', 74-5.

16   M. Liversidge, *Bristol High Cross* (BHA, 42, 1978).

17   *Gentleman's Magazine*, 13 (1743), 496-7; J. Wood, *A Description of the Exchange of Bristol* (Bath, 1745); Barrett, *History*, 461-4. The best introduction to Bristol's civic ritual is E. Fawcett and E. Ralph, eds, 'Mugleworth's Diary', *TBGAS*, 61 (1939), 224-68 (the civic sword-bearer's diary for the 1720s).

18   Barrett, *History*, 66-7, 73-80, 95-7; 'A Citizen', *A Short Historical Account of Bristol Bridge* (Bristol, 1759); 'A.Y.' in *FFBJ*, 19 Apr. 1760.

19   The changing topography is discussed in Sacks, 'Trade, Society and Politics'; P. Slack, 'The Local Incidence of Epidemic Disease: The Case of Bristol, 1540-1650', in id., ed., *Plague Reconsidered* (Matlock, 1977), 49-62; A. Gomme, M. Jenner and B. Little, *Bristol: An Architectural History* (1979); E. Baigent, 'Economy and Society in Eighteenth-Century English Towns: Bristol in the 1770s', in D. Denecke and G. Shaw, eds, *Urban Historical Geography* (Cambridge, 1988), 109-24 and id., 'Assessed Taxes as Sources for the Study of Urban Wealth', *Urban History Yearbook* (1988), 31-48, both based on E. Baigent, 'Bristol Society in the Later Eighteenth Century' (unpublished DPhil thesis, University of Oxford, 1985); C. B. Estabrook, 'Urban and Rustic Bristol: Social Spheres and Cultural Ties in an English City and its Hinterland, 1660-1780' (unpublished PhD thesis, Brown University, 1991), chap. 1.

20   V. Waite, *The Bristol Hotwell* (BHA, 1, 1960). For the idea of an 'urban renaissance' see P. N. Borsay, *The English Urban Renaissance: Culture and Society in the Provincial Town, 1660-1770* (Oxford, 1989).

21   BRO, Common Council Proceedings, July 1733; Barrett, *History*, 82-113, 294; Latimer, *Eighteenth-Century Annals*, 223; Barry, 'History and Antiquities', 71.

22   J. Barry, 'The Parish in Civic Life', in S. Wright, ed., *Parish, Church and People* (1988), 152-70.

23   J. Barry, 'Cultural Patronage and the Anglican Crisis: Bristol, c.1689-1775', in J. Walsh et al., eds, *The Church of England, c.1689-c.1833* (Cambridge, 1993), 191-208; Barry, 'History and Antiquities'.

24   For example, Barrett, *History*, 58, 243, 278-9, 295, 339, 387-8, 449, 579-80.

25   J. W. Raimo, 'Spiritual Harvest: the Anglo-American Revival in Boston, Massachusetts and Bristol, England, 1739-42' (unpublished PhD thesis, University of Wisconsin, 1974); Barry, 'Parish in Civic Life'.

26   *An Account of the Hospitals, Almshouses and Public Schools in Bristol* (Bristol, 1775);

Barrett, *History*, esp. 610-23; T. J. Manchee, ed., *Bristol Charities*, 2 vols (Bristol, 1831); W. K. Jordan, 'Forming of the Charitable Institutions of the West of England', *American Philosophical Society Transactions*, n.s. 50, pt 8 (1960); Barry, 'Cultural Life', 33-6, 178-81.

27 Barry, 'Popular Culture', 74-6; id., 'Cultural Life', 136-7, 313; M. Fissell, *Patients, Power and the Poor in Eighteenth-Century Bristol* (Cambridge, 1991); id., 'Charity Universal? Institutions and Moral Reform in Eighteenth-Century Bristol', in L. Davison et al., eds, *Stilling the Grumbling Hive: The Response to Social and Economic Problems in England 1689-1750* (Stroud, 1992), 121-44; J. Barry, ed., 'The Society for the Reformation of Manners 1700-5', in J. Barry and K. Morgan, eds, *Reformation and Revival in Eighteenth-Century Bristol* (BRS, 45, 1994), 1-62; J. Barry, '"Begging, Swearing and Cursing": The Reformation of Manners and the Politics of Religion in Bristol, 1689-1715', in id., *Religion in Bristol, 1640-1775* (forthcoming).

28 H. More, *Essays on Various Subjects* (1777); id., *Thoughts on the Importance of the Manners of the Great* (1788).

29 Barry, 'History and Antiquities', 60-3.

30 A. S. Catcott, *The Antiquity and Honourableness of the Practice of Merchandize* (Bristol, 1744). Cf. W. Goldwin, *The Honourableness, Usefulness and Duty of Merchants* (Bristol, 1715); *The Bristol Merchants Triumphant* (n.d., c.1733) A. Hooke, *Bristollia* (1748), preface; play prologue reprinted in *Oracle and Country Advertiser*, 31 Aug. 1745; essays in *FFBJ*, 22-29 Aug. and 3-10 Oct. 1767.

31 E. Gander and F. Ware, 'The Heraldry of Some of the Citizens of Bristol between 1662 and 1683', *TBGAS*, 30 (1907), 273-82, together with many reports on heraldic devices found in homes reported in the same journal; T. F. Fenwick and W. C. Metcalfe, *Visitation of the County of Gloucestershire, 1682-3* (Exeter, 1884); G. D. Squibb, ed., *The Visitation of Somerset and the City of Bristol 1672* (Harleian Society, n.s., 11, 1992).

32 For the 'Ancient and Honourable Society of Free and Accepted Masons' see A. C. Powell and J. Littleton, *History of Freemasonry in Bristol* (Bristol, 1910); Barry, 'Cultural Life', 171, 177, 179-81, 315.

33 D. Defoe, *A Tour Through the Whole Island of Great Britain* (revised edn, 1778), vol. 2, 235-53, at 239.

34 Sacks, 'Trade, Society and Politics', 228-35, 495-504, 752 et seq.; J. R. Holman, 'Apprenticeship as a Factor in Migration: Bristol, 1675-1726', *TBGAS*, 97 (1979), 85-92; A. Yarborough, 'Geographical and Social Origins of Bristol Apprentices, 1542-65', *TBGAS*, 98 (1980), 113-30; id., 'Apprentices as Adolescents in Sixteenth-Century Bristol', *Journal of Social History*, 13 (1979), 67-82; J. Vanes, *Education and Apprenticeship in Sixteenth-Century Bristol* (BHA, 52, 1982); I. K. Ben-Amos, 'Failure to Become Freemen: Urban Apprentices in Early Modern England', *Social History*, 16 (1991), 154-72; id., 'Service and the Coming of Age of Young Men in Seventeenth-Century England', *Continuity and Change*, 3 (1988), 41-64; id., *Adolescence and Youth in Early Modern England* (New Haven and London, 1994).

35 Barry, 'Cultural Life', 172, 181, 317.

36 I. K. Ben-Amos, 'Women Apprentices in the Trades and Crafts of Early Modern Bristol', *Continuity and Change*, 6 (1991), 227-52; the reports of the celebrations of Queen Anne's coronation in Bristol Central Library, Bristol Collection, 9167 under 1701, reprinted in *FFBJ*, 5 Sept. 1761; *Two State Martyrs* (1643), 9; R. Purnell et al., *Church of Christ in Bristol* (1657), 21, 47; *Bristol Weekly Intelligencer*, 16 June 1750.

37 Barry, 'Popular Culture', 73-4.

38 Barry, 'Cultural Life', 319-21. See, for example, the elaborate rituals associated with the mock execution of Stephen Fecham, reported in *Gloucester Journal*, 28 March 1732

and, in more detail, in Bodleian, MS Gough Somerset 2, fos 166, 169.

39   See Steve Poole's chapter in this volume on this theme; Barry, 'Politics of Religion', 168-9.

40   See refs in n.9 and P. McGrath, *John Whitson and the Merchant Community of Bristol* (BHA, 25, 1970); R. H. Quilici, 'Turmoil in a City and an Empire: Bristol Factions 1700-75' (unpublished PhD thesis, University of New Hampshire, 1976), 140-84; W. Minchinton, 'The Merchants of Bristol in the Eighteenth Century', in *Sociétés et Groupes Sociaux en Aquitaine et en Angleterre* (Bordeaux, 1979), 185-200; K. Morgan, 'Bristol West India Merchants in the Eighteenth Century' *TRHS*, 6th ser., 3 (1993), 185-208; Barry, 'Cultural Life', 323-4.

41   J. Barry, 'Bourgeois Collectivism: Urban Association and the Middling Sort', in J. Barry and C. Brooks, eds, *The Middling Sort of People: Culture, Society and Politics in England 1550-1800* (Basingstoke, 1994), 84-112.

42   See, e.g., *Case of Creditors of J. G. Pedley* (Bristol, 1783), introduction; Sacks, *Widening Gate*.

43   Barry, 'Cultural Life', 324-38. A composite picture of Bristol's political history from c.1600-1800 can be obtained from: Sacks, 'Corporate Town'; id., *Widening Gate*; id., 'Bristol's "Wars of Religion"', in R. C. Richardson, ed., *Town and Countryside in the English Revolution* (Manchester, 1992), 100-29; Barry, 'Politics of Religion'; Barry, '"Begging, Swearing and Cursing"'; Quilici, 'Turmoil in a City'; L. Colley, *In Defiance of Oligarchy* (Cambridge, 1982), 138-40, 166-7; N. Rogers, *Whigs and Cities* (Oxford, 1989), chap. 8; P. T. Underdown, 'The Parliamentary History of the City of Bristol 1750-1790' (unpublished MA thesis, University of Bristol, 1948); J. E. Bradley, *Religion, Revolution and English Radicalism* (Cambridge, 1990), chaps 6-7; J. A. Phillips, *The Great Reform Bill in the Boroughs*, (Oxford, 1992), chap. 2; Steve Poole, 'Popular Politics in Bristol, Somerset and Wiltshire 1791-1805' (unpublished PhD thesis, University of Bristol, 1993).

44   See above n. 27.

45   W. R. Savadge, 'The West Country and the American Mainland Colonies' (unpublished DPhil thesis, University of Oxford, 1973); P. T. Underdown, *Bristol and Burke* (BHA, 2, 1961).

46   Barry, 'Cultural Life', 337-8; Barry, 'History and Antiquities'.

THE ECONOMIC DEVELOPMENT OF BRISTOL, 1700-1850

Kenneth Morgan

Visitors to Bristol in the eighteenth century were impressed by the commercial vitality of the city. Bristol was 'the greatest, the richest, and the best port of Trade in Great Britain, London only excepted', and traded 'with more entire independency upon London than any other town in the country'.[1] Bristolians were remarkable for their 'sharp and hard dealings'.[2] Even the clergy, it was claimed,

> talk of nothing but trade and how to turn a penny ... all are in a hurry, running up and down with cloudy looks and busy faces, loading, carrying and unloading goods and merchandises of all sorts from place to place; for the trade of many nations is drawn hither by the industry and opulency of the people.[3]

Eighteenth-century historians of Bristol concurred that the growth of the city and the port stemmed from trading advantages found in its citizens and location.[4] The port was also central to the city's industrial evolution, for much handling of raw materials and processing of manufactured goods associated with trade and shipping took place around the quays in the city centre. Many Bristolians participated in industrial ventures as well as in trade. Merchant partners in the local brewing industry, for instance, were involved in glassmaking, distilling, sugar refining, and the confectionery and tobacco industries, while Bristol shipowners and merchants invested in copper and brass works and gunpowder mills in North Somerset.[5]

The prosperity of Bristol centred around its thriving merchant community, which had an elite society, the Society of Merchant Venturers, as its vehicle for lobbying MPs on economic and political issues.[6] West India merchants and planters were the richest sector among Bristolians; they were exceptionally cohesive as a group and their fortunes were substantial by provincial standards.[7] The wealth of Georgian Bristol was manifested in other ways. After 1750, Bristol became a significant provincial banking centre with partners in private banks frequently drawn from the local mercantile and industrial elite.[8] By the time of the American Revolution, several wealthy parishes in the centre of the city – All Saints, Christ Church, St Ewen, St Mary-le-Port, St Nicholas and St Werburgh – were associated with the work and residence of domestic and overseas traders.[9] The prosperity of the city was reflected in the increased number of published maps, plans and directories that listed prominent businessmen.[10] The increase in the wealth of Bristol led to topographical expansion and new building schemes in industrial suburbs and middle-class residential areas such as Clifton and Redland.[11] Numerous merchants made sufficient money to invest in country houses and land in the immediate environs of the city and farther afield.[12] Yet by the end of the Georgian era Bristol had undergone a sharp decline in prosperity. Matthews's *Bristol Directory* in 1828 noted that 'Bristol for centuries ranked as the second city in England in respect of riches, trade and population; but the present extent of its foreign commerce will bear no comparison with that of the port of Liverpool; and it appears to be exceeded in population by the manufacturing town of Manchester.'[13]

The demography, commerce and industry of Bristol experienced significant change between the late Stuart period and the early Victorian era, and its economic significance declined within a national context. In 1700 Bristol, with approximately 20,000 inhabitants, was the third largest city in England after London and Norwich. By the 1730s, Bristol overtook Norwich to become the second city in the land. By 1800, with a population of some 60,000, Bristol was only the sixth largest British city (but larger than any of the five leading English provincial cities of 1700). Half a century later the city's population was some 137,000 and it had slipped further down the league table of British urban centres to seventh position.[14] Bristol's status as a port experienced a similar trend. In 1700 Bristol was the second-largest port in the kingdom. A century later it had fallen to eighth place among the outports in vessels, tonnage and men.[15] By 1855, Bristol was the sixth largest English port in the coastal trade but only the twelfth largest in overseas trade.[16]

The relative demographic and commercial eclipse of Bristol has been investigated by historians seeking to analyse the city's economy in the eighteenth and nineteenth centuries. There is, however, no consensus over the extent of the decline, its timing, or its causes. This is partly because some economic indicators we would like to have (especially caches of business records) have not survived in abundance; partly because it is always difficult to discuss the economic development of a particular place within a changing national context; partly because historians have tended to write either about the eighteenth- or the nineteenth-century parts of the story but not both; and partly because Bristol's changing economic status is a complex matter. For some, Bristol's economic decline was primarily commercial. William Hunt was perhaps the first historian to express this view. By 1800, he argued, Bristol was at its commercial height but before long it entered a period of decline owing to the shift of commerce to the north-west of England, the rapid rise of Liverpool, the national drawbacks of Bristol as a port, the decline of the local West India trade, and heavy dock dues that drove away trade from the city.[17] A. J. Pugsley emphasized Bristol's over-commitment to the West India trade in the early nineteenth century as a factor inhibiting capital from being put into local enterprises, but he provided little evidence to prove his assertion.[18] W. E. Minchinton and Alan F. Williams independently noted that the decline of the port began towards the end of the eighteenth century but was induced more by developments outside Bristol and its hinterland (notably the shift in the economic centre of gravity to the north-west) than by the situation at Bristol itself.[19] Martin Daunton and David Large have suggested that lack of sufficient development in Bristol's hinterland was a root cause of Bristol's relative commercial decline.[20]

In recent years, three separate analyses have appeared of the problem under discussion. Bernard Alford argued that the first signs of Bristol's economic decline appeared with the problems of the port, notably expensive dock dues. To the technical problems of port improvement were added the over-dependence of traders on West India and Irish commerce, the declining national importance of industries in the hinterland, and the apathy and inefficiency of a mercantile elite that influenced local businesses to the extent that, by the 1830s, 'these men were to a degree unable and to a degree unwilling to promote the necessary kinds of change and adaptation to meet such difficulties.'[21] In contrast to this interpretation, Brian Atkinson considers that Bristol's economic decline in the first half of the nineteenth century was influenced more by secular developments such as changes in trading patterns and technological advance rather than by complacency and lack of enterprise. He does not regard business conservatism as a fundamental factor in Bristol's decline.[22] Charles Harvey and Jon Press have recently supported a more optimistic view of Bristol's economic performance in the nineteenth century. They point to the long-term resilience of many industries in and around the city, and emphasize that Bristol was much more than just a decaying maritime centre.[23]

To evaluate which approach best fits Bristol's economic development from 1700 to 1850, this essay examines the problems associated with the port and trade of Bristol, the merchant community, the various industries in and around the city, and weighs up these endogenous factors with exogenous developments. An attempt is made to place Bristol's changing economic fortunes within a regional and national context. When making comparisons with other ports and their industries and hinterlands, particular emphasis is laid on developments at Liverpool and Glasgow, which were Bristol's leading competitors among the west-coast outports and towns that initially lagged behind Bristol in population, commerce and industry but overtook it during the century after 1750. An analysis of Bristol's fluctuating economic fortunes from the late Stuart period until the mid-Victorian era is useful generally for the light thrown on the integration of different sectors of the local and national economy.

Throughout our period, Bristol's economic life experienced major problems because of the failure to modernize the port. Ships entering the River Avon from the Bristol Channel had to contend with 7 miles of winding river, fast currents, fitful winds and an exceptional tidal range of 45 feet before reaching the quays in the city centre. Many ships came to grief while passing Horseshoe Bend or were stranded in the narrow gorge by St Vincent's Rock. In the heart of the port shipping congestion was already a problem by the early eighteenth century. It became worse as the volume of trade and size of ships increased. Many people realized that the port needed improvement. Responsibility for doing this lay with the Society of Merchant Venturers, which leased the quays from the city. Unfortunately, the changes they made did not solve the situation. By 1712 the Society had extended the quay wall along the River Frome and had erected cranes. A decade later they had built a wharf on Welsh Back for loading corn and other goods from market boats and had constructed a separate quay on St Augustine's Back for timber and naval stores. These developments, however, did not match the need for accommodation. A wet dock was built at Sea Mills between 1712 and 1717, but merchants considered it too far from the city and so it was little used. The Merchant Venturers' lease to run the port was renewed in 1764 on condition that further improvements were made. They duly extended the quay on the east bank of the Frome, constructed a new quay on the Grove and on St Augustine's Back on the west bank of the same river, and lengthened the quay on the north bank of the Avon to Welsh Back. In 1770 they purchased William Champion's dock, built on the right bank of the Avon near Rownham five years earlier. But none of these schemes provided a safe anchorage at a time when, with expanding trade, it was crucial for Bristol to cope with a larger volume of shipping.[24]

Various schemes were suggested for improving the port in the last third of the eighteenth century, but none got off the ground. In 1767, William Champion suggested that a floating harbour should be built to enable large vessels to use the port with ease. This would be constructed by building lock gates across the Avon at its confluence with the Frome. The opponents of port improvement, including influential members of the Merchant Venturers and the Common Council, stated that the costs would be at least double the £30,000 Champion suggested. The proposals were therefore dropped. A spate of other port improvement schemes proposed between 1787 and 1793 came up against a Corporation and Society of Merchants reluctant to fund the projects and opposed to change.[25]

The situation continued to deteriorate and, after much procrastination, it was agreed that William Jessop's report of 1802 should be implemented. This recommended the creation of a Floating Harbour in the centre of Bristol and the digging of a New Cut or course for the Avon. Jessop revised his scheme in 1803, and was appointed chief engineer for the Floating Harbour. Working under the auspices of the Bristol Dock Company, formed by Act of Parliament in 1803, he was responsible from that date for the operation of the port. The harbour was built between 1804 and 1809. A huge dock of over 70 acres, it was a significant engineering achievement that has become a permanent recognizable feature of the port of Bristol. It included an entrance in Rownham Meads of 4 acres (the Cumberland Basin) with two locks at the western end; the exclusion of spring tides from the Floating Harbour; the installation of further locks at Totterdown and Engine Mills; the construction of a new channel at Trim Mills (i.e. Bathurst Basin); and the building of the New Cut and a feeder canal linking up with the old river. The whole project took longer to construct and cost far more than the £212,000 anticipated. It did not solve the problem of port congestion. Though ships in the Float were now able to stay upright at all states of the tide, the harbour was costly to maintain because it tended to silt up. The Bristol Dock Company had to find £580,000 in capital by 1809 for construction of the harbour, and only recouped some of this money by bringing in extra dues on ships and foreign goods as well as feeder canal tolls.[26]

Soon there were widespread complaints about the high level of duties on shipping and trade at Bristol. Comparisons were made with cheaper rates charged elsewhere. Merchants using the port of Bristol had to pay town dues, mayor's dues, water bailiff's fees, quay warden's fees, corn treasurer's fees, various dues owed to the Merchant Venturers (for wharfage, tonnage, carriage, cannage, cranage and plankage) as well as the sums owed to the Bristol Dock Company.[27] Public agitation over this situation was led by the Bristol Chamber of Commerce, formed in 1823 to provide united action by the business community against the high dues. A paper drawn up by the Chamber in 1823 showed that the charges on 44 selected imports would be £515,608 at Bristol, £231,800 at Liverpool, £210,098 at London and £147,587 at Hull.[28] By presenting carefully prepared estimates, the Chamber of Commerce revealed Bristol's unfavourable position. As a body it proved much more vigorous in its campaigns than 'a self-interested Corporation and a lethargic and complacent Society of Merchant Venturers'.[29] In 1835, the Chamber's annual report noted that Bristol's customs charges were still expensive; dues for articles of high value (including brandy, rum, tobacco, sugar and wine) were more than double the rate at Liverpool.[30] In that year, the City Corporation ordered a large reduction of the town dues, which were wholly abolished for exports.[31] In 1836 a committee was set up by the City Council, the Merchant Venturers, the Chamber of Commerce and the Great Western Steamship Company to look into harbour grievances.[32]

Several engineers attempted to improve the problems of tidal scouring, lockage and silting at the port. Foremost among their achievements was Brunel's redesign of the south entrance lock to the Cumberland Basin, which increased its width from c.35 to 54 feet and enabled ships to enter the harbour at half-tide.[33] But the problems of congestion and high dock dues continued. Symptomatic of the problems was the fate of Brunel's two famous vessels, the S.S. *Great Western* and the S.S. *Great Britain*. The former, a timber-hulled paddle steamer of some 1340 tons, could not use the Floating Harbour and had to lie at Kingroad, a safe anchorage near the mouth of the Avon. Yet the Bristol Dock Company demanded full payment of port dues for the ship, so after 1842 it was moved entirely to Liverpool. The *Great Britain*, a screw-propelled iron steamer, was placed immediately at Liverpool because it was too large for the port of Bristol.[34] By maintaining an upriver site, Bristol could not accommodate large ships attempting to use the Avon. This problem was not surmounted even after the city docks were transferred to the Corporation in 1848, when Bristol was the most expensive port in Britain.[35] Suitable sites for dock elaboration did not emerge until the late 1870s with the geographical shift of the port down the Avon to the confluence with the Bristol Channel and the construction of deep water docks at Avonmouth and Portishead.

The situation at Liverpool was very different partly because it had a deep water estuary frontage and access to the Irish sea, but also because the city corporation there invested large sums of money in port development and helped to build five wet docks on the Mersey during the eighteenth century. The pace of dock construction at Liverpool quickened thereafter. Between 1811 and 1825 dock water space on the Mersey increased by 80 per cent.[36] Better organization and finance of the docks at Liverpool stimulated the rise of Merseyside even if they cannot be claimed as indispensable to the growth of Liverpool's trade.[37] These developments were paralleled at Glasgow where, from the late seventeenth century onwards, considerable expense and civic initiative led to the improvement of docks at Port Glasgow, then the headport and principal customs station on the Clyde.[38]

Problems with her port were only one factor in Bristol's relative economic decline; difficulties also emerged in overseas trade. Extensive trading did, of course, occur. Bristol's foreign trade rose considerably in absolute terms between 1700 and 1850, as figures cited below will show. Bristolians traded with British ports and with the Severn Valley basin, making use of coasting vessels, flat-bottomed trows and small wherries; there was extensive trade with Ireland; commerce continued with many European regions from the Mediterranean to the Iberian Peninsula and from the Baltic to France; and substantial growth occurred in trade with the wider Atlantic world. Among Bristol exports were window glass, bottles, beer, cider, Hotwell water, refined sugar, copper and brassware, wrought iron and leatherware plus hardware and metalware from the industrial west midlands and textiles, primarily woollens, from a number of English regions. Vessels bound across the Atlantic sometimes also took cargoes of convicts and indentured servants and picked up provisions at southern Irish ports. On the import side, Bristol took sugar, rum, molasses, tobacco, rice, deerskins, wine, brandy, oil, fruit, dairy produce, linen, yarn, timber and naval stores (pitch, tar, turpentine).[39] Many commodities were carried in vessels built at various sites in the dock area of the city, where they received stiffening in their construction to make them 'shipshape and Bristol fashion'.[40]

But, as with the port, there was relative decline: the trade of other ports increased at a faster rate than Bristol's commerce. The changing position of Bristol's foreign trade is difficult to pin down precisely, nevertheless, because of the varied and incomplete statistics available. And while there was decline, it was more in terms of volume – the capacity of shipping using the port – than of value. The tonnage of merchant shipping owned at Bristol rose from 15,500 in 1709 to 19,000 in 1751 and to 43,000 in 1792. This absolute increase is quite impressive for the second half of the century, but it was accompanied by relative decline. Bristol slipped from being the second English outport in terms of merchant shipping owned in 1709 to fourth in 1751 and to seventh in 1792, even though throughout the 1700s she was the largest port in the south-west for shipownership.[41]

A similar story emerges from statistics on the volume of Bristol's merchant shipping. Table 1 shows that the rank order of Bristol dropped markedly for inward and outward overseas shipping in the period from 1709 to 1841, and that despite an absolute growth in volume over the course of the eighteenth century, there was a slight reduction in tonnage in the first half of the nineteenth century. Accurate details on the volume of coastal shipping using the port of Bristol are unavailable for most of the eighteenth century, but the number of coastal vessels leaving Bristol rose from 449 in 1698/9 to 453 in 1752 and to 575 in 1788/9.[42] Table 2 shows that the volume of coastwise shipping at Bristol increased a good deal between 1791 and 1855, but was again accompanied by relative decline.

TABLE 1: Tonnage of foreign-going vessels entering and clearing Bristol in selected years, 1709-1841, with their rank order among English/British ports.

	Vessels inwards		Vessels outwards	
	Tons	Rank Order	Tons	Rank Order
1709	19,800	2	21,200	4
1751	30,400	5	27,300	6
1791	79,000	4	71,000	5
1841	75,000	8	70,000	10

Note: The rank order for 1709 and 1751 is for English ports. The rank order for 1791 and 1841 is for British ports.

Sources: 1709, 1751: BL, Add. MS. 11, 256, cited in P. J. Corfield, *The Impact of English Towns, 1700-1800* (Oxford, 1982), Table VI, 40. The figures are in tons burden. 1791, 1841: PRO, Customs 17/13 and BPP, 1842 (259), cited in G. Jackson, 'The Ports', in M. Freeman and D. Aldcroft, eds, *Transport in Victorian Britain* (Manchester, 1988), Table 19, 246-7.

TABLE 2: Tonnage of coastal vessels entering and clearing Bristol in selected years, 1791-1855, with their rank order among British ports.

	Vessels inwards		Vessels outwards	
	Tons	Rank Order	Tons	Rank Order
1791	103,000	4	68,000	6
1841	311,000	4	258,000	10
1855	400,600	4	340,000	10

Sources: 1791, 1841: PRO, Customs 17/13 and BPP, 1842 (259), cited in G. Jackson, 'The Ports', in M. Freeman and D. Aldcroft, eds, *Transport in Victorian Britain* (Manchester, 1988), Table 20, 248-9. 1855: BPP, 1856 LVI, 384-5, cited in P. Bagwell and J. Armstrong, 'Coastal Shipping' in M. Freeman and D. Aldcroft, eds, *Transport in Victorian Britain*, Table 6, 176.

In terms of the value of trade, however, Bristol did rather better. Between 1750 and 1757, annual average customs duties at Bristol amounted to £289,365, comfortably ahead of Liverpool's £201,862. In 1781 Bristol's gross customs receipts comprised £243,370, just ahead of Liverpool, the second outport, with £241,587.[43] The amount accruing to Bristol from customs duties increased very significantly by the first half of the nineteenth century. Between 1833 and 1848, gross customs receipts for inward and outward trade at Bristol averaged around the £1 million mark.[44] In 1856 gross customs duties at Bristol amounted to £1,193,000, making it third in the value of customs collected at British ports.[45] These revenues were boosted by the high number and range of dutiable goods imported into Bristol, for it was on the import rather than the export side that the money accumulated: exports paying duty regularly amounted to only between a quarter and a third of the gross customs receipts collected at Bristol between 1833 and 1848.[46]

The statistics cited point to a paradox: a port whose trade grew absolutely in the period 1700-1850 yet declined relatively, but one where the value of trade increased and retained its comparative position. It is worth exploring Bristol's trade in more depth to examine the implications of these findings for the city's overall economic growth in the Georgian and early Victorian eras. Three crucial aspects of Bristol's commercial connections were the Americanization of its trade, its significance as an industrial centre, and its role as a metropolis of the west, all of which enabled her to maintain a prominent place among the outports in the eighteenth century; by 1850, they had not developed as fully as had been hoped.

Bristol had been interested in Atlantic voyages for a couple of centuries by 1700, as the widening gate of commercial activities brought its merchants into ever-increasing contact with the Atlantic wine islands and the maritime world of North America, the West Indies and west Africa.[47] The eighteenth century saw the heyday of Bristol's role as a significant Atlantic maritime centre at a time when British trade was becoming Americanized in terms of commodities, shipping and geographical orientation. Already by the 1720s Bristolians were trading with all 13 British colonies on the north American mainland, with the Canadian maritime provinces, with the British sugar islands in the Caribbean, and with the slave coast of west Africa from the River Gambia to Angola. But there were entrepreneurial problems associated with two of the most significant Atlantic trades in which Bristol was involved – tobacco and slaves. These difficulties certainly hindered Bristol's commercial prosperity with regard to its rivals, and it can be argued that they had a negative influence on the city's overall economic development.

Bristol's tobacco trade with the Chesapeake region remained static from 1722 until 1773, with imports remaining around the 4 million lb. mark; it declined after the American Revolution to annual levels of no more than 2.5 million lb. by 1800. By 1855 tobacco imports had slipped further to 1.8 million lb. Bristol was passed in the level of tobacco imports by her main provincial rivals, by Glasgow in the 1720s, by Liverpool in 1738, and by Whitehaven in 1739.[48] Bristolians specialized in high quality, sweet scented tobacco from the York and James rivers in Virginia, tobacco that was more suited to the home market than the coarser, darker oronoco leaf exported from other parts of Virginia and Maryland. Liverpool and (especially) Glasgow merchants forged ahead of Bristol, however, by adopting more aggressive marketing strategies, by shipping tobacco more efficiently, by using factors on the spot in the Chesapeake to purchase tobacco directly, by catering for the re-export market in France and Holland, which was much bigger than the home market, and by claiming drawbacks for this reshipped tobacco.[49]

Bristol's commitment to the triangular trade was substantial. It dispatched some 2114 slaving vessels between the end of the Royal African Company's monopoly in 1698 and the abolition of the British slave trade in 1807. Bristol pulled ahead of London, its main early rival in the slave trade, only to be overtaken by Liverpool in the 1740s. Bristol's share of the volume of the English slave trade (in terms of total tonnage) declined from 42 per cent in 1738-42 to 24 per cent in 1753-57 to ten per cent in 1773-77 and to a mere one per cent in 1803-07.[50] By the end of the British slave trade, Bristol's involvement in the Guinea traffic had virtually finished; after 1807 she played a prominent role in the palm oil trade with west Africa but there was no overlap with slave trading.[51]

Various reasons account for Bristol's declining role as a slave-trading port. Liverpudlians apparently paid their captains and crew less than their equivalents at Bristol; they adopted more aggressive marketing strategies; they sold slaves at levels that undercut Bristol; they smuggled slaves effectively from the Caribbean islands to Spanish America; and they had the geographical advantage in wartime of sending ships into the north Atlantic around the north of Ireland, a relatively safe route, whereas Bristolians dispatched ships into the Bristol Channel and the English Channel, where they were prime targets for enemy privateers.[52] In both the tobacco and slave trades, the lost ground was never recovered. Some Bristol slave merchants converted their vessels to privateers in wartime in search of new profits; they were often successful, but privateering only brought short-term financial gains because it involved the capture of prize cargoes without any commodity trade to stimulate labour and industry in the port of Bristol.[53]

The major success story among Bristol's Atlantic trades in the eighteenth century was the sugar trade with Jamaica, the Leeward and the Windward Islands. Specializing in the most valuable single commodity imported into Britain in the period 1670-1820, Bristol remained the leading British outport in the sugar trade until overtaken by Liverpool in 1799. Sugar imports at Bristol rose significantly during the eighteenth century to reach almost 270,000 cwt in 1800; they were 502,817 cwt in 1848 and 630,354 cwt in 1855.[54] This was the most lucrative trade at Bristol and one in which the greatest accumulation of wealth occurred. Leading firms – the Brights, the Meylers, the Miles family, the Daniels, the Protheroes and the Pinneys – were prominent in this commerce. They weathered eighteenth-century wars successfully; they catered for a home market in which there was an ever-rising demand for sugar; and they were an unusually close-knit group of businessmen connected by social and family ties.[55] Yet various contemporary comments suggest that this merchant group had lost much of their competitive edge by around 1800, by which time they were content to rest upon their laurels and over-committed to West India trade. A visitor to Bristol in 1790 found that the leading traders were 'principally rich respectable West India Merch[an]ts who do not go out of their usual line of business and averse to speculation'.[56] John Wesley, a frequent visitor to Bristol, felt generally that Bristolians were renowned for their love of money but also for their love of ease.[57]

Bristolians continued to trade significantly in West India commerce, however, because many were both merchants and planters, and therefore much of their capital was tied up in Caribbean mortgages, annuities and plantations and was not all that easy to repatriate. Charles Pinney, a leading Bristol merchant, stated in 1830 that five-eighths of the city's trade was with the West Indies. Three years later another Bristol merchant declared that Bristol would be a fishing port without the West India trade.[58] Caribbean-linked trade at Bristol was intertwined with sugar refining, shipbuilding, several port industries, the employment of seamen and a number of maritime crafts, and was central to Bristol's economic livelihood. Bristol had followed the trend towards specialization at the outports in the eighteenth century, with Glasgow concentrating on tobacco, Liverpool on slaves, and Bristol on sugar.[59] The West India connection continued at Bristol well into the nineteenth century.

Sugar importation was linked to sugar manufacture at Bristol's refineries, and this reminds us that, as Sir Frederick Eden put it, the city was 'not more a commercial than a manufacturing town'.[60] Much industrial activity was based around the port, though the restricted size of the quays and docks set limits to the development of a large-scale urban infrastructure. Bristol's main industries were sugar refining, rum distilling, glass manufacture, zinc, copper and brass-ware, lead works, and smaller enterprises in bricks and tiles, soap boiling, leather, earthenware, porter brewing, the storage and blending of wine and sherry, ceramics, cocoa and chocolate manufacture, tobacco manufacture and clay tobacco-pipe making.[61] These industries tended to cater more for the home market than for foreign sales. In terms of their connections with overseas trade, they were always more prominent on the import than on the export side. By the 1850s, Bristol was mainly an import centre taking foodstuffs and general commodities; by the 1930s, it was still predominantly an import centre specializing in foodstuffs, timber and petroleum.[62] Bristol remained relatively insignificant as an export centre throughout its modern history, ranking fifteenth among British ports for exports in 1857.[63]

The industrial history of Bristol was dominated by concentration on a specialized group of manufactures linked heavily to the port's trade, especially on the import side. Over time internal business problems arose with several of these industries as well as stiff external competition. Two of Bristol's leading industries, sugar refining and glassmaking, experienced problems in the first half of the nineteenth century. The number of sugar refineries in Bristol numbered 20 from 1724 to 1780. Seven refineries closed their doors during the 1780s owing to shortages in the supply of raw sugar. Despite a revival in prosperity between 1790 and 1812, the number of local refineries plummeted thereafter.[64] Increased world supplies of sugar, a fall in prices and a rise in import duties squeezed profits in sugar sales after the end of the Napoleonic Wars. The number of sugar refineries at Bristol fell from 14 in 1818 to six in 1838.[65] By 1852, only two were left. To some extent, this pattern reflected national trends, because there was a secular decline in the number of sugar refineries nationwide: more than 200 refineries operated in Britain in the first half of the nineteenth century, but only 16 remained by 1900.[66] The sugar houses of Bristol also declined in the nineteenth century because of adherence to outdated techniques and poor adaptation to mechanization. Steam power only came to Bristol at Conrad Finzel's refinery on the Counterslip when the West India trade was already in decline.[67]

In and around the city at the beginning of the eighteenth century, there were five glasshouses making bottles, one making bottles and window glass, and three producing flint glass and ordinary glass. This was the largest concentration of glasshouses (i.e. glass-making kilns) outside London. Bristol emerged as a centre for this industry because it was an established trading centre with accessible raw materials for making glass (sand, limestone and red lead). It also possessed local supplies of coal. Bristol's glass industry flourished for much of the century, with the manufacture of flint glass for bottles, coloured decorative glass, notably the famous 'Bristol blue', and opaque white glass. Problems for the industry occurred, however, in the 1770s: a number of glasshouses came up for sale and some of the best-known glass-makers and merchants withdrew from business after the War of Independence terminated trade with the important North American market. Towards the end of the century, a heavy excise on flint glass plus a tax on bottles also hindered the productivity of glass-making.[68] By 1800 only four glasshouses were still working in Bristol. By 1838, with six glasshouses out of 106 throughout England, Bristol was no longer an important centre for glass-making.[69] Bristol's glass-making industry did not show the vitality of west Lancashire, and lacked its advantages towards concentration of production in terms of raw materials, transport, associated industries and a rapidly growing market in its region.[70]

Several of Bristol's other industries declined in the nineteenth century as a result mainly of fiercer competition from other parts of the country. This can be illustrated by reference to soapmaking, pottery production, and the manufacture of brass and copper. In 1722 and 1739 some 62 Bristol freemen were listed as soapmakers or soapboilers. By the early nineteenth century, Bristol soapmaking firms made candles as well as olive-oil based soaps for personal use and cheaper tallow-based soaps for household cleaning. The main markets for soap at this stage were still local. The industry flourished at Bristol until the 1820s and 1830s, when it was the third largest soap producing centre in the United Kingdom, following London and Liverpool and accounting for c.3600 tons of soap out of an annual national production of around 45,000 tons. But Bristol's annual production remained static at about 3500 tons of soap between 1819 and 1841 while its share of the national market fell from around 8 per cent to 4.8 per cent.[71]

Potteries flourished at Temple Back and Redcliff in the eighteenth and nineteenth centuries. They were notable for producing Bristol Delft, a distinctive white and coloured glaze on an earthenware body. For a few years in the 1770s, high quality porcelain manufacture was established at Bristol before the patent rights were sold to a Staffordshire company. This marked the beginning of decline for Bristol's potteries, most of which were too small to compete with large-scale pottery production, with its economies of scale, in north Staffordshire.[72] Besides pottery, Hanoverian Bristol was a notable centre for the non-ferrous metal industries. Industrial archaeologists have located over 30 sites in and around the city that were once copper works. The Warmley Company, which smelted copper ore to make brass and also produced spelter, was the most advanced establishment of its kind by 1769, when its owner went bankrupt.[73] Yet the small brass and copper works in the Bristol area became less competitive as newer and larger concerns elsewhere took a greater share of the national market. Bristol was too distant from supplies of copper ore from Anglesey and failed to use steam power and compete with Birmingham's metal trades in adapting to industrialization.[74]

Several of Bristol's other industries performed quite well over the long term, but were either unimportant in a national context in the period 1700-1850 or reached their height in the later nineteenth and early twentieth centuries. The common brewing firm, Georges, was founded in the late eighteenth century, when Bristol had a large and growing market for beer. Faced with an increase in the malt tax and beer duties and rapidly rising raw material prices in the war years between 1793 and 1815, Georges expanded their product line from a reliance on porter to pale ale and began to tap new markets. The firm underwent steady growth from 1815 to 1830; the removal of beer duties and the move towards free trade, coupled with rising working-class incomes, stimulated demand thereafter; and by the 1860s Georges was producing beer for publicans. But Georges was never more than a medium-sized provincial firm.[75]

The cocoa and chocolate business was a success story in the long term in Bristol. Founded by Joseph Fry in the 1750s, the manufacture of cocoa and chocolate grew in the second half of the eighteenth century. By 1843 J. S. Fry & Son was producing 28 different types of chocolate and cocoa; its sales rose tenfold from £11,041 in 1836 to £102,747 in 1867, taking advantage of the doubling of per capita cocoa consumption in Britain between 1841 and 1868. This increase in the firm's trade was based partly on internal improvements, such as more sophisticated manufacturing techniques, but also resulted from rising real incomes, lower rates of duty on cocoa and falling prices.[76] The foundation of Mardons and Robinsons in the city in the mid-1840s reflected a growing demand for the printing and packaging of mass-produced goods made in Bristol, such as boots and shoes, cigarettes, pipe tobacco, cocoa and chocolate. But the printing revolution in Bristol was a phenomenon of the second half of the nineteenth century and of the twentieth century.[77]

Tobacco manufacturing began in Bristol in the seventeenth century, but flourished particularly after the formation in 1786 of the firm that eventually became known as W. D. & H. O. Wills. By the turn of the nineteenth century, tobacco manufacture was a small industry catering to snuff takers and smokers of strong tobacco in clay pipes; cigarettes were a later development. Though there were some hard times in Wills's's industrial development in the 1810s and 1820s, tobacco manufacturing survived in Bristol long after tobacco imports had declined. It was an enterprise requiring neither major technical changes nor large supplies of coal and iron. By 1900 Wills was the largest producer of tobacco goods in the United Kingdom, but most of the firm's growth came after 1850.[78]

This broad-based manufacturing activity was very much linked to exports and imports at Bristol, and hence to the fortunes of the port, though of course these industries also supplied the home market. What Bristol lacked was heavier industrial development or a large staple industry, such as coal, cotton or iron, that could transform the industrial fortunes of the port by being linked to an interlocking network of services and commercial organizations, such as happened in Liverpool and south Lancashire.[79] The only serious development of cotton manufacture at Bristol was the Great Western Cotton factory at Barton Hill, opened in 1838. This establishment survived financial crises to maintain production and moderate prosperity until World War One, but it was an isolated attempt to develop textile manufacture in Bristol.[80]

By having its trade and industry so geared towards imports, Bristol developed as more of a consumption centre than as an entrepôt for foreign trade, like Liverpool or Glasgow, with a surplus of mass-produced industrial goods for export. Specialization in sugar for so many years helped to boost sugar refineries, rum distilling, brewing and cocoa and chocolate manufacture but probably retarded growth in other sectors of the urban economy. A consumption centre based around processing of tropical produce and the distributing trades failed to generate significant multiplier effects. It did not require the structural economic change necessitated by other ports concerned with a growing volume of exports to worldwide markets, ports that tapped an expanding demographic and industrial hinterland based on higher rates and younger ages of marriage, rising wage labour in factories, and productivity gains in industry.

If Bristolians failed to capitalize fully on their Atlantic trading connections and industrial development, they also did not expand the city's role as a 'metropolis of the west.' Bristol remained a significant magnet for the trade and industry of a wide region between 1700 and 1850. Linked by the River Avon to the Bristol Channel and the ports of the south-west in one direction, and to the river and canal network of the Severn and Wye basins in the other, Bristol dispatched goods via the coasting trade to a region that comprised five largely rural counties – Gloucestershire, Somerset, Wiltshire, Devon and Cornwall. Improvements to turnpike roads in and around Bristol, with their associated carriers' networks, stimulated inland trade. By 1750 Bristol already had 96 separate carriers sending wagons to 117 different towns. With these transport links, Bristol was the main market for the agricultural produce of the area, taking wheat from the west midlands, barley from Wales and Gloucestershire, peas and beans from Gloucestershire, cider and perry from Devon and Herefordshire, and dairy products from various areas.

Bristol also served as the main market for industrial raw materials. In some instances it served as a distribution point, as in the case of

Cornish tin en route to tinplate works in South Wales. But it also provided raw materials for local industries, including Cornish tin and Anglesey copper for local brass and copper works, unrefined sugar from the West Indies for local sugar refineries, and tobacco for processing in snuff mills. Bristol's role as the chief market of the west was manifest in the thriving bustle of its fairs, where many commercial deals were struck. The second function of Bristol as a 'metropolis of the west' was as a source of capital for its hinterland. Much of this finance was poured into copper, tin and ironworks in South Wales, into the Coalbrookdale ironworks in Shropshire, and into shares in canals and turnpikes. Bristol also became a regional centre of provincial banking, marine insurance and fire insurance.[81]

While Bristol's hinterland continued to contribute to the city's role as a metropolis of the west, it failed to grow sufficiently to enable Bristol to assume national economic importance by 1850. This may well have been the true Achilles' heel holding back much of Bristol's economic development. Liverpool's hinterland industrialized much more rapidly in the late eighteenth and early nineteenth centuries and was better integrated with transport services via canals and river navigations, enabling home demand and foreign demand to be harnessed together effectively.[82] At Glasgow, too, the city's hinterland was integrated towards the urban centre. This resulted from improvements to the Clyde navigation and by the construction, by 1820, of the Forth and Clyde canal, linking Glasgow to the Firth of Forth and enabling her businessmen to trade both eastwards and westwards in Scotland.[83] Part of the problem in the Bristol area was that much of the hinterland consisted of scattered agricultural settlements that lacked the demographic growth and large labour force associated with industrialization. In the Somerset-Wiltshire border area in the late eighteenth century, only the small coalfield area around Radstock and Midsomer Norton experienced a genuine upturn in demographic and economic fortunes, with the exploitation of new coal seams helping to provide employment opportunities and economic growth. Communities experiencing no significant structural change were demographically stable and lacked the springs of growth. They included the textile area of Bradford-upon-Avon, Trowbridge, Westbury, Warminster, Frome and Radstock, and the agricultural parishes with a varied farming economy between the coalfield and the textile districts.[84]

But even the industrial parts of Bristol's hinterland had mixed fortunes. The Mendip leadmining industry had declined throughout the eighteenth century. It lingered on in a semi-moribund condition until 1850, when it became extinct. The industry was highly under-capitalized and its metal, though good for shot and bullets, was unsuitable for sheeting and plumbing and inferior to that of Yorkshire, Derbyshire and Flintshire.[85] Zinc mining on the Mendips also came to an end by the early nineteenth century. The Somerset coalfield increased its output and demographic growth in the later eighteenth century, but was dwarfed by the growth of coalmining in other regions, notably South Wales, the west midlands, south Lancashire and the north-east. The Somerset coalfield's share of United Kingdom coal output fell from 3.5 per cent of production in 1800 to much less than 1 per cent by 1850. The shift of industry towards the major coalfields benefited the hinterlands of Cardiff, Liverpool, Newcastle and Sunderland more than Bristol.[86]

Textile production also slumped in the Bristol area. The west of England woollen industry had passed its peak by 1800 and failed to make the adjustment to power-driven mills sufficiently quickly to compete with woollen manufacture in other regions, notably Yorkshire. The West Country industry concentrated on high quality products rather than on the cheaper woollens and worsteds produced in the West Riding.[87] The failure of the Wiltshire woollen industry to introduce machinery before the 1790s, an inability to secure improved transport for the carriage of coal from nearby coalfields, and inadequate marketing when compared with the aggressive salesmanship of the West Riding of Yorkshire's woollen industry all suggest that there was a deficiency of entrepreneurship in the Bristol area in the classic period of the early industrial revolution.[88] The decline of the gunpowder, copper, brass and glass industries in north Somerset after 1800 resulted not just from growing industrial competitiveness in the North but from a loss of vigour on the part of Bristol merchants who had been important investors in these enterprises.[89]

It has been argued that Bristol was not so adaptable to industrial change as Liverpool and that, by contrast with their north-western rival, Bristolians invested more in South Wales than in their own hinterland by the late eighteenth century.[90] Certainly, Bristolians invested substantially in the ironworks, copper smelting and tinplate works of South Wales and were active in the industrial development of Cardiff.[91] Whether this was a case of over-investment, draining capital away from Bristol, is impossible to prove from the surviving evidence, but it is a strong possibility. It was not the case that sufficient capital for investment was unavailable at Bristol, for it was a provincial city where mercantile fortunes were accumulated. In the decade after 1783, with business confidence boosted by access to cheap credit and peacetime recovery, Bristolians were very active in investments in speculative building schemes in Bristol and Clifton and in the canal mania of the early 1790s. But the historian of these activities, J. R. Ward, has suggested that this is a case of idle assets finding employment in a situation, not replicated at Liverpool, in which comparable investment opportunities were lacking in Bristol's own hinterland.[92]

On top of these difficulties, Bristol's transport connections with her hinterland lagged behind those of Liverpool. A contemporary observer noted in 1774 that 'if we consider domestic trade, or inland Navigation, Bristol is without rival.'[93] But this situation changed rapidly. Many canal schemes were drawn up for the Bristol area in the 1790s, but only three systems were constructed. The Thames and Severn Canal was completed by 1789 but the Wiltshire and Berkshire branch canal, linking the Thames and Avon rivers, only began to operate in 1809, and the Kennet and Avon Canal was not completed until the following year.[94]

An integrated system of canals never came into being in the Bristol region. By 1800 Liverpool was the focus of a group of waterways superior to those serving other English ports. Already by the 1790s Liverpool was connected to the Severn via a network of waterways; certainty of dispatch, along with lower transport costs and a shorter distance from the industrial midlands, gave it the advantage over Bristol for securing metalware and hardware from the Birmingham and Black Country area.[95]

How, by way of conclusion, should we weigh up the relative importance of endogenous and exogenous factors in Bristol's economic development between 1700 and 1850? Clearly, there is much evidence of entrepreneurial decline in and around the city in the second half of this period, both in trade and industry. Bristol's merchants were outpaced in the tobacco and slave trades during the eighteenth century because their business decisions did not match the vigour, enterprise and marketing skills of Liverpudlians and Glaswegians. Bristol's potteries and copper and brass manufacture also suffered from poor entrepreneurial decisions; and there is further evidence of this problem in hinterland industries such as gunpowder, woollens and glassmaking. Though it would be superficial to label Bristol's businessmen entrepreneurial failures, the sheer number of scattered examples of failing to meet internal business problems cannot be ignored.

For several historians, the crux of the matter is the complacency of the successful West India merchant elite and its influence on policy-making at Bristol. The Bristol West India interest was heavily represented on Bristol's old Corporation by the early 1830s.[96] Many of its members, through representation in the Society of Merchant Venturers, were firmly opposed to dealing quickly with the need to improve the port and to cut high port dues. Hunt considered that the West India merchants were imbued with a club spirit that permeated the entire Bristol merchant community, the Dock Company and the Common Council.[97] Richard Pares agreed with this view. He concluded, from a detailed examination of the Pinneys and their business associates, that such a comfortable, cosy clique would not want to wage commercial war with one another.[98] This line of argument has been extended by W. G. Neale to include the merchants, shipowners and manufacturers of Bristol as a whole, whom he characterizes as an inbred oligarchy opposed to fresh avenues of enterprise.[99] Alford has broadened this view by stating that the whole commercial ethos of Bristol by the 1830s was stagnant, and that there may have been a case of third generation entrepreneurial failure.[100]

A more optimistic view of entrepreneurial performance in early nineteenth century Bristol has been taken by Atkinson, who states correctly that insufficient evidence is currently available to prove the third generation failure thesis. Moreover, in several respects the 1830s showed considerable vision on the part of Bristol businessmen and engineers in relation to the creation of the Great Western Railway, Temple Meads station, the Great Western Steamship Company and the Great Western Cotton factory. Bristol West India merchants, deterred from new investments in the Caribbean in the era of slave emancipation, were among the investors in these enterprises. In Peter Marshall's succinct phrase, the original Bristol subscribers to the Great Western Railway were willing 'to replace slaves by sleepers'. That not all of these enterprising schemes of the 1830s were successful is not so much an example of commercial sluggishness, but merely of mistakes and lack of resources.[101] Harvey and Press have also taken a more optimistic view of Bristol's industrial performance. They note the success of innovations in light industries such as Frys and Wills and make the valid point that, although Bristol was the national centre for no single industry, it was home to a diverse set of industries, some of which did well in the long run and helped to produce a strong local and regional economy more in tune with recent economic historians' views on the evolutionary process of industrial and economic change in modern Britain.[102] The existence of various smaller industries in Bristol in the first half of the nineteenth century presumably helped labour to be mobile during periods of economic recession and absorbed with relative ease in prosperous times.[103]

It is noteworthy, however, that the industries which survived well at Bristol in the later nineteenth century and into the twentieth century were those that were independent of the West India connection.[104] For, as we have seen, though the West India merchants did deploy their capital in enterprising ways – in railway shares, sugar refining, banking and investments in South Wales – they were not tempted to put large amounts of money into exports because of the import-led nature of Bristol's overseas trade and the lack of available opportunities for substantial export growth in the city's hinterland. The West India merchants acted in a rational way. While it is fair to accuse them of sluggishness over port improvements, they certainly did not lack enterprise; it was just that the enterprises with which they were mainly concerned were not the ones most likely to lead to rapid structural economic change at Bristol and the building of an integrated infrastructure in the city and its hinterland.

While recognizing, in terms of endogenous factors, that entrepreneurial weaknesses existed at Bristol by the 1830s without there being a wholly stagnant ethos, many local problems faced by the Bristol business community were not susceptible to easy solutions; more powerful exogenous factors were present that boosted the regional growth of the north-west and the west midlands and the industrial areas of Scotland more than the Bristol region. It is difficult to see what Bristolians could have done to improve the port fully in the centre of the city to overcome problems of congestion and tidal range, though one could argue that the movement of facilities to the mouth of the Avon should have come earlier. Certainly municipal control of the docks in itself, though hard-won, was not the solution to the problem. Yet the lack of textile growth in and around Bristol, the limited use of steampower, the relatively poor quantity and quality of available local coal, the lack of a fully-fledged transport system, a predominantly agricultural hinterland, and the rise of urbanization elsewhere in the country – all factors central to the birth of industrialization in Britain – meant that by 1850 Bristol was no longer, as in 1700, a centre of national economic importance but one of local and regional significance. By the mid-Victorian period, it had not generated linkages to transform the city from a commercial to a fully industrial centre. Though Bristol experienced relative economic decline in the period under discussion, the adaptability of its modest range of industries and its need to continue as a consumption centre for a large urban cluster enabled it to undergo steady, gradual, if rather unexciting, economic growth in the later Victorian period and beyond.

Notes

1   D. Defoe, *A Tour Through the Whole Island of Great Britain* (1724-26), quoted in P. T. Marcy, *Eighteenth Century Views of Bristol and Bristolians* (BHA, 16, 1966), 14.

2   Entry for 6 Sept. 1777, in A. Oliver, ed., *The Journal of Samuel Curwen, Loyalist*, 2 vols. (Cambridge, Mass., 1972), 399-400.

3   T. Cox, *Magna Britannia et Hibernia: Somersetshire* (1720-31), quoted in W. E. Minchinton, *The Port of Bristol in the Eighteenth Century* (BHA, 5, 1962).

4   J. Barry, 'The Cultural Life of Bristol 1640-1775' (unpublished DPhil thesis, University of Oxford, 1985), 301-02.

5   G. Channon, 'Georges and Brewing in Bristol', in C. Harvey and J. Press, eds, *Studies in the Business History of Bristol* (Bristol, 1988), 166, and B. J. Buchanan, 'Capital Investment in a Regional Economy: Some Aspects of the Sources and Employment of Capital in North Somerset, 1750-1830' (unpublished PhD thesis, University of London, 1992), 268-78, 281-2, 310-11.

6   W. E. Minchinton, 'The Merchants of Bristol in the Eighteenth Century', in *Sociétés et Groupes Sociaux en Aquitaine et en Angleterre* (Bordeaux, 1979), 185-200, and P. McGrath, *The Merchant Venturers of Bristol* (Bristol, 1975). For examples of the Merchant Venturers' lobbying see W. E. Minchinton, ed., *Politics and the Port of Bristol in the Eighteenth Century: The Petitions of the Society of Merchant Venturers 1698-1803* (BRS, 20, 1963).

7   K. Morgan, 'Bristol West India Merchants in the Eighteenth Century', *TRHS*, 6th series, III (1993), 185-208.

8   C. H. Cave, *A History of Banking in Bristol from 1750 to 1899* (Bristol, 1899) and P. Ollerenshaw, 'The Development of Banking in the Bristol Region, 1750-1914', in Harvey and Press, eds, *Studies in the Business History of Bristol*, 55-82.

9   E. Baigent, 'Economy and Society in Eighteenth-Century English Towns: Bristol in the 1770s', in D. Denecke and G. Shaw, eds, *Urban Historical Geography: Recent Progress in Britain and Germany* (Cambridge, 1988), 109-24, and id., 'Assessed Taxes as Sources for the Study of Urban Wealth: Bristol in the Later Eighteenth Century', *Urban History Yearbook* (1988), 31-48.

10   J. H. Bettey, *Bristol Observed: Visitors' Impressions of the City from Domesday to the Blitz* (Bristol, 1986), 80-1.

11   M. D. Lobel and E. M. Carus-Wilson, *Historic Towns: Bristol* (1975), 23; Walter Ison, *The Georgian Buildings of Bristol* (1952); Donald Jones, *A History of Clifton* (Chichester, 1992), chaps 4-9; A. Gomme, M. Jenner and B. Little, *Bristol: An Architectural History* (1979).

12   Minchinton, 'The Merchants of Bristol in the Eighteenth Century', 196; Morgan, 'Bristol West India Merchants in the Eighteenth Century', 201; P. K. Stembridge, *Goldney: A House and a Family* (Bristol, 1969); J. H. Bettey, 'From Quaker Traders to Anglican Gentry: The Rise of a Somerset Dynasty', *PSANS* (1992), 1-9; P. Bright, *Dr Richard Bright (1789-1858)* (1983), chap. 1; M. Elton, *Annals of the Elton Family: Bristol Merchants & Somerset Landowners* (Stroud, 1994); N. Kingsley, *The Country Houses of Gloucestershire, II, 1660-1830* (Chichester, 1992), 50, 108, 157, 234, 269, 291.

13   Quoted in Bettey, *Bristol Observed*, 105.

14   Lobel and Carus-Wilson, *Historic Towns: Bristol* (1975), 21; M. J. Daunton, 'Towns

and Economic Growth in Eighteenth-Century England', in P. Abrams and E. A. Wrigley, eds, *Towns in Societies: Essays in Economic History and Historical Sociology* (Cambridge, 1978), 266; H. A. Shannon and E. Grebenik, *The Population of Bristol* (Cambridge, 1943), 6, and B. R. Mitchell with P. Deane, *Abstract of British Historical Statistics* (Cambridge, 1962), 24. The nineteenth century population figures for Bristol include people living within the city boundaries established in 1835.

15   W. E. Minchinton, ed., *The Trade of Bristol in the Eighteenth Century* (BRS, 20, 1957), ix.

16   D. Large, ed., *The Port of Bristol 1848-1884* (BRS, 36, 1984), Table II, xiv.

17   W. Hunt, *Bristol* (Bristol, 1895), 208-09.

18   A. J. Pugsley, 'Some Contributions towards the Study of the Economic Development of Bristol in the Eighteenth and Nineteenth Centuries' (unpublished MA thesis, University of Bristol, 1921), chap. 7. Cf. C. M. MacInnes, 'Bristol', in C. Northcote Parkinson, ed., *The Trade Winds: A Study of British Overseas Trade during the French Wars, 1793-1815* (1948), 66, and id., 'The Port of Bristol' in H. A. Cronne, T. W. Moody and D. B. Quinn, eds, *Essays in British and Irish History in Honour of James Eadie Todd* (1949), 212-13.

19   Minchinton, 'The Port of Bristol in the Eighteenth Century', 157-8; A. F. Williams, 'Bristol Port Plans and Improvement Schemes of the Eighteenth Century', *TBGAS*, 81 (1962), 180.

20   Daunton, 'Towns and Economic Growth', 266-7; Large, *Port of Bristol*, ix.

21   B. W. E. Alford, 'The Economic Development of Bristol in the Nineteenth Century: An Enigma?', in P. McGrath and J. Cannon, eds, *Essays in Bristol and Gloucestershire History* (Bristol, 1976), 252-83, at 263.

22   B. J. Atkinson, 'An Early Example of the Decline of the Industrial Spirit? Bristol Enterprise in the First Half of the Nineteenth Century', *Southern History*, 9 (1987), 71-89.

23   C. Harvey and J. Press, 'Industrial Change and the Economic Life of Bristol since 1800', in Harvey and Press, eds, *Studies in the Business History of Bristol*, 1-32.

24   Minchinton, 'The Port of Bristol in the Eighteenth Century', 127-60; McGrath, *Merchant Venturers*, 150-69; MacInnes, 'The Port of Bristol', 204-05; Charles Wells, *A Short History of the Port of Bristol* (Bristol, 1909), 20-33; and G. Farr, 'Sea Mills Dock, Bristol', *Mariners' Mirror*, 35 (1939), 349-50.

25   For fuller details see Williams, 'Bristol Port Plans and Improvement Schemes', 138-88.

26   R. A. Buchanan, 'The Construction of the Floating Harbour in Bristol, 1804-9', *TBGAS*, 88 (1969), 184-204; Wells, *Short History of the Port of Bristol*, 34-53, and J. Lord and J. Southam, *The Floating Harbour: A Landscape History of Bristol City Docks* (Bristol, 1983).

27   W. G. Neale, *At the Port of Bristol: Volume One: Members and Problems 1848-1899* (Bristol, 1968), 5.

28   J. Latimer, *The History of the Society of Merchant Venturers of the City of Bristol* (Bristol, 1903), 236.

29   McGrath, *Merchant Venturers*, 294-303, at 294; J. Latimer, *The Annals of Bristol in the Nineteenth Century* (Bristol, 1887), 103-05; and G. Bush, ed., *Bristol and its Municipal Government, 1820-1851* (BRS, 29, 1976), 47-8.

30   *Annual Reports of the Bristol Chamber of Commerce*, 26 Jan. 1835, 15.

31   Latimer, *History of the Society of Merchant Venturers*, 244.

32   Neale, *At the Port of Bristol*, 5-7.

33   See three studies by R. A. Buchanan: 'I. K. Brunel and the Port of Bristol', *Transactions of the Newcomen Society*, 42 (1969-70), 41-55; *Nineteenth Century Engineers in the Port of Bristol*, (BHA, 26, 1971), and 'Brunel in Bristol', in McGrath and Cannon, eds, *Essays in Bristol and Gloucestershire History*, 230-2.

34 Buchanan, 'Brunel in Bristol', 243-4; G. Farr, *The Steamship Great Western*, (BHA, 8, 1963), and id., *The Steamship Great Britain*, (BHA, 11, 1965).

35 Large, *Port of Bristol*, vii. For the struggle between the City Council and the Dock Company over municipalization of the docks see Bush, *Bristol and its Municipal Government*, 165-73.

36 F. E. Hyde, *Liverpool and the Mersey: An Economic History of a Port, 1700-1970* (Newton Abbot, 1971), 10-15, 72-8; G. Jackson, 'The Ports', in D. H. Aldcroft and M. J. Freeman, eds, *Transport in the Industrial Revolution* (Manchester, 1983), 200-01, and J. Bird, *The Major Seaports of the United Kingdom* (1963), 281-2.

37 G. Jackson, *The History and Archaeology of Ports* (Tadworth, Surrey, 1983), 47-8.

38 J. R. Kellett, 'Glasgow', in M. D. Lobel, ed., *Historic Towns of the British Isles* (1969), I, 9.

39 For these developments see Minchinton, 'The Port of Bristol in the Eighteenth Century' and id., *The Trade of Bristol in the Eighteenth Century*; McGrath, *Merchant Venturers*, 124-49; K. Morgan, 'The Organization of the Convict Trade to Maryland: Stevenson, Randolph and Cheston, 1768-1775', *William and Mary Quarterly*, 3rd series, 42 (1985), 201-27; id., 'Bristol and the Atlantic Trade in the Eighteenth Century', *EHR*, 107 (1992), 626-50, and id., *Bristol and the Atlantic Trade in the Eighteenth Century* (Cambridge, 1993); C. M. MacInnes, *Bristol: A Gateway of Empire* (Bristol, 1939), 188-281; H. B. Jameson, 'Bonded Servants on the North American Continent in the Eighteenth Century: some new evidence from Bristol', *TBGAS*, 99 (1981), 127-40; A. Crawford, *Bristol and the Wine Trade* (BHA, 57, 1984), 20-7; S. McIntyre, 'The Mineral Water Trade in the Eighteenth Century', *Journal of Transport History*, n.s., 2 (1973-4), 4-6; P. T. M. Woodland, 'Bristol Merchants and the Overseas Trade in Cider c.1773-1818', *TBGAS*, 106 (1988), 173-88; P. Mathias, *The Brewing Industry in England, 1700-1830* (Cambridge, 1959), 193-4; W. R. Savadge, 'The West Country and the American Mainland Colonies, 1763-1783, with special reference to the Merchants of Bristol' (unpublished BLitt thesis, University of Oxford, 1952); R. H. Quilici, 'Turmoil in a City and an Empire: Bristol's Factions, 1700-1775' (unpublished PhD thesis, University of New Hampshire, 1976), and G. R. Cane, 'The Trade between Bristol and Ireland, 1791-1793' (unpublished MA thesis, University of Exeter, 1976).

40 G. Farr, *Bristol Shipbuilding in the Nineteenth Century* (BHA, 27, 1971); id., *Shipbuilding in the Port of Bristol* (Greenwich, 1977); and id., *Records of Bristol Ships 1800-1838* (BRS, 15, 1950).

41 BL, Add. MS. 11,255 and Add. MS. 38,432, cited in P. J. Corfield, *The Impact of English Towns, 1700-1800* (Oxford, 1982), Table V, 36-7. The figures are tons burden for 1709 and 1751 and measured tons for 1792.

42 W. E. Minchinton, 'Bristol – Metropolis of the West in the Eighteenth Century', *TRHS*, 5th series, 4 (1954), 71.

43 W. Barrett, *The History and Antiquities of the City of Bristol* (Bristol, 1789; facs. repr. 1982), 187; Liverpool Central Library, Holt and Gregson Papers, X, fos 276-7, duplicated in XIX, fos 99-100.

44 *Annual Reports of the Bristol Chamber of Commerce*, 1833-48.

45 Large, *Port of Bristol*, Table VII, xx.

46 Estimated from data in *Annual Reports of the Bristol Chamber of Commerce*.

47 D. H. Sacks, *The Widening Gate: Bristol and the Atlantic Economy, 1450-1700* (Berkeley, 1991).

48 J. M. Price and P. G. E. Clemens, 'A Revolution of Scale in Overseas Trade: British Firms in the Chesapeake Trade, 1675-1775', *JEcH*, 47 (1987), App. A, Tables 13 and 14, 39-

40; Large, *Port of Bristol*, Table VI, xix.

49 On these points see Morgan, *Bristol and the Atlantic Trade in the Eighteenth Century*, chap. 6; J. M. Price, 'The Rise of Glasgow in the Chesapeake Tobacco Trade, 1707-1775', *William and Mary Quarterly*, 3rd series, II (1954), 179-99; T. M. Devine, *The Tobacco Lords: A Study of the Tobacco Merchants of Glasgow and their Trading Activities c.1740-1790* (Edinburgh, 1975) and id., 'The Golden Age of Tobacco', in T. M. Devine and G. Jackson, eds, *Glasgow. Volume 1: Beginnings to 1830* (Manchester, 1995), 145-6.

50 D. Richardson, 'The Eighteenth-Century British Slave Trade: Estimates of its Volume and Coastal Distribution in Africa', *Research in Economic History*, 12 (1989), app., 185-95.

51 M. Lynn, 'Bristol, West Africa and the Nineteenth-Century Palm Oil Trade', *Historical Research: The Bulletin of the Institute of Historical Research*, 61 (1991), 359-74.

52 Morgan, *Bristol and the Atlantic Trade*, chap. 5; G. D. Ramsay, *English Overseas Trade during the Centuries of Emergence: Studies in some Modern Origins of the English-Speaking World* (1957), 156-7; D. Richardson, 'The Bristol Slave Trade in the Eighteenth Century' (unpublished MA thesis, University of Manchester, 1969), id., *The Bristol Slave Traders: A Collective Portrait* (BHA, 60, 1985), and id., *Bristol, Africa and the Eighteenth-Century Slave Trade to America, Vol. 1: The Years of Expansion 1698-1729, Vol. 2: The Years of Ascendancy 1730-1745, Vol. 3: The Years of Decline 1746-1769* (BRS, 38, 39, 42, 1986-90).

53 Morgan, *Bristol and the Atlantic Trade*, chap. 1; D. J. Starkey, *British Privateering Enterprise in the Eighteenth Century* (Exeter, 1990), 88-9, 101-2, 113, 121, 141, 165, 181, 200, 221, 271.

54 Morgan, *Bristol and the Atlantic Trade*, 189-90; Large, *The Port of Bristol*, Table VI, xix.

55 Morgan, *Bristol and the Atlantic Trade*, chap. 7, and id., 'Bristol West India Merchants in the Eighteenth Century'; R. Pares, *A West-India Fortune* (1950). The business activities of one prominent member of this group are illustrated in K. Morgan, ed., 'Calendar of Correspondence from William Miles, a West Indian merchant in Bristol, to John Tharp, a planter in Jamaica, 1770-1789' in P. McGrath, ed., *A Bristol Miscellany* (BRS, 37, 1985), 79-121.

56 Historical Society of Pennsylvania, Philadelphia, Robert Phillips to Phillips, Cramond & Co., 7 April 1790, Cramond, Phillips & Co. correspondence. See also University of Melbourne Archives, Parkville, Victoria, Australia, Bright & Milward to Henry Bright, 15 June 1773, box 16, Bright Family Papers.

57 Entry for 15 Sept. 1786 in N. Curnock, ed., *Journal of John Wesley*, 8 vols. (1909-16), VII, 209.

58 MacInnes, *Bristol: A Gateway of Empire*, 358, 370.

59 Price, 'Rise of Glasgow', 190.

60 F. M. Eden, *The State of the Poor*, 3 vols. (1797), II, 183.

61 Minchinton, 'The Port of Bristol in the Eighteenth Century', 133; R. A. Buchanan, 'Industry', in J. S. Moore, ed., *Avon Local History Handbook* (Chichester, 1979), 46-54; W. J. Pountney, *Old Bristol Potteries* (Bristol, 1920); G. Harrison, *Bristol Cream* (1955); I. C. Walker, *The Bristol Clay Tobacco-Pipe Industry* (Bristol, 1971); id., *Clay Tobacco Pipes, with particular reference to the Bristol Industry*, 4 vols. (Ottawa, 1977), vol. B, 451-759; B. Little, *The City and County of Bristol: A Study in Atlantic Civilization* (1954), 166-73; A. C. Powell, 'Glassmaking in Bristol', *TBGAS*, 47 (1925), 211-57; F. Buckley, 'The Early Glasshouses of Bristol', *Journal of the Society for Glass Technology*, IX (1925), 36-61; and studies cited in the footnotes below.

62 F. Walker, 'The Port of Bristol', *Economic Geography*, 15 (1939), 109-24.

63 Large, *Port of Bristol*, xv.

64   I. V. Hall, 'A History of the Sugar Trade in England with Special Attention to the Sugar Trade of Bristol' (unpublished MA thesis, University of Bristol, 1925), 68.

65   R. Stiles, 'The Old Market Sugar Refinery, 1684-1908', *BIASJ*, 2 (1969), 12.

66   A. Murray, 'A Staple Consumer Industry on Merseyside: Sugar Refining in the Nineteenth Century and the Emergence of Henry Tate and Company', in B. L. Anderson and P. J. M. Stoney, eds, *Commerce, Industry and Transport: Studies in Economic Change on Merseyside* (Liverpool, 1983), 62-4.

67   Little, *The City and County of Bristol*, 259. I. V. Hall, in a series of articles, has studied the fortunes of individual sugar refineries at Bristol: see esp. 'Whitson Court Sugar House, Bristol, 1665-1824', *TBGAS*, 65 (1944), 1-97, and 'The Daubenys: Part 1', *TBGAS*, 84 (1965), app. II, 137-40.

68   C. Weeden, 'The Bristol Glassmakers', in C. Witt, C. Weeden and A. Palmer Schwind, *Bristol Glass* (Bristol, 1984), 27-31; J. H. Bettey, ed., 'A Bristol Glassworks c. 1730', in McGrath, ed., *A Bristol Miscellany*, 15-20.

69   C. Weeden, 'The Bristol Glass Industry: its rise and decline', *Glass Technology*, 24 (1983), 251-5, and 'Bristol Glassmakers: their role in an emergent industry', *BIASJ*, 17 (1984), 24, 27.

70   B. W. E. Alford, 'The Flint and Bottle Glass Industry in the Early Nineteenth Century: A Case Study of a Bristol Firm', *Business History*, 10 (1968) 12-21; C. Weeden, 'The Ricketts Family and the Phoenix Glasshouse, Bristol', *Glass Circle*, 4 (1982), 84-101.

71   J. Somerville, *Christopher Thomas Soapmaker of Bristol: The Story of Christopher Thomas & Bros, 1745-1954* (Bristol, 1991), 14, 18, 30; S. J. Diaper, 'Christopher Thomas & Brothers Ltd.: The Last Bristol Soapmakers. An Aspect of Bristol's Economic Development in the Nineteenth Century', *TBGAS*, 105 (1987), 224, 226.

72   H. Owen, *Two Centuries of Ceramic Art in Bristol...* (1873); F. S. McKenna, *Champion's Bristol Porcelain* (Leigh-on-Sea, 1947); A. D. Selleck, *Cookworthy: A Man of No Common Clay* (Plymouth, 1978); R. Jackson, P. Jackson and R. Price, 'Bristol Potters and Potteries, 1600-1800', *Journal of Ceramic History*, 12 (Stoke-on-Trent, 1982); R. A. Buchanan and N. Cossons, *The Industrial Archaeology of the Bristol Region* (Newton Abbot, 1969), 149-50.

73   J. Day, *Bristol Brass: A History of the Industry* (Newton Abbot, 1973), and id., 'The Costers: Copper Smelters and Manufacturers', *Transactions of the Newcomen Society*, 47 (1974-76), 47-57; H. Hamilton, *The English Brass and Copper Industries to 1800* (2nd edn., 1967), 108-10, 154-6, 300; R. Jenkins, 'The Copper Works at Redbrook and at Bristol', *TBGAS*, 63 (1942), 145-67.

74   Buchanan & Cossons, *Industrial Archaeology of the Bristol Region*, 121.

75   Channon, 'Georges and Brewing in Bristol', 167-9, 171.

76   S. Diaper, 'J. S. Fry & Sons: Growth and Decline in the Chocolate Industry, 1753-1918', in Harvey and Press, eds, *Studies in the Business History of Bristol*, 33-8.

77   D. Bateman, 'The Growth of the Printing and Packaging Industry in Bristol, 1800-1914', in Harvey and Press, eds, *Studies in the Business History of Bristol*, 84, 94, 96, 103, and A. P. Woolrich, *Printing in Bristol* (BHA, 63, 1986), 9, 11.

78   B. W. E. Alford, *W. D. & H. O. Wills and the Development of the U.K. Tobacco Industry, 1786-1965* (1973).

79   F. Walker, 'The Industries of Bristol', *Economic Geography*, 20 (1946), 1.

80   S. J. Jones, 'The Cotton Industry in Bristol', *Transactions of the Institute of British Geographers*, 13 (1947), 66-79; Buchanan and Cossons, *Industrial Archaeology of the Bristol Region*, 137-9.

81   Minchinton, 'Bristol – Metropolis of the West', 69-89; T. S. Willan, 'The River Navigation and Trade of the Severn Valley, 1600-1750', *EcHR*, 8 (1937), 68-79; P. T. Marcy,

'Bristol's Roads and Communications on the Eve of the Industrial Revolution, 1740-1780', *TBGAS*, 87 (1968), 149-72.

82   J. Langton, 'Liverpool and its Hinterland in the late Eighteenth Century', in Anderson and Stoney, eds, *Commerce, Industry and Transport*, 1-25.

83   J. F. Riddell, *Clyde Navigation: A History of the Development and Deepening of the River Clyde* (Edinburgh, 1979), chaps 2-7; G. Jackson, 'New Horizons in Trade', in Devine and Jackson, eds, *Glasgow, vol. 1*, 220-1.

84   S. Jackson, 'Population Change in the Somerset-Wiltshire Border Area, 1701-1800: A Regional Demographic Study', *Southern History*, 7 (1985), 119-44.

85   J. W. Gough, *The Mines of Mendip* (1930), 157-205.

86   F. Walker, *The Bristol Region* (1972), 212-13.

87   Walker, *The Bristol Region*, 206-12; Jackson, 'Population Change', 119-44; K. G. Ponting, *The Woollen Industry of South-West England* (Bath, 1971), 39, 45; S. J. Jones, 'The Growth of Bristol', *TIBG*, 11 (1946), 77; J. de Lacy Mann, *The Cloth Industry in the West of England from 1640 to 1880* (Oxford, 1971), chap. 6.

88   B. J. Buchanan, 'Aspects of Capital Formation: Some Insights from North Somerset, 1750-1830', *Southern History*, 8 (1986), 88.

89   Buchanan, 'Capital Investment in a Regional Economy', 256-7; B. J. Buchanan and M. T. Tucker, 'The Manufacture of Gunpowder: A Study of the Documentary and Physical Evidence Relating to the Woolley Powder Works near Bath', *Industrial Archaeological Review*, 5 (1981), 185-202.

90   Daunton, 'Towns and Economic Growth', 267-9.

91   A. H. John, *The Industrial Development of South Wales, 1750-1850* (Cardiff, 1950), 8, 25, 31-2, 166; A. Raistrick, *Quakers in Science and Industry* (1950), 148-51, 213-14; R. O. Roberts, 'Dr John Lane and the Foundation of the Non-Ferrous Metal Industries in the Swansea valley', *Gower*, IV (1951), 19-24; W. E. Minchinton, *The British Tinplate Industry: A History* (Oxford, 1957), 18-19; M. Elsas, ed., *Iron in the Making: Dowlais Iron Company Letters, 1782-1860* (Cardiff, 1960), vii.

92   J. R. Ward, *The Finance of Canal Building in Eighteenth-Century England* (Oxford, 1974), 138-42, and id., 'Speculative Building at Bristol and Clifton, 1783-1793', *Business History*, 20 (1978), 3-18.

93   J. Campbell, *Political Survey of Britain* (1774), 147.

94   Walker, *The Bristol Region*, 229-30.

95   BRO, Bright MSS, Acc. 11168/2c, [Richard Bright], 'Draft of Particulars of the Trade of Bristol, 1788'.

96   Bush, *Bristol and its Municipal Government*, 24-5.

97   Hunt, *Bristol*, 209, 211.

98   Pares, *A West-India Fortune*, 212.

99   Neale, *At the Port of Bristol*, 31.

100   Alford, 'Economic Development', 262-6.

101   Atkinson, 'An Early Example of the Decline of the Industrial Spirit', 74-81; P. Marshall, *Bristol and the Abolition of Slavery: The Politics of Emancipation* (BHA, 37, 1975), 27; and G. Channon, *Bristol and the Promotion of the Great Western Railway* (BHA, 62, 1985).

102   Harvey and Press, 'Industrial Change and the Economic Life of Bristol', 1-28. Cf. for the nation N. F. R. Crafts, *British Economic Growth During the Industrial Revolution* (Oxford, 1985) and C. H. Lee, *The British Economy Since 1700: A Macroeconomic Perspective* (Cambridge, 1986).

103   These points were made in an untitled pamphlet by 'A Merchant', Dec. 1831, deposited at the Bristol Reference Lib., and cited in A. P. Hart, 'The Bristol Riots of 1831

and the Mass Media' (unpublished DPhil thesis, University of Oxford, 1979), 78-9.
104 See fn. 103.

TO BE A BRISTOLIAN: CIVIC IDENTITY AND THE SOCIAL ORDER, 1750-1850

Steve Poole

> Whenever convulsions take place in a community, they will almost always be traceable to one cause, namely, an unnatural state of society, arising from misgovernment[1]

It is surely no coincidence that contemporary history writing has become so preoccupied with ideas about past 'communities'. Against a background of social alienation, fracturing continents and puzzlingly non-ideological 'small wars', the historiography of our urban areas has embraced the rediscovery of civic identity with a ready enthusiasm. This essay attempts to show how such a concept may throw new light on our understanding of an old problem; the politics of public order at Bristol in the Age of Revolutions.

The terrible destruction of the 1831 reform riots has cast a formidable shadow over much writing on the Bristol crowd. Eyewitnesses to Jacobite rioting in 1714 had minimized the disturbance (despite fatalities) and drawn a clear line between the city's 'very good protestants' and the more culpable 'filthy ruffians' of Kingswood.[2] But the reality of 1831 made such distinctions ridiculous, for the working class had become infiltrated by 'the roughs and wastrels of adjoining countries ... ostensibly in search of work', whose disorderly nature had 'brought disgrace upon the fair name of this great city'.[3] A new generation of chroniclers absolved themselves from guilt by amplifying the barbarity of the lower orders. 'The violence of the Bristol mob had long been notorious,' indeed it was 'the most dangerous in England'.[4] To these Whiggish champions of modernity, the reform riots were the result of steadily mounting local antipathy between the citizens and their 'self-electing, secretive, inaccessible and extravagant' Corporation: 'The ruffian incendiary walked abroad in safety, but walked in safety only because men of all parties refused to rally round those in whom they could place no confidence.'[5] According to this meritocratic analysis, bourgeois consensus, police reform and a consequently tepid Chartist movement were all part of the happy result. Some twentieth century historians have done little to challenge this view. Bristol was either 'a turbulent port containing all the ingredients

76

for a riot', or a place where such serious disorders simply 'exemplify the persistence of older (pre-industrial), backward-looking patterns of behaviour'.[6]

It is small wonder then that the roots of social and political antagonism in Bristol seem to have become located solely in the bourgeois ideology of the Chamber of Commerce, a body founded in 1823 and deeply hostile to Corporate inertia over stagnating trade.[7] This essay will argue that the reform riots were not simply a consequence of the elite's stubborn refusal to embrace modernity, but of their failure to maintain social consensus around an idealized civic world; a world of reciprocal duties and shared aspirations hovering tentatively between collectivism and the free market. Indeed, between 1753 and 1831, serious public disorder outside election times is more noticeable by its absence than its frequency. This simple fact, which flies in the face of all the rhetoric about the Bristol 'mob', is largely incomprehensible without a proper understanding of the culture of the 'civis' and its role in averting social disturbance.

Responsibility for the maintenance of social order lay with the Corporation. In each of the city's 12 wards, an appointed magistrate and a volunteer chief constable supervised between seven and 30 regular volunteer day constables and a slightly smaller number of nightwatchmen. For crowd control, this skeleton force could be supplemented by the enrolment of special constables or the ad hoc *posse comitatus*, normally men from the middling orders whose presumed attachment to property was expected to be enough to make them leap to its defence. In practice, their relatively small numbers required consent at *both* ends of the constable's nightstick, as the refusal of some officers to police a Radical meeting in 1816, or their wholesale abdication during the reform riots was to show.[8] This is how matters remained until 1836 when a professional force of 227 waged, uniformed and properly equipped constables was installed in four new purpose-built police stations.[9]

In cases of emergency, militia regiments could normally be relied upon to restore order, but there were legal restraints upon their use at election times (when rioting was most likely) and few magistrates saw military action as much of a substitute for cultural hegemony. The mayor's request for military support to prevent Church and King riots in 1791 provoked his fellow magistrate George Daubeny to fear disturbance 'in consequence of the attention of the multitude being excited by the means taken to prevent it'.[10] Yet, when a Bristol crowd physically prevented the collection of tolls on the city bridge in 1793,

Daubeny was instrumental in ordering militia to the scene. The deaths of a number of respectable tradesmen, caused as the militia opened fire, did irreparable damage to relations between citizens and Corporation, and made magistrates more hesitant about military intervention in subsequent years.[11] Food rioting in 1795 went unchecked for 48 hours before soldiers were introduced, and in 1800 troops cleared a crowd before the Riot Act had been read because the magistrates failed to appear.[12]

In a city where crowds might physically resist impressment, and where even army enlistment had to be abandoned in 1794 because of the 'turbulent, riotous, and mutinous state' of recruits, the militia were not popular guests.[13] Neither could their reliability be guaranteed. The East Devon militia played a leading role in the 1795 food riot, and the Northamptonshire refused to fire when ordered to break up a mutiny amongst Irish Fencibles at Pill docks. Irish soldiers, continually 'repeating their situations and distresses to the common people here', were more a cause for concern than comfort to the authorities.[14] The Bristol Volunteers, the 'Home Guard' of the French Wars, promised greater security. Recruitment snowballed rapidly following the disclosure of French plans to raze the city to the ground in 1797, but officers were soon 'mortified' by their men's 'remissness and inattention to parade duty'.[15]

Major problems of law enforcement were centred upon deep-seated antagonisms between the city and its outlying areas. In 1729, the clothier Stephen Fechem fled the city when a Kingswood coroner found him liable for the manslaughter of several weavers from beyond Lawford's Gate, members of a crowd who had attacked his house during a wages dispute. The civil power, whose own forces had proved inadequate in preventing bloodshed, felt obliged to plead Fechem's case with central government.[16] Further judicial inactivity occurred in 1749 when a Kingswood crowd protesting against new turnpike tolls in the surrounding country attacked the city's Temple Gate in a bid to release prisoners taken the previous day. A sword-wielding Turnpike Commissioner, John Brickdale, took the law into his own hands and led a posse of tradesmen out of the gate and into a fierce sortie with colliers that would not be forgotten four years later when a similar but far more serious rupture took place.[17]

A large crowd of weavers and colliers stormed the city bridewell in 1753 to secure the release of a Kingswood community leader, Job Phipps, taken by the authorities in an initial skirmish over the price of bread a few days before. The 'very nervous and unavoidably agitated' mayor vacillated over the use of his small troop of Scots Greys and instead permitted a hastily convened force of armed tradesmen to conduct a disorderly rout which left four colliers dead and a trades- man taken back to Kingswood as a hostage. A Kingswood coroner subsequently found a case of unlawful killing against four of the Bristol middling sort, including John Brickdale. Fearing recrimina- tions, Brickdale quit his business and fled the city, leaving the Corporation with the costly and time-consuming task of overturning the verdict in the Court of King's Bench. Alarmingly, outrage at the tradesmen's behaviour had also resonated amongst the poorer classes *within* the city, for the mayor detected 'a strong inclination ... among the lower sort of our citizens to join (the rioters)' making containment 'too hard a task for our present force'.[18]

The 1753 episode was serious because it was directly caused by the administrative practice of the Corporate elite within the city bound- aries (in this case, over the regulation and control of the markets). Also, the unprecedented scale of its social violence had not only involved the Corporation in an unwanted lawsuit and emphasized policing deficiencies, but severely disrupted trade and commerce for several days. Given the impossibility of immediate improvements in policing, and magistrates' unease about becoming any more reliant upon soldiers, Corporation initiatives now developed in two directions. First and foremost, deliberate attempts at regulation and intervention were introduced in the provisions market, including interference with the Assize of Bread and incentives to encourage co-operative enter- prise amongst the merchant class. Charitable relief measures were simultaneously extended from the city into Kingswood, which was incorporated into the new parish of St George's in 1754, and the evangelical Richard Hart installed as minister. This mixture of modern and traditional market practice was instrumental in successfully avert- ing serious disturbances in the market during a number of scarcity periods later in the century, particularly in the prolonged dearth of 1766-7.[19] Second, there was a detectable renewal of emphasis on the virtues of collective responsibility and citizenship, a reinvigoration of the consensual civic ethos, intended to minimize political factionalism and its accompanying distractions and disorders.

Outsiders and 'Factious Aliens'

> Community of interests begets community of action;
> dissolve the common connection and each party

struggles for itself; re-unite it, the struggle is for one
and all.[20]

Perhaps the strongest expression of Bristolian self-absorption lay in
the consignment of outsiders to the margins of civilization. Local
Jacobites expressed antipathy to 'all foreigners' whilst visitors'
complaints that Bristolians were 'remarkably insolent to Strangers'
were commonplace. Only freedom of the city conferred the right to
trade within its walls, and outsiders were formally excluded in the
qualifying oath.[21]

The idea of the city as a self-regulating social organism united by
commercial interest was theoretically challenged by outsiders with no
respect for market practice and whose inherently 'disorderly' nature
placed them at odds with 'respectable' mores. Beyond the civic boundary of Lawford's Gate to the east, the mono-economic communities of
miners and weavers were continually represented in this way, from
their 'bravadoing halloos and shouting clamours' to their taking beer
'without paying any money'.[22] These 'underground workmen who are
but little known and on that account very desperate fellows', shared a
'strange dialect'[23] and their dysfunctional behaviour stood in stark
contrast to civic reason and gentility. The mayor was said to have
initially received them 'mildly' and 'very civilly' in 1753 for example;
it was their unreciprocating attitude that made subsequent dispersal
necessary. When this happened, the formulaic and theatrical 'brisk
movement' of the constables' staves 'afforded a pleasant diversion to
the spectators'.[24] Sometimes colliers or weavers would be referred to
generically as 'country people', a rationalization that eased the admis-
sion of women and others into their disorderly ranks. Unsurprisingly,
several accounts of the 1831 riots conflate unsupportable allegations of
the involvement of colliers with large numbers of 'abandoned
females', and approach roads crowded with 'country people' and
strangers.[25]

It is in this context that we should consider the lurid fascination
exhibited by Bristolians with the activities of the criminal underclass of
Cock Road in the nearby parish of Bitton who were 'the terror of the
inhabitants of Bristol' at the end of the Napoleonic wars. Protected by
the same close-knit family networks as the miners and weavers, the
businesslike depredations of the Cock Road gangs were a direct affront
to the respectability of legitimate commerce. Indeed, urban nightmares
seemed confirmed when an 'immense mob' of colliers prevented the
arrest of some Cock Road men in 1817, all, it was emphasized,

'WITHIN FOUR MILES OF THE SECOND CITY IN THE EMPIRE'. Bristolian Methodists quickly saw the potential in such 'scarce humanized uncivilized natives' for challenging missionary work, for here were a people 'still in a state of native ignorance ... wild as the untaught Indian brood'. Bricks and bibles were hurriedly transported to build Sunday School outposts, but for most Bristolians the lawlessness of the country people simply confirmed the growing need for strong and effective police protection. The city authorities appear to have played this card for all it was worth. In 1831, the Poor Law Commissioners accused the Corporation's discriminatory relief practices in the neighbouring outparish of St George's of 'sadly misrepresenting (the villagers) as turbulent and troublesome; while they are religious, orderly and peaceable'.[26]

As long as they followed the rules of the civic orthodoxy, inwardly migrating outsiders might become accepted Bristolians. It helped if they were white. In 1816 for instance, a year of acute hardship and unemployment, the mayor was anxious to rid his work-hungry city of 'the number of foreign seamen, blackmen, and men of colour' then competing with 'native' Bristolians for jobs[27]. It also helped if they were not Irish. Bristol had no Irish 'ghetto', but the 4000 strong Irish-born community living there by the middle of the nineteenth century was certainly the largest in the south west.[28] Many of the poorer families found cramped accommodation in the lowly lodging houses of Marsh Street and Host Street, close to the Quay 'where they live, as it were, in clusters'. Like the colliers and weavers, the Irish were resented as much as anything else for running a community within a community; for putting their own national identity before the interests of the civis. An Irishman called upon to give evidence at a trial of election rioters in 1830 for instance, was reluctant to talk for 'he should certainly have been murdered if he told of a countryman.'[29] Tensions turned to violent anti-Irish rioting in 1810, 1825, and 1829. Two-thirds of the prisoners taken after the 1831 riots were declared, falsely, to be Irish by *Felix Farley's*[30] and an 'Irish mob' was blamed for instigating running battles with the police during the 1841 election.[31] Tory papers watched with mounting horror as 'miserable' Irish migrants, 'carrying with them the seeds of disease and death', arrived in steadily rising numbers after the famine of 1846; a Trojan Horse of typhus and gastric fever.[32]

Radicalism, Disorder and the Corporation

> Let every man keep his own house in order, and the
> city will remain orderly.[33]

Civic virtue was not constructed entirely by geography, but also by recognized norms of behaviour. The interrelationship between politics and declining commerce may be measured by elite reactions to popular radicalism after 1790. Commercial decline produced two distinct but broadly liberal popular responses. First, the entrepreneurial bourgeoisie demanded Corporate intervention to 'revive our drooping commerce', an object attainable only through a 'feeling of mutual confidence which alone can unite us all'.[34] However, a second, more radical response sought a complete redefinition of Bristolian civic identity. The political iconoclasts who made up this group were roundly attacked by both the Corporation and its entrepreneurial critics, but it was the authorities' preoccupation with quietening radicalism that led eventually to their complete alienation from the business community. The Corporation's abiding fear of popular sovereignty only made their behaviour more exclusive, causing further outrage amongst the meritocratic bourgeoisie. The architects of Bristolian radical protest equated commerce with vulgarity, avarice and corruption. It was 'a sense of justice, not the spirit of commerce' that would 'tranquillise the dissensions of mankind', argued the scientist and physician Thomas Beddoes.[35] Coleridge's fellow poet and pantisocrat at Bristol, Robert Lovell, satirized the city's commercial values in a savage condemnation of the Corporation's 'sordid' privileging of private wealth and slavery over social welfare. Popular identification with an ethos so unprincipled, argued Lovell, and a Corporation concerned only with 'the *name*, the important air, the fur-clad gown and magisterial chair', should invoke not pride but shame.[36]

The defenders of civic culture hit back with relish. Radicals seeking a public enquiry into the Corporation's role in the 1793 Bridge riot were lambasted as 'a few factious aliens', drawing Coleridge's sneering retort that if shooting unarmed civilians was a Bristolian virtue, 'I glory that I am an alien in your city.'[37] Moreover, Radicalism was presented as proof that reformers wanted to destroy the very substance of the city. Benjamin Hobhouse, an independent Whig candidate at the 1796 election thought it best to package himself as a 'native and a member of the Society of Merchants', yet he could not escape vilification for his alien 'frenchified' politics, nor a heavy drubbing at the polls.[38] Similar arguments would re-emerge in 1831 when the reform riots became a Radical plot to destroy by fire Bristol's 'greatest source of wealth – the West India interest'.[39] Radicals disliked being dismissed as outsiders and Cobbett defended them in 1812:

> Who were to burn the city? Not the horses or dogs of
> Bristol; not any banditti from a foreign land; not any
> pirates who had chanced to land upon the coast. No,
> no ... they were, in fact, the People of Bristol.[40]

And that, of course, was unthinkable.

The Corporation strove to steer its anti-Radicalism away from national issues and the attention of central government. It gave no encouragement to loyalist Whigs and Tories who wanted to form an anti-Jacobin association in 1792, making Bristol the only major British town not to do so.[41] An anonymous threat to incendiarize the docks was handled with remarkable circumspection in 1793, and Radicalism was declared completely 'ineffectual' a few months before the riot on Bristol Bridge.[42] The Home Secretary, increasingly frustrated by the Corporation's long silences about the progress of Radical clubs, was forced to rely upon 'reports circulated in Town', for news of this major disturbance. In fact, the Corporation was preoccupied with an attempt to silence its critics inside the city and 'under the utmost perplexity' about rumours that they were to be prosecuted for murder. After the policing disasters of 1729, 1749 and 1753, this was familiar and unsettling political territory. Despite earlier statements, the Recorder was now certain the riot had been sparked 'by a conspiracy' for 'seditious' purposes by 'hidden leaders'; the mayor was happy to back any explanation which located the problem with marginal and alien elements, exonerated the Corporation, and denied the suggestion of legitimate commercial grievances amongst the middling sort.[43]

In 1794, the mayor officially denied the existence of Radical clubs,[44] despite Whitehall intelligence of contacts between Bristol and London Radicals and despite the Bristol Constitutional Society's published 'Address' which made its reforming objects perfectly plain. A copy already graced the desk of the Treasury Solicitor in Whitehall, who was considering a prosecution for seditious libel.[45] Support for the Corporation's non-confrontational stance came from sections of the merchant elite who feared the destabilizing effects of repression. The damaging effects of the war with France on trade and popular discontent even drove some of them into the Radical-led peace movement by

1795, and the Corporation's dogged refusal to endorse petitions opposing the war nearly cost it merchant support. The food riots of 1795, the first in Bristol for forty-two years, signalled the failure of both merchant enterprise and civic paternalism within a restricted national economy. With trade in decline and visible rents in the social fabric, the construction and appropriation of civic identity would now become permanently contested ground.[46]

Yet, in 1797 the peace movement was effectively silenced by the shock of the bungled French invasion attempt and an understandable renewal of interest in the defence of Bristol. 'However different opinions may have been respecting the conduct of the administration,' commented the local press with some relief, 'there appears no difference in the grand object of repelling the French foe.'[47] The Corporation gladly played the patriotic card, vigorously promoting the Volunteers and tacitly permitting a rampaging crowd of loyalists to besiege and ransack the rooms of the Constitutional Society for two full days. When Radicals tried to hold an outdoor meeting, 'a stop was put to it', and the mayor reiterated, without elaboration, the low Radical profile to Whitehall.[48] Despite evidence that Bristol's Radicals were involved with the insurrectionary underground,[49] judicial repression remained muted until after the Irish Rebellion of 1798. Faced with floods of disaffected fugitives, the Corporation stopped and interrogated arrivals with such efficiency that Whitehall had to advise the mayor to 'exercise discretion'. After comprehensive surveillance, the mayor personally led a party of militia to capture two United Irish suspects in 1799.[50] In the light of the generally restrained reception given to indigenous Jacobins, the Corporation's response to Radicalism had apparently become mediated by geography.

Corporation tactics were influenced by the Radical mass platform at the end of the war. Although some magistrates favoured prosecuting leaders, the majority 'did not think themselves justified in searching for their papers'.[51] The preferred route lay in public humiliation through overwhelming opposition. Hunt's 1816 meeting was therefore surrounded by four troops of lancers from Weymouth and Trowbridge, nearly 500 yeomanry, 100 infantrymen and over 1200 special constables. The select vestries urged casual spectators to stay at home or risk 'letting the world believe that because they were listeners to their jargon, they were also promoters and abettors of their principles and conduct'. The thousand or so Radicals who did turn out were left looking like a minority faction, hopelessly 'overawed by the civil and military power'.[52] Radical leaders and platform orators may not have been harassed, but vendors of Radical papers were. In 1817 two men were prosecuted and fined for selling Cobbett's *Political Register*, and a printer, Joseph Arnold, for publishing local copies of the satirical 'Political Litany'. In 1820 a printer was prosecuted for advertising a Radical illumination (organized, unsurprisingly, by 'a mere stranger amongst us, a quondam London bagman') and many news vendors were now considered too afraid to handle Radical titles. Two more prominent publishers were gaoled in the 1830s.[53]

Contemporary chroniclers coming to terms with the events of 1831 gave leading roles to outsiders. Not only colliers but 'agents', 'emissaries' and 'tall men in long cloaks and fur caps' from Orleanist France were imagined hoodwinking the loyal Bristolian working class into burning their own city.[54] Such tales deny agency amongst the indigenous poor whilst locating real responsibility in the Corporation's alienation from the capitalist bourgeoisie. Yet if the crowds who commanded the streets for three days in 1831 merely represented either disinterested and disorderly nihilism or a physical manifestation of the middle class agenda, how are we to read their actual behaviour? Queen Square, two sides of which were destroyed by fire, was systematically looted and expropriated. Yet, despite contemporary images of anarchic chaos, the polite way in which residents were ordered to leave, the decoration of William III's statue with a cap of liberty, the introduction of circle dancing on the grass and the systematic liberation of the city's four gaols, suggest a degree of organization, not mindless hooliganism.[55] The destruction of the Square, a showpiece monument to mercantile enterprise, was not coincidental and arguments that it was done because the Corporation owned it are unconvincing. However slim the purchase of Radical anti-mercantilism, we need hardly doubt the disaffection of the nineteenth-century working class with the idea of a local commonwealth. Capitalism had brought few improvements to the cramped and insanitary living conditions of the poor, and the elite had largely emigrated to the suburbs. Social unity was an increasingly untenable illusion.

In the years following 1831 the assumption of linkage between the lower orders, Radicalism and disorder was difficult to dispel. The stagnation of Reform politics showed in the return of two Tory MPs at the first post-Reform Act election. With the help of a little judicious gerrymandering, the Tories even managed to retain a grip on the Council after the first municipal elections in 1836.[56] The close ties established between the Chamber of Commerce and the trade unions during the campaign to free the Dock Company from Corporate Tory control in the 1820s proved difficult to break in the cautious climate of the later 1830s.[57] These factors ensured liberal ascendancy in 'opposition' politics in the Chartist years, securing the support of the trades at the 1837 election and for the founding of the Anti-Corn Law League. Chartist efforts to agitate the League were not helped by the Welsh origins of its most prominent local leader, William Morgan; and still less by the violent climax of the South Wales rising in 1839, prompting League supporters to yell 'Go to Newport' at Morgan.[58] Moreover, the national and Westminster-centred focus of Chartist demands were arguably of only marginal relevance to popular politics in Bristol. The Reform agitation of the earlier nineteenth century had been almost entirely about using Parliament as a jemmy to lever open a closed and rotten Corporation. Despite the excitement generated by the Reform crisis in 1831, the resulting Act barely changed an already relatively open franchise. Municipal reform thus largely took the wind from the Chartists' sails; although the inadequacy of the 1835 act continued to form the basis of much Chartist oratory.[59] Chartists were lampooned in the press as Irish rebels mixing 'Repale' with 'the Paple's Charter', and their regular use of meeting rooms owned by the 'blasphemous' Owenite socialists allowed the configuration of all three groups into an irreligious triumvirate.[60] The police displayed supreme indifference when an Anglican/Tory campaign to 'Drive out Socialism' culminated in a mob attack on the Owenite Hall of Science. 'First they kick up a row', commented a Superintendent, 'then send for us to put it down'. As in earlier years, marginalization and crowd action was followed by prosecution of the unstamped press; this time of Owenite missionary Charles Southwell's openly anti-Christian *Oracle of Reason* in 1842. Southwell was gaoled and Owenism saddled with an atheist stigma from which it never fully recovered.[61]

Politics and Public Space

An important side effect of the conflict over radicalism lay in literal and emblematic contests over 'contested ground'. Magistrates had always done their best to prevent Radical meetings in public houses, but the Corporation's veto on Radical use of the Guildhall on numerous occasions between 1795 and 1840 caused indignation and several attempts to disrupt 'loyalist' meetings. Radicals saw their exclusion as nothing less than 'a wanton and daring encroachment upon their rights as freemen'.[62] Barred from accommodation at his 'usual' inn when he came to fight the 1812 election, Henry Hunt threatened to turn the Exchange into his headquarters. Built in the eighteenth century with £50,000 of freemen's money, the Exchange had long been a locus for crowd activity at election times, but Hunt emphasized popular ownership: 'The mayor and Corporation are only Guardians and Trustees of this property; it does not belong to them but to you.'[63] This atmosphere of contention was also the cause of a lingering controversy over the use of the nearby Commercial Rooms. Rules forbidding the discussion of 'political subjects' were invoked in 1817, 1819 and 1820 to obstruct Radical access but loyalist meetings were accommodated.[64]

The exclusion of Radicalism from public buildings effectively facilitated the mass platform in open spaces like Queen Square and Brandon Hill where access could not be effectively prevented. The importance to civic geography of the large tree-lined square, centrally located between the Quay and the Back, and framed by the grand houses of the elite, has already been suggested. Thomas Beddoes urged 'the People' to 'convene' there in 1795 to protest against Pitt's anti-Radical legislation, and it would later host meetings of the Political Union and the Chartists. Its post-1830 use during elections spectacularly mapped the essence of citizenship. Milling crowds around the polling booths gave it 'the appearance of a large fair ... the flags, the banners, the music, the colours ...' And while the men dutifully conducted their public business below, 'the windows of the surrounding houses were crowded with Ladies, who appeared highly to participate in the interest of the day.' Despite lapses into factional brawling, elections offered a sharp and reassuring contrast to the horror of the Reform riots. It was not association with the merchant elite that made the Square such an arena for popular rights, but its association with constitutional liberty via the central equestrian statue of William III. For the constitution of 1688 charted territory no less contested than that of the civis. Whilst the Corporation celebrated the 1788 centenary by decorating the statue with a canopy and coloured lamps, Thomas Beddoes believed it should be 'draped in black mourning til our liberties be secure'. The anonymous Bristolians who attached a bloody loaf to the railings together with a scribbled note denouncing corruption and war during the near famine of 1800 were never discovered. Yet the centrality of the Square to the 1831 riots overshadowed subsequent popular use and an 1832 Reform meeting deliberately avoided it, opting instead for the less 'provocative' Brandon Hill.[65]

Bristolians had enjoyed access rights to Brandon Hill, an area of rising scrub to the west of the city, since the mid-sixteenth century. Reminded by populist orators that this was 'our own Brandon Hill', Radical groups made it a regular location for large outdoor meetings after the end of the French Wars, its use peaking during the early phases of Chartism and provoking a short war over its policing which was emblematic once again of the wider contest for possession of the civis. Chartists disputed the right of the Corporation to regulate the hill with its 'armed Bourbon police force...' and new police station built at its very foot, and introduced their own 'constabulary force' of 45 'officers', a 'superintendent' and four 'inspectors' to steward meetings, each armed with a stave. In 1839 the Corporation changed tack, beginning large scale 'improvements' to the site with wide gravel terraces and 'winding walks'. The process of gentrification was completed in 1898, with the deeply symbolic erection of Cabot's Tower on the summit; a monument to commercial pre-eminence in a thoroughly bourgeois pleasure garden.[66]

Popular celebrations on 5 November are a useful index to changing attitudes over the 'ownership' of civic space. Inclusive protestant pageants were deliberately encouraged by the Corporation at central outdoor locations like College Green or the Exchange in the 1740s and 1750s to encourage the dispersal of popular support for Jacobitism. Despite some rowdiness, unifying spectacles like these were thought to bestow 'decency, sobriety and good order' on the civis as a whole.[67] Consequently, convictions for the indiscriminate throwing of fireworks in the streets were few in the eighteenth century, although the magistrates made an annual show of warning people not to do it.[68] Encouragement was stepped up once again to counter Radicalism in the 1790s despite the destructive sacking of two Tower Lane brothels for fuel in 1792.[69] But the growing desire of urban elites to 'reform' plebeian recreations, coupled with the consignment of the effigies of prominent anti-reformers to local bonfires in 1831, caused a change of heart in the nineteenth century. Arrests and prosecutions for street fireworks rose rapidly in number.[70] Bonfire crowds were forced out of traditional central territories and relegated to border districts like Kingsdown, 'a species of debatable ground or no man's land' in which revellers might more easily evade the jurisdiction of the police and magistrates.[71] But Kingsdown was a respectable suburb, and the annual divisive and violent confrontations between celebrants and police were not to the taste of residents who found themselves caught up in the fighting.[72] Consequently, squibbing in Queen Square and on

Brandon Hill was officially rehabilitated after about 1850.[73] Compromise was rewarded with regulation. Whilst effigy-burning crowds ranged freely through nearby towns in 1867, squibbing at Bristol was boisterous but undirected and individualistic. Indeed, bonfire night had become 'decidedly dull' in the opinion of the *Bristol Times*.[74]

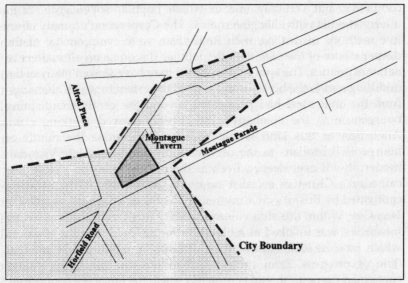

Figure 1: Kingsdown's 'debatable ground'. Banished from the city centre, nineteenth-century bonfire crowds gathered instead outside the Montague Tavern, annually engaging the police across the county boundary for possession of the city margins.

Conclusion

The search for consensus and stability in a town where rapid growth had made society increasingly unmanageable by force of law alone, nourished elite endorsement of the civic ideal. Loose identification with a common commercial interest was strengthened most forcefully by the descriptive exclusion of geographic and ideological 'outsiders'. In practice, this mercantile definition of 'civis' held good until it was interrupted by two factors in the early nineteenth century, Bristol's relative economic decline and the Corporation's adoption of laissez-faire.[75] The inability, or unwillingness, of the Corporation to act decisively to improve the harbour effectively isolated the elite from the majority of citizens and turned the interpretation of the civis into a battlefield. This 'abdication' of responsibility by Bristol's patrician governors lent added impetus to a respectable, locally focused Radicalism which contested elite dominance of the civic tradition and questioned its commercial basis. Jacobin Radicalism eulogized not trade but 'liberty', a commodity no better defined or delineated than commerce, but certainly one in which popular sovereignty stood utterly at odds with elite governance. The Corporation's quietly effective methods of dealing with Radicalism were symptomatic of the deeper desire of the elite to stifle popular discourse on all matters of national politics. The apocalypse of 1831 may have shaken many of the middling sort to the bone – but it proved the extent to which alienation from the civic ideal had permeated beyond the gently complaining bourgeoisie to the combative and 'liberty'-starved working class. Alienation of this kind would continue to exercise the minds of bourgeois Bristolians as the divisive individualism of late Victorian modernity bit ever deeper. Even as the century drew to a close, the cathedral's Christian socialist canon, S. A. Barnett, felt sufficiently captivated by Bristol's civic mythology to use it as the basis for his *The Ideal City*. Within this slim volume, the city that was 'encompassed by memories' was invoked as a blueprint for national urban renewal, in which timeless ideals of municipal citizenship might still secure that 'line of progress' from rural to urban life. 'A true municipality,' confirmed Barnett, 'should completely grasp the life of the community and in doing so express the communal idea; one for all, all for one.'[76]

Notes

1   G. Pryce, *A Popular History of Bristol from the Earliest Period to the Present Time ... Impartially Written* (Bristol, 1861), 467.

2   *The Bristol Riot ... By a Gentleman who Attended the Commission* (1714). The quotation from Seyer's *Memoirs of Bristol* appears with caustic annotation in Pryce, *A Popular History of Bristol*, 437.

3   J. F. Nichols and J. Taylor, *Bristol Past and Present*, 3 (1882), 167.

4   W. Hunt, *Bristol* (1886), 200; W. Sturge, *Some Recollections of a Long Life* (Bristol, 1893), 21, quoting Harriet Martineau.

5   'A Rated Burgess', *Lessons from History on the Operation of the Close Corporate System in this City on its Trade and Prosperity ...* (Bristol, 1835), 29.

6   M. Brock, *The Great Reform Act* (1973), 250; E. P. Thompson, *The Making of the English Working Class* (1963), 81. For George Rudé too, the riots represented a 'hangover from the past': *The Crowd in History, 1730-1848* (revised edition, 1981), 149. See also G. Bush, *Bristol and its Municipal Government, 1820-1851* (BRS, 29, 1976), 159; J. Cannon, *The Chartists in Bristol* (BHA, 10, 1964), 15; R. Walters, *The Establishment of the Bristol Police Force* (BHA, 36, 1976), 16-17; D. Large, *Radicalism in Bristol in the Nineteenth Century* (Bristol, 1981); S. Thomas, *The Bristol Riots* (BHA, 34, 1974), 10; G. Amey, *City Under Fire:*

The Bristol Riots and Aftermath (Guildford, 1979), 177; M. Harrison, *Crowds and History: Mass Phenomena in English Towns, 1790-1835* (Cambridge, 1988), 289-291; J. Caple, *The Bristol Riots of 1831 and Social Reform in Britain* (Lewiston, U.S., 1990).

7   For a taste of the invective, see 'A Burgess', *Letters, Essays, Tracts and other Documents Illustrative of the Municipal History of Bristol and of the Trade of its Port* (Bristol, 1836).

8   PRO, Home Office (hereafter HO), 42/158, J. Haythorne to Sidmouth, 5 Jan. 1817. John Cossens, a leading member of the post-war Radical circle at Bristol and described as 'a very dangerous fellow' by a government spy in 1817, was also a city constable: HO 42/163, W. Lloyd Caldecot to Sidmouth, 4 Apr. 1817.

9   Walters, *Establishment of the Bristol Police*, 16-17.

10   PRO, HO 42/19, Daubeny to Nepean, 25 July 1791. See also BRO, Town Clerk's Letter Boxes, 1791, bundle 27, anonymous letters dated 21-31 July 1791.

11   The best account of the Bridge riot will be found in Mark Harrison, *Crowds and History*, 271-88. Henry Hunt's election address of 1812 was peppered with references to those 'unarmed citizens unmercifully and indiscriminately shot by an armed Military' in 1793. See *An Account of Mr Hunt's Public Reception in Bristol with a Full Report of his Second Address* (Bristol, 1812), 10.

12   For the 1795 riots see the *Courier*, 11 June 1795; *BMerc*, 8 and 15 June 1795; PRO, War Office (hereafter WO) 1/1092, Rooke to Wyndham, 7 June 1795. For the 1800 riot see PRO, HO 42/51, Rooke to Portland, 19 Sept. 1800.

13   *FFBJ*, 19 April 1755 and 2 April 1803; PRO, WO 1/1081, W. C. Wilmott to Lewis, 5 July 1794.

14   Steve Poole, 'Popular Politics in Bristol, Somerset and Wiltshire, 1791-1805' (unpublished PhD thesis, University of Bristol, 1993), 260-1; PRO, WO1/1092, Rooke to Lewis, 19 July 1795.

15   Volunteering was an essential component of middle class 'urban consciousness'; see J. E. Cookson, 'The English Volunteer Movement in the French Wars, 1793-1815: Some Contexts', *HJ*, 32, (1989), esp. 868 & 874. One Bristol recruit admitted enlisting 'for the purpose of bringing custom to his shop': *BG*, 13 and 20 June 1797. See also P. Pickle, *To the Mock Volunteers or Bristol Heroes* (Bristol, 1794); BRL, Volume of Notices Relating to the Bristol Volunteers, 1797-1810; *Rules and Regulations to be Observed by the Bristol Armed Volunteer Association* (Bristol 1797), and for a more uplifting account, J. Brown, *The Rise, Progress and Military Improvement of the Bristol Volunteers* (Bristol 1798). The French orders are reproduced in H. F. B. Wheeler and A. M. Broadley, *Napoleon and the Invasion of England: The Great Terror* (1908), 39-41. Clandestine plots to incendiarize the docks were the stuff of recurrent paranoid nightmares amongst the merchant class. These fears were founded in the partially successful attempts of a republican pro-American arsonist, James 'the Painter' Aitken, to do precisely that in 1777: J. Aitken, *The Life of James Aitken, Commonly Called John the Painter, an Incendiary* (1777); BRL, Jefferies Collection, vol. 12, unidentified news cutting, 171.

16   PRO, State Papers (hereafter SP) 36/16, J. Yorke to Duke of Newcastle, 20 Dec. 1729.

17   N. Rogers, *Whigs and Cities: Popular Politics in the Age of Walpole and Pitt* (Oxford, 1989), 292-3; R. Malcolmson, 'A Set of Ungovernable People: The Kingswood Colliers in the Eighteenth Century', in J. Brewer and J. Styles, eds, *An Ungovernable People: The English and their Law in the Seventeenth and Eighteenth Centuries* (1979), 106-11.

18   Steve Poole, 'Scarcity and the Civic Tradition: Market Management in Bristol, 1709-1815', in A. Charlesworth and A. Randall, eds, *Markets, Market Culture and Popular Protest in Eighteenth Century Britain* (Liverpool, forthcoming).

19   This argument is presented in detail in Poole, 'Scarcity and the Civic Tradition'.

20   'A Rated Burgess', *Lessons from History*, 25.

21   P. K. Monod, *Jacobitism and the English People, 1688-1788* (Cambridge, 1989), 174; Thomas Cox (1727), quoted in P. Marcy, *Eighteenth Century Views of Bristol and Bristolians* (BHA, 16, 1966), 16; the burgesses' oath ran, 'You shall not colour the goods of any Foreigner or Stranger, or know any Foreigner or Stranger to buy and sell with another Foreigner'.

22   UBL, Paget Papers DM106/492, broadside, *The Colliers of Kings-wood in an Uproar* (Bristol, 1738).

23   PRO, SP 36/122 pt.1, Clements to Newcastle, 21 May 1753. For the dialect see Pryce, *Popular History of Bristol*, 441.

24   *FFBJ*, 26 May 1753; Pryce, *Popular History of Bristol*, 438.

25   *FFBJ*, 26 May 1753; PRO, SP 36/122, Thomas Farr to Roger Holland, 6 June 1753; BRL, Jefferies Collection, unidentified Newspaper cutting, XII, 181; A. P. Hart, 'The Bristol Riots and the Mass Media' (unpublished DPhil thesis, University of Oxford, 1979), 25-9, 101-2. The 'country people' were not irredeemable, however. When they poured into the city to help repel the French in 1797, the press welcomed them as a 'loyal peasantry': *FFBJ*, 4 March 1797.

26   A. Braine, *History of Kingswood Forest* (London & Bristol, 1891), 92-4; *FFBJ*, 27 Feb., 3 April 1813, 8 Oct. 1814, 3 June 1815; *BG*, 2 Feb., 7 April 1814; *Bath & Cheltenham Gazette*, 18 June 1817; *First Report of the Poor Law Commissioners* (1834), app. A, 1, 514. Two monographs exist on the Cock Road gangs, I. Wyatt, 'The Cock Road Gang', *Gloucester Historical Studies*, 4 (1970), and P. Lindegaard, 'The Mark of Cain: The Cock Road Gang', *Avon Past*, 9 (1983). For an excellent contextual study see R. Wells, 'Popular Protest and Social Crime: the Evidence of Criminal Gangs in Rural Southern England, 1790-1860', in B. Stapleton, ed., *Conflict and Community in Southern England: Essays in the Social History of Urban and Rural Labour from Medieval to Modern Times* (Stroud, 1992). The Corporation had been warned by the Home Office about the imminent arrival of criminal outsiders at the city's fringes unless it reformed its police as long ago as 1792. The new Metropolitan Police Bill had had the effect of 'driving the convicts from the metropolis': PRO, HO 42/21, Dundas to Noble, 12 Sept. 1792.

27   PRO, HO 43/25, Beckett to Haythorne, 9 Nov. 1816.

28   D. Large, 'The Irish in Bristol in 1851: A Census Enumeration', in R. Swift and S. Gilley, eds, *The Irish in the Victorian City* (1985), 37-41; 'Some streets literally swarm with them', noted a disapproving *FFBJ*, 6 June 1829.

29   *FFBJ*, 9 July 1825; *BG*, 21 Oct. 1830.

30   *FFBJ*, 12 Nov. 1831.

31   *FFBJ*, 9 July 1825, 3 July 1841; *BMerc*, 15 Feb. 1829, 6 & 13 April 1829.

32   *BMerc*, 15 May, 19 June 1847.

33   *BG*, 2 Sept. 1830.

34   'A Rated Burgess', *Lessons from History*, 5.

35   Beddoes quoted in D. Stansfield, *Thomas Beddoes: Chemist, Physician, Democrat* (Lancaster, 1984), 117.

36   Robert Lovell, *Bristol: a Satire* (Bristol, 1794). Thorne's 'Bristolia' ('Majestic Bristol! to thy happy port/ Prolific COMMERCE makes its lov'd resort...') is reprinted in E. Martin and B. Pickard, eds, *Six Hundred Years of Bristol Poetry* (Bristol, 1973), 19. The theme is taken up again by Henry 'Orator' Hunt in 1812. Arriving in Bristol to contest the election as an independent radical, Hunt found the 'merchants and gentry, as they are called, the most corrupt, the most vulgar, the most ignorant, the most illiberal and the most time-serving race that are to be found in Europe... The Corporation is the richest in the world,

perhaps, except London,; while the freemen, whose property goes to enrich the said Corporation, are the very poorest freemen in the world': H. Hunt, *Memoirs of Henry Hunt Esquire, Written by Himself*, 3 (1822), 41.

37 A. W., *A Letter to Edward Long Fox, M.D.* (Bristol 1795); S. T. Coleridge, *An Answer to a Letter to Edward Long Fox* (Bristol, 1795). The radical pamphleteer Thomas Lee was attacked for being an outsider in 1807, see Large, *Radicalism in Bristol*, 6.

38 BRL, untitled election handbill, 25 May 1796.

39 The extent of the Corporation's links with the slave trade are clear from the enormous sums of compensation paid out after emancipation to alderman Thomas Daniel, chairman of the West India Company, and Charles Pinney, mayor of Bristol during the riots. See Hart, 'Bristol Riots and the Mass Media', 30-33.

40 William Cobbett, 'To the Independent Electors of Bristol', reprinted in Hunt, *Memoirs*, 3, 58-67.

41 The Mayor hosted two public meetings which pledged loyalty to King and Constitution and committed the magistrates to the prosecution of Jacobins, but despite the pleading of several Tory populists, the process was taken no further. A Clifton Loyal Association and a 'True Briton Society' failed to get off the ground early in 1793. *FFBJ*, 8, 15 and 22 Dec. 1792, 12 Jan. and 2 Feb. 1793. BL Add. Ms. 16,927, Reeves Papers, Duke of Brunswick to Moore, 5 Dec. 1792.

42 Poole, 'Popular Politics', 66-7; BRO, Quarter Session and Assize Papers, May 1792 – March 1793, 'Address of the Grand Jury', April 1793.

43 BRL, Manuscript Diary of William Dyer, entries for 19-30 Sept. 1793; PRO, HO 42/26, Dundas to Morgan, n.d. Oct. 1793, Morgan to Dundas 7 Oct. 1793; HO 42/27, Farqueson to Dundas, 10 Nov. 1793, Morgan to Dundas, 11 and 19 Nov. 1793; BRL, Holograph Letter B18588, R. Burke to J. Noble, 25 Nov. 1793.

44 BRO, Corporation Letter Book, J. Morgan to H. Dundas, 21 May 1794.

45 *Annual Register*, 1792, 2 (1821 edition), 153; BL Add. Ms. 16927, Reeves Papers, Brunswick to Moore, 5 Dec. 1792; BL Add. Ms. 27812, Place Papers, London Corresponding Society Journal, 31 Oct 1793; PRO Treasury Solicitor (hereafter TS) 11/958/3503, report of Lynham, 5 Nov. 1793; Two letters from the BCS to the LCS were reproduced in the *Second Report of the Committee of Secrecy* (1794); Bristol Constitutional Society, *Address to the People of Great Britain* (Bristol, 1794). For the Treasury Solicitor's copy see TS 24/2/13.

46 For merchant unease about repression see UBL, Pinney Papers, Family Letter Book, 1795-6, Azariah Pinney to William Wordsworth, 26 Nov. 1795.

47 *BG*, 22 Feb. 1797.

48 PRO, HO 43/9, Duke of Portland to J. Harvey, 7 Aug. 1797; BRO, Corporation Letter Book, J. Harvey to Portland, 8 Aug. 1797. Sources for the riot, which went completely without comment in the newspaper press, and which was not reported to Whitehall, are limited to: (John King) *A Statement of the Facts Relative to the Riot at Union Street, Bristol... With Some Free Observations on the Conduct of the Civil Power on that Occasion* (Bristol, 1797); BRO, Town Clerk's Letter Boxes, 1796 Box, unnumbered bundle, J. King to J. Harvey, 20 Mar. 1797 (wrongly dated); and the trial report of one rioter privately prosecuted by King in *FFBJ*, 19 July 1797.

49 An admittedly sketchy picture emerges from the following sources: PRO Privy Council (hereafter PC) 1/42/A140, William Bennett to William Wickham, two letters, 30 April 1798 and James Major to William Wickham, 30 April 1798; PC1/43/A152, Papers seized from Henry Hastings; PC1/44/A161, list of prisoners taken in London with dates of release, 1798-9; *FFBJ*, 28 April 1798; *The Times*, 26 May 1798. Government knowledge

of the plot to establish a cell of United Britons in Bristol and to furnish it with pikes was entirely due to a leading member (William Bennett) turning King's evidence. For the narrative see Poole, *Popular Politics*, 107-12.

50   A detailed account of the activities and harassment of Irish migrants in Bristol after the rebellion is given in Poole, 'Popular Politics', 112-122. Fugitive Irish nationalists were again on the run in Bristol in 1828: PRO, HO 52/5, J. McDonagh to R. Peel, 27 June 1828.

51   PRO, HO 42/161, J. Davison to Sidmouth, 12 March 1817; HO 42/157, T. Daniel to Sidmouth, 19 & 22 Dec. 1816.

52   BRO, Harford Papers, 28048/C.62, J. S. Harford to J. Harford, 6 Jan. 1817; *Cobbett's Political Register*, 11 Jan. 1817; *BMerc*, 31 Dec. 1816; *FFBJ*, 21 Dec. 1816, 4 Jan. & 1 Feb. 1817.

53   Fifteen independent printers in the city had refused to print radical material themselves. PRO, HO 42/155, R. Baker to Sidmouth, 27 Nov. 1816; HO 42/156, W. Lloyd Caldecot to Sidmouth, 5 Dec. 1816; HO 42/159, J. Haythorne to Sidmouth, 9 Feb. 1817; BRO, Town Clerks Letter Box, 1817, R.F.M. to Haythorne, n.d., *FFBJ*, 13 Nov. 1819; *BG*, 23 Nov. 1820; *Courier*, 16 Nov. 1820; Large, *Radicalism in Bristol*, 12.

54   Hart, 'Bristol Riots and the Mass Media', 25-9, 101-2.

55   *BMerc*, 1 Nov. 1831; *FFBJ*, 5 Nov. 1831; Caple, *Bristol Riots of 1831 and Social Reform*, 27-31. For polite knocking and dancing, see eyewitness report in Pryce, *Popular History of Bristol*, app. LXXIV, 618.

56   Large, *Radicalism in Bristol*, 19.

57   Large, *Radicalism in Bristol*, 10.

58   *FFBJ*, 9 Jan. 1841; D. McNulty, 'Bristol Trade Unions in the Chartist Years', in J. Rule, ed., *British Trade Unionism; The Formative Years, 1750-1850* (1988), 226-33.

59   See Caple, *The Bristol Riots of 1831*, 107-131. His survey of radical politics in Bristol between 1784 and 1831 is sketchy and at times incomplete (the intense activism of the 1790s is barely glimpsed), but the argument that support for Reform was motivated by local concerns is strongly made. For the preoccupation with municipal politics in Chartist oratory, see William Morgan's speech at the Owenite Hall of Science reported in *FFBJ*, 16 Jan 1841.

60   *FFBJ*, 2, 9 and 16 Jan. 1841, 9 Dec. 1843. The Owenites had actually been present since 1834, but it was not until 1840 that support grew sufficiently to justify building a Hall of Science.

61   *FFBJ*, 23 Jan. 1841, 6 & 27 Feb. 1841. Southwell's trial is reported in the editions of 15 and 22 Jan. 1842. See also Large, *Radicalism in Bristol*, 14-15.

62   For a very full coverage of these meetings see L. Patton and P. Mann, eds, *The Collected Works of Samuel Taylor Coleridge, 1, Lectures, 1795, on Politics and Religion* (Cambridge, 1971). This circle of respectable Radicals – physicians like Beddoes and Long Fox, the poets Coleridge and Lovell, and the banker Edye – interrupted further loyalist meetings at the Guildhall in 1797: *BMerc*, 6 Feb. 1797, *Courier*, 27, 28 and 29 April 1797. For later controversies see *BMirr*, 9 Oct. 1819; *Bath & Cheltenham Gazette*, 29 Nov. 1820, 27 Dec. 1820; D. McNulty, 'Working Class Movements in Somerset and Wiltshire, 1837-48' (unpublished PhD thesis, University of Manchester, 1981), 80, 130, 412; Hunt, *Memoirs*, Vol 3, 97-102.

63   Henry Hunt, *Memoirs*, 3, p.95; *An Account of Mr Hunt's Public Reception at Bristol, with a Full Report of his Second Address* (Bristol, 1812), 9.

64   *BMirr*, 8 March 1817; *Bath Chronicle*, 28 Oct. 1819; *BG*, 26 Oct. & 30 Nov. 1820.

65   Thomas Beddoes, *A Word in Defence of the Bill of Rights Against Gagging Acts* (Bristol, 1795); *FFBJ*, 1 & 8 Nov. 1788. For the bloody loaves incident see BRO, Corporation Letter

Book, J. Morgan to Portland, 26 Feb. 1800; *BMerc*, 12 May 1832; *BMirr*, 29 July 1837. When a reform crowd pulled down a royal statue in 1813, it was not the centrally located monument to William III, but an image of the incumbent monarch, George III, in the newly built Portland Square close to the city limits: *BMerc*, 29 March and 10 May 1813; *FFBJ*, 27 March 1813. Various corroborative sources for the tricolour incident are given in Hart, 'Bristol Riots and the Mass Media', 29.

66 *Bristolian*, 26 Dec 1829; Walters, *Establishment of the Bristol Police Force*, 16-17; McNulty, 'Working Class Movements', 107-9; *FFBJ*, 24 Aug. 1839. For the Hill's historical origins see Arrowsmith's *Dictionary of Bristol* (Bristol, 1906), 306-7.

67 *Bristol Oracle and Country Advertiser*, 9 Nov. 1745; *Bath Journal*, 11 Nov. 1745; *Bristol Weekly Intelligencer*, 10 Nov. 1750.

68 BRO, Petty Sessional Convictions, 1728-1795. Two prosecutions are recorded in 1758, two more in 1769 and one in 1782.

69 Note the absence of coverage in *Bonner and Middleton's Bristol Journal*, 11 Nov. 1786, 10 Nov. 1787, 8 Nov. 1788 (an anomaly because it was Jubilee year), 7 Nov. 1789, 6 Nov. 1790 and 12 Nov. 1791. 1788 was an exception, but it was also the centenary year of the Glorious Revolution. The emphasis changed suddenly in 1792 when a preponderance of 'bells, flags, bonfires and fireworks' made a reappearance. See also 10 Nov. 1792, 9 Nov. 1793 and 8 Nov. 1794. For Tower Lane, see BRO, Quarter Session Papers, 1792, information of Alice King and others, 10 Nov. 1792.

70 *BG*, 10 Nov. 1808; *Bristol Liberal*, 5 Nov. 1831. In 1837, 24 men were fined for illicit squibbing, and five more for acts of violence, *BMerc* 11 Nov. 1837.

71 *BMirr*, 9 Nov. 1822, 10 Nov. 1838; *BMerc*, 7 Nov. 1835.

72 *BMerc*, 11 Nov. 1822, 12 Nov. 1836, 18 Feb. 1837, 10 Nov. 1838, 9 Nov. 1839; *BMirr*, 11 Nov. 1837; *FFBJ*, 13 Nov. 1841.

73 *WDP*, 9 Nov. 1863, *BMirr*, 8 Nov. 1856, *BTM*, 6 Nov. 1866.

74 *BTM*, 7 Nov. 1867. Bristol avoided serious bonfire night rioting in subsequent years, unlike Frome in 1871, 1877, and 1888; Bath in 1876, 1879 and 1881, Exeter in 1879, or Westbury in 1881: *WDP*, 8 Nov. 1871; *Bath Chronicle*, 9 Nov. 1876, 8 Nov. 1877, 13 Nov. 1879, 10 and 17 Nov. 1881; *BTM*, 7 Nov. 1879, 7 Nov. 1888; *Salisbury Journal*, 12 Nov. 1881.

75 The abandonment of paternalism was nowhere more evident than in approaches to the politics of bread. When a Radical councillor urged his colleagues to petition government against the Corn Laws in 1839, he was firmly reminded that public questions like this were the concern of Parliament, but not of a local Corporation; *FFBJ*, 9 Feb. 1839.

76 Barnett's complete text is republished in H. E. Meller, ed., *The Ideal City* (Leicester, 1979), 55-67.

I would like to thank Jonathan Barry for his helpful comments on an earlier draft of this chapter, and the British Academy for the Postdoctoral Research Fellowship that made it possible.

PROTESTANTS, CATHOLICS AND JEWS: RELIGIOUS DIFFERENCE AND POLITICAL STATUS IN BRISTOL, 1750-1850

Madge Dresser

By the mid-eighteenth century, Bristol was not only a 'city of churches', but a city of chapels, a 'mass-house' and a synagogue as well. Such religious diversity was a sign of economic vibrancy but did it contribute to civic harmony? Had Bristolians laid aside 'religious bickering' and division for the 'manly and rational' activity of commerce as one contemporary observer had been led to suggest?[1]

This image of religious tolerance engendered by a mutual respect for Mammon, however much it may accord with conventional notions of increasing secularization, is not altogether convincing. Throughout the period under consideration, religious affiliation formed the basis for one's political identity. Bristol's official religious life, intertwined as it was with the civic culture, was deeply Anglican. The vast majority of Bristolians saw themselves as Protestants of a particular type. To be a fully participating actor in Bristol's civic life assumed an identity that was Christian, Protestant and loyal to the Established Church. Did not the great early eighteenth century patron of Bristol, Edward Colston, take great pains to ensure no Catholic or Dissenter could benefit from the schools or charities he so generously endowed?[2]

Essentially masculine and based on notions of property ownership this older culture also limited the participation of all women and men without property. Nevertheless, Anglican women and the poorest 'free born Englishman' were part of Bristol's corporate life in a way that religious minorities, particularly the Catholics and Jews, were not. As the tide of liberalism gathered strength restrictions on such minorities were swept away. Dissenting Protestants such as Congregationalists, Presbyterians, Baptists, Unitarians and Quakers managed to gain their full political and civil rights in 1828, Roman Catholics in 1829. Jews had to wait until 1858. What response from Bristol's citizens and its press did Jews, Dissenters and Catholics encounter when they sought full political status? What does this response tell us about the relationship between religious beliefs and the city's political culture?

These questions do not appear to have been addressed for this period in any detail by historians of Bristol with the notable exception of Jonathan Barry whose focus is on the period before 1775 and the

96

generalized surveys of Bryan Little and Rupert Davies.[3] Yet Helen Meller, in her study of Bristol in the period 1870-1914, identified the emergence in the late nineteenth century of a common 'religious sub-culture' which underlay the assumptions of the governing elite – an elite which by then was 'drawn from the Church of England, the Quakers, Congregationalists, Baptists, Wesleyans, even Roman Catholics ...'.[4] I would argue that this religious subculture had long been established and, though no longer exclusively Anglican, was still essentially Protestant. This chapter seeks to examine the religious dimensions of this civic subculture as evidenced in the debates over the political rights of religious minorities which so engaged local attentions in the years between 1750 and 1850. In so doing, it is hoped to demonstrate the enduring, if complex, relationship between the religious and political identity.

Anglican Dominance?

As Jonathan Barry has shown, in 1750 the Anglican Church was the dominant religious power in Bristol.[5] The overwhelming number of inhabitants saw themselves as Anglican, and the Church of England was established firmly at the structural centre of political and cultural life. If the Corporation included prominent dissenters, the Anglicans were still in the majority, and parish government remained an important force in civic life. By 1753 only Quakers and Jews were exempt from marrying in church. Until 1836 births, marriages and deaths were registered with the parish. Though the livings attached to Bristol's parish churches and Cathedral were so modest as to make pluralism endemic, church rates were still exacted from all, Anglican and non-Anglican alike.

The Corporation had church livings in its gift, and celebrated civic affairs with Cathedral services and church processions. The churches and the civic associations that clustered around them set the tone for much of Bristol's cultural life. Even in 1750, however, the challenge to Anglican hegemony was becoming apparent from an important proportion of prosperous and respectable dissenting Protestants.[6] The Presbyterians being 'occasional conformers' could take the Anglican sacrament and hold office. Other Dissenting groups could, by virtue of annually passed Indemnity Acts, be exempted from the penalties for holding office without taking the Sacrament. Yet because the discriminatory Test and Corporation Acts had not been rescinded, such toleration was temporary, potentially expendable and in any case effectively debarred most Dissenters from full participation in political life.[7] Disproportionately represented amongst the middling ranks of this commercial city, the Dissenters resented what they saw as the oppressive privilege and unwarranted complacency of the Anglican church and, as we shall see, actively sought to limit its power.

The Methodists constituted another challenge to Anglican supremacy. Bristol had been an important starting point for the 'great awakening' of evangelical fervour which had swept England and America from 1739. The Wesley brothers, John and Charles, lived for much of our period in Bristol and established a spiritual headquarters in Broadmead. The great orator George Whitfield commanded audiences of many thousands wherever he preached and his patron, the Countess of Huntingdon, established Methodist chapels in Bath and Bristol. Whilst Wesleyan Methodism stayed uneasily within the Anglican church until after John Wesley's death in 1791, Anglican divines rightly saw the whole tenor and approach of Methodism, with its alarming displays of religious enthusiasm and its emphasis on personal salvation and vigorous evangelizing to the poor and outcast, as a threat to their way of conducting religious life.[8] But the attitude of the Anglican clergy and the populace at large to the Methodists, though sometimes violently hostile up until the 1770s, was not monolithic. Though suspected by some of Catholic leanings, the Methodists were at least home-grown if somewhat wayward products of the Reformation.[9]

Bristolians and the 'Jew Bill'

Bristolians were less tolerant of foreign imports and there was local consternation at Bills introduced in 1747 and 1751 to naturalize foreign Protestants.[10] But it was the proposed Bill for the Naturalisation of the Jews in 1753 which provoked the most widespread and furious opposition both within Bristol and the country as a whole.[11] There had been confusion over the status of British-born Jews who, though excluded from the franchise and political office, were enabled by Common Law to own and inherit land. The Bill itself proposed that a wealthy minority of foreign-born Jews should enjoy similar rights without having to take the Anglican Sacrament.[12] From the spring of 1753 until early the following year, the story dominated the city's main newspaper, the Tory *Felix Farley's Bristol Journal*. Jews were a rarity in early eighteenth-century Bristol. The city's flourishing medieval community had been punitively taxed until 1290 when they and all their co-religionists were expelled from the country.[13] Since then, apart from reports of a handful of secret Jews fleeing the Inquisition in the mid-sixteenth century and settling in London and Bristol[14], there had been no Jews in England until they were formally re-admitted by Cromwell. By 1753 a synagogue was established in the Temple area and some 40 Jewish men and women reported by 1766.[15] Thus what most Bristolians would have known about both the Jews and the proposed Bill was what they would have gleaned from press and the pulpit.

Felix Farley's Journal ran a major propaganda campaign against the 'Jew Bill' and the Jews in general, co-ordinating negative foreign reports about Jews from as far apart as Germany and Algeria, with editorials, letters, doggerel, spoof stories and domestic reportage. The main thrust of the case made against the Bill centred around the essentially Christian nature of the English Constitution. Some supporting arguments were derived from medieval conceptions of the Jew as Christ-killer, ritual murderer of gentile children and usurer.[16] Other arguments had a more modern ring as anxieties were expressed about 'swarms' of Jews coming to take over England, threatening both the land and jobs of the local population.[17] The term 'Jewish Power' was repeatedly set in threateningly bold gothic script unlike the rest of the text.

Judaism was portrayed as a vengeful[18] and gold-obsessed religion[19] whose followers (always assumed to be male) were actively contemptuous of Christianity and intent on imposing male circumcision on the host-community.[20] Whether pedlars, stock-jobbers or wealthy merchants, these 'scheming' and 'Subtil' 'Shylocks' would swell the country's number of coin clippers, fraudsters and receivers of stolen goods.[21] The incorporation of Jews into political life (which the Act did not provide for but which its critics felt with some justice would inevitably follow) would hasten the deepening decline of ethical standards in English political life. Jews became the symbols (and scapegoats) for the corruption endemic in pre-reform England. In the words of *Felix Farley's Bristol Journal*, '... is not every man who sells his Vote, and every Trustee who betrays his Trust, a Jew? Nay is he not a Judas?'[22] This onslaught of propaganda was effective in mobilizing local opinion. A spoof petition reported in the Bristol column of the *Journal* illustrates how the Bill was seen as only the beginning of an onslaught against established religion. Purporting to be from 'the Turks on behalf of themselves and other good Musselmen' the alleged petitioners asked for a clause to be added to the Jew Bill so that they too could be naturalised and flock to England with their 'slaves, Janisseries, numerous wives and concubines'.[23] Once the Bill became law, some 1600 of Bristol's 'gentlemen, clergy, Freeholders and Burgesses' (out of a total population of some 45,000) met at the Bush Tavern to sign a petition expressing their 'great alarm' at 'the engrafting into our community [of] those avowed Enemies of our Saviour'.[24]

Voices of toleration do not seem to have been representative of the city's Anglican majority. Josiah Tucker, 'the Jew Chaplain' as he was later to be called, was reportedly burned in effigy ('in full cannonicals') for his arguments favouring Jewish naturalization on ethical and economic grounds.[25] Sir Robert Nugent's support for the Act provoked such an outcry in Bristol that he voted for its repeal, just before the 1754 election.[26] As no Bristol newspapers seem to have survived for the week immediately after repeal, we do not know the nature or extent of public reaction to the news, but the week before and after saw gleeful reports of anti-Jewish processions elsewhere. In Bicester, 'All principal inhabitants' gathered in the 'largest' illumination 'ever known' to burn an effigy 'the Jew' and in Devizes a detailed account approvingly described with unconscious irony how people of different 'perswasions' laid 'Party and Prejudice' entirely aside to unite in 'expressing their Joy' as

> The effigy of a Jew was carried thro' every street, attended with all sorts of Rough musick: several men carried torches, that the Inhabitants might see the Effigy and read the Paper that was stuck on its Breast, containing these words: *No Jews! ... Christianity forever!...* They made a Halt two of three times in every street, drank and repeated the above amidst the acclamations of a great number of people. A large Fire was made, and they burnt the Body of the Jew and set his head on the Top of the Pillory. The Bells rang and Drink was given to the populace ... loyal toasts were made ...

This communal custom clearly acted as a bonding ritual for the people of Devizes and by the prominence given to it in *Felix Farley's Journal* underlined the essentially Christian nature of the Bristol civis and the 'otherness' of the Jew.[27]

But what of Bristol's Jews themselves? It is perhaps not coincidental that the robbery and murder of a Jewish Bristol pedlar in

Monmouthshire occurred at the height of the repeal campaign. The city's Jewish community placed an advertisement in *Felix Farley's Bristol Journal* decrying the 'horrid and barbarous Murder' (its anguished tone in distinct contrast to that of the paper's own brief report) and offering a reward for the killer's capture. Generally though, the Jews residing in Bristol were allowed to get on with their lives. Excluded from becoming freemen, they were nonetheless able to pursue their livelihoods which included, so far as can be surmised, hawking and peddling, glass-making, engraving, pawnbroking, shop-keeping, ship-broking and probably tailoring and apothecary work.[28] Despite the persistence of negative stereotypes in the popular culture, a writer to the editor of *Sarah Farley's Journal* gave a favourable account of a Bristol synagogue service in 1786 stressing its decorousness and loyal prayers for the welfare of King George III.[29] But the issue of civil rights for Jews did not re-emerge until 1830. In the meantime, the debate over Jewish naturalization had encouraged both Protestant Dissenters and Roman Catholics to lobby for changes in their own political status.

The Position of Roman Catholics

> From the so-called Reformation until the accession of
> George II, in no commercial city of the British empire
> was Catholic faith more discouraged and depressed
> than in Bristol.[30]

The 'Glorious Revolution' of 1688 had enshrined Protestantism as a cornerstone of the British Constitution as a bulwark against the absolutist ambitions of the Catholic Stuarts. This 'majestic edifice of national liberty which stands alone in Europe like a beacon in the midst of the waters'[31] was opposed in the popular mind by a corrupt and repressive Papacy just waiting to reassert its tyranny over free-born Englishmen.

Local expression of hostility to Catholics drew on Parliament's formidable armoury of anti-Catholic legislation. Catholics were legally proscribed from teaching and public worship and priests and teachers transgressing this faced the threat of life imprisonment. In 1719, for example one Mr Townsend was seized at Bristol and sent to Gloucester 'as a popish priest' after 'reading or speaking to a company of foreigners'.[32] Anti-Catholic feeling in the first half of the century had a distinctly political dimension, given the Jacobite threat. At the beginning of the eighteenth century, Bristol as well as London, Norwich and York, could boast of 'loyal mughouses', fiercely partisan meeting places where the Protestant Ascendancy was toasted and Popery condemned.[33] Certainly by 1735 both the dominant Whig faction in Bristol's Corporation, with its significant sprinkling of English Presbyterians, and the Bishop of Bristol, Thomas Secker, who himself came from a Dissenting background, had no wish to encourage 'the papists'.

But around this time Abraham Darby and Richard Champion, the Quaker proprietors of Bristol's brassworks in the Baptist Mills area, needed to import highly skilled Rhenish and Flemish workers to help them beat foreign competition. These workers refused to stay unless they could worship freely as Catholics. It was at this point that, as one mid-Victorian Catholic chronicler tartly remarked, 'Bristol cupidity overcame Bristol stupidity'[34] and a Catholic chapel was opened in the room of a private home near the brass works at Hook Mills, at the foot of Ashley Hill.[35]

Yet even after the failure of the Jacobite rebellion of 1745 what Linda Colley has characterized as a 'vast superstructure of anti-Catholic sentiment'[36] still informed local attitudes. Josiah Tucker had reportedly been burnt in effigy also in 1751 on the wild suspicion he had gone to Rome expressly to 'beg pardon of the Pope' for his former anti-Papist rhetoric. And there was a fear that increasing numbers of good Protestant subjects were being lured away from an unduly complacent Anglican Church in order to embrace the 'evidently erroneous doctrines of Rome'. As *Felix Farley* warned its readers, 'When *Shepherds* sleep, the *Sheep* will be devoured by the *Wolves*'.[37]

Fragmentary evidence shows at least two well-born women who came to live in Bristol were attracted to Catholicism in their youth in the 1770s, but the pressures against such flirtations were immense. Fanned by the re-publication of such popular anti-Catholic texts as Foxe's *Book of Martyrs* and Bunyan's *Pilgrim's Progress*, popular resentment against Catholics was further inflamed by successive wars with France and Spain,[38] fulsomely reported in the local press and broadsides. During the Seven Years War (1756-1763) sentiment was such in the genteel Bristol suburb of Kingsdown that a successful dancing master was 'compelled to decamp' once residents learned he was 'a Papist'.[39]

The highest ranks of Bristol society were however willing to turn a blind eye to Catholic worship so long as it was discreet and did not proselytize. Dr Thomas Newton, Bishop of Bristol (1761-81) once summoned Bristol's lone Catholic priest, Fr. Scudamore, to the Mayor's residence in order to dissuade him from opening a 'mass-house' in the aristocratic resort of Hotwells. Catholic worship in such a public place, he was told, was 'an affront so contemptuous a defiance of all law and authority that no government would endure [it]'. Despite the reportedly frank and friendly nature of the meeting, Newton who took advice from a government minister about the matter, seems to have been prepared to use the full force of anti-Catholic legislation, should friendly persuasion fail. It is no wonder that Scudamore agreed to abide by the Bishop's wishes.[40]

The general opinion in Bristol seems to have been that Catholics, like Jews, were 'enemies to our own Constitution'. Opposition to the Catholic Relief Act of 1778 (which enabled Catholics to own and inherit property, stopped the prosecution of priests on the evidence of an informer and ended the penalty of life imprisonment for running Catholic schools) was considerable. The anonymous author of one handbill complained to the 'Gentlemen, Clergy, Freemen and Freeholders ... of Bristol', that ever since they had learned that Edmund Burke, their Irish-born MP, supported

> ... the late act for repealing a small part only of the severe laws against the Papists, you call him a Catholic and at once settle his education at St. Omer's though he has never seen the place.[41]

This statement reminds us that by the late 1770s the Catholic question was increasingly conflated with the vexed relationship between Ireland and England. Burke's support for the relaxation of damaging restrictions imposed on Irish trade to the colonies was seen to threaten Bristol's colonial interests. The increasing numbers of impoverished Irish immigrants flowing into Bristol and other English ports during this period, also fed into anti-Catholic attitudes. Around half of Bristol's 400-500 Catholics were Irish and most of the Irish were poor, those Catholics around the quayside parish of St Stephen's being described as 'Irish sailors, their wives or females of the worst denomination'.[42]

1780 marked the year of the Gordon riots in London. 10,000 soldiers were needed to quell this anti-Catholic disturbance in which 285 people died. The unrest also had repercussions in the West Country. For in Bath, on 12 June 1780 a 'most alarming riot' began with an attack on the house of the local Roman Catholic priest which adjoined a newly built Roman Catholic chapel. It was staunchly asserted by the local Bristol papers that the riot was the product of a London-based conspiracy.[43] This ignored the fact that in Bath as well as in Bristol local branches of Gordon's Protestant Association (which urged the repeal of the Catholic Relief Act) seemed to have sprung up 'spontaneously and to have had little direction from the centre' though Burke claimed only four or five Bristolians were formal members.[44]

In any case, an attack on Bristol was anticipated soon after. A crowd had reportedly gathered 'near the Romish chapel' [by then in Silver Street]. The Corporation called on The Duke of Beaufort's Volunteers and the Monmouthshire Militia to stand guard. Fr. Scudamore partially dismantled his chapel in order to avoid its destruction by 'evil-disposed persons'.[45] So charged was the atmosphere in the city that even the supremely Protestant Moravians were fearful of their Bristol chapel being mistaken for 'a mass house' given the 'destructions and burnings of the Roman Catholic Chapels and Houses and the threatenings of the Mob'.[46]

Dr Newton was then both the Bishop of Bristol and Dean of St Paul's in London. Though he had opposed the Catholic Relief Act, he too had been forced to flee his London residence during the riot. He blamed the riots partly on the provocative behaviour of the 'Papists' and the persecuting spirit of the Dissenters, and partly on Wilkes and 'the mob'.[47]

Burke who had publicly condemned the riot and the militant Protestantism which engendered it, stood down from his Bristol seat that same year. The evidence suggests his unpopularity amongst Bristolians over his pro-Catholic stance was a major factor in his resignation.[48] Whilst the American question dominated both the general elections of 1780 and a local election in 1781, patriotic sentiment was explicitly bound up with loyalty to Protestantism, though precisely which sort of Protestantism varied according to whether one was a Whig or a Tory. Both were anti-Catholic and the Tory candidate George Daubeny implored voters to 'Stand up for the Church' whilst his Whig opponent, Henry Cruger, ran on a 'no Popery' ticket.

Colin Haydon observed that the Gordon riots made anti-Catholic bigotry unfashionable in polite circles at least. With the French Revolution of 1789, Catholics came in for increasing sympathy as the victims of atheistic mob rule. The local leader of Bristol's Catholics, Robert Plowden, was sometimes assisted by two French emigré priests whose evident cultivation was said to have helped to allay anti-Catholic prejudice.[49] Plowden himself came from a prominent English

Catholic family and proved an able advocate for the rights of local Catholics. A Protestant source saw Plowden as having 'conciliated the respect, esteem and favour of the public' during his thirty-year residence.[50] As a result of his leadership and the increased commercial and political confidence of a growing Catholic population, a chapel was opened at Trenchard Street in 1790 a year before the Act legalizing limited forms of Catholic public worship and chapel building was passed.[51] But the Irish Rebellion of 1798 soon revived accusations of Catholic subversion. As King George III refused to countenance further movement towards Catholic emancipation after the Act of Union between Britain and Ireland in 1800, agitation over Catholic rights appears to have subsided somewhat until the renewed campaign for emancipation in 1812-13.[52]

Dissenters and Citizenship

Events in France had revived Dissenters' hopes of full political equality along with growing Establishment alarm at their Radicalism. The supposed Radicalism of Bristol Dissenters seems to have been overstated by their Anglican Tory opponents. Of all the denominations the Unitarians and the Quakers were perhaps the most estranged from the Anglican establishment, despite the fact that their members were amongst the most prosperous of Bristol's residents. The Lewin's Mead congregation of English Presbyterians (who had previously differed little from Anglicans except for their rejection of the episcopal structure) evolved towards a more radical, Unitarian faith under the ministry of John Prior Estlin (1770-1817).[53] One of their number, Richard Bright, chaired the local branch of the Association of Protestant Dissenters Committee which was established in 1790 to lobby for the Repeal of the Test and Corporation Acts. The reforming style of this Committee (which also included Bristol Baptists, Congregationalists, and probably Quakers) was evidenced by their expressed admiration of religious liberty in the new French regime.[54] The Quaker refusal to pay tithes, church rates or 'taxes devoted to military purposes' led to regular distraints on their property which were recorded from the mid-1790s onwards.[55] There were, however, real and growing tensions between those Dissenters who embraced radical theories of natural law to substantiate their claims for religious freedom, and those who argued for full civil rights on the grounds of their loyalty and respectability.[56] For example the hugely popular young Baptist preacher Robert Hall extolled in dazzlingly erudite sermons the views of such English Radicals as Joseph Priestley, Richard Price and Mary Wollstonecraft. Hall's religious radicalism seems to have led to irreconcilable differences with Dr Caleb Evans the Baptist minister. Hall left Bristol in 1791 for Cambridge just as the backlash against the Revolution was about to break. From the Napoleonic Wars, religious as well as political radicalism was viewed as unpatriotic and even seditious. As loyalist sentiment gathered force, invective replaced advice. In 'Old Mother Church', a ditty 'to be sung to the tune of "God Save the Queen"', Dissenters (like the Catholics before them) were likened to ravening wolves and Priestley was associated with both Guy Fawkes and the French mob:

> Old Mother church disdains
> The vile dissenting Strains
> That round her ring
> ....
> Sedition is their Creed
> Feign'd Sheep but *Wolves* indeed
> How can we trust;
> Gunpowder PRIESTLEY wou'd
> Deluge the Throne with Blood
> And lay the Great and Good,
> Low in the dust.[57]

Such was the worry about the connections between Radicalism, the French Revolution and Dissent that the Bill for the repeal of the Test and Corporation Acts was lost by a bigger margin in 1790 than in 1789 though both the Tory and Whig MPs for Bristol seem to have voted in favour of repeal, possibly a reflection of the strength of Dissent amongst the city's electorate.[58] But during the war year of 1812 even traditional Whig Parliamentary candidates like Bristol's Edward Protheroe opposed the progressive Whig candidate Sir Samuel Romilly (who was of Huguenot stock) and his Bristol Unitarian allies on the question of the repeal.[59] Henry Hunt's public and 'whole-hearted' support in the Bristol press for the 'emancipation' of the whole of Protestant Dissent also cast a subversive shadow over supporters of repeal.[60] Careful to distinguish himself from 'French Whigs' Protheroe feared that 'Dissenters if further tolerated would endanger the State'.[61] By 1800 worries about religious sedition had become so intense that even legal toleration of trinitarian Dissenters was under threat.[62] The repeal of the Test and Corporation Acts was, for the moment at least, out of the question.

Such loyalist fervour had also helped to amplify the increasing influence of evangelical ideas upon the old Dissenting sects.[63] Whilst evangelicals in both Anglicanism and nonconformity were 'radical' in their stress on itinerancy, their vociferous campaigns against such social evils as the slave trade, their concern to convert and educate the poor and marginalized, their emphasis on the primacy of faith over good works and the advocacy by many of them of spiritual rather than political equality, inclined them away from political Radicalism and was accompanied by an increasingly rigid anti-Catholicism.

Wesleyan Methodism's anti-Catholic inclinations were similarly reinforced in this era, despite its break with the Established Church in 1795. An increasingly public anti-Catholicism served to make Methodism both respectable and popular.[64] Thus when a Bill for Catholic Emancipation was presented to Parliament in 1812, Bristol's Wesleyan Methodist Society circulated an open letter against it, insisting on the political threat posed by allowing Catholics into public office and pointing in lurid terms to the Roman Church's 'lust for domination'.[65]

Bristol's Wesleyans were not alone in seeing Catholics as potential political subversives, induced by their religion to serve the political ambitions of the Pope. Given that under the terms of the 1778 Catholic Relief Act any Catholic holding office would have had to swear allegiance to the King and forswear the Pope's authority in civil matters, why did so many Protestants refuse to be reassured? The fact that at this time Catholic regimes on the Continent, including the Papacy itself, were still associated with repressive behaviour cannot fully explain why a speaker at a meeting in 1812 of 500 Bristolians opposing the Emancipation could declare himself 'a firm friend of toleration'.[66] Fear of Catholicism lay deeply rooted at the heart of Protestant nationalism.[67]

Thus when the Radical *Bristol Mercury*, and its Unitarian allies, argued that religious liberties would be more threatened 'not by conceding these [Catholic] claims but by refusing them',[68] they were trying to use rational means to address inchoate and often irrational fears. One of the most influential expressions of anti-Catholic feeling in this period written by the popular Independent minister of Castle Green, William Thorp, illustrates how rational justifications of an anti-Catholic position were the icing on a much more complicated cake.[69] For Thorp, 'The simple question, sir, is this: – are Roman Catholics eligible to places of power and national confidence – in a Protestant

Government?' His answer tells us much about the politics of religious exclusion:

> Would you appoint a Quaker to be Genralissimo of
> the military forces...? A Jew to be Secretary of State?
> Or a Mahometan to be Lord Chief Justice in a Court of
> English Judicature?

To Thorp and his intended audience, the absurdity of such appointments was so evident because religious and cultural uniformity was assumed as a basic principle of English political identity. The savage anti-Catholic imagery which soon slipped into Thorp's rhetoric also shows how prejudice and fear operated alongside more legitimate anxieties about Papal influence. Thorp described Catholicism as 'motivated by a malignant spirit':

> Oh Popery, Popery!... A serpent whose poison is
> instant death, lurking undiscovered until he hath
> inflicted the fatal wound; a hungry lion sharp set and
> ready to seize his prey; the vapour of pestilence which
> depopulates an empire; a fury entwined with scorpi-
> ons, an ideal monster that is sour, livid, full of scars,
> wallowing in gore ... is harmless and inoffensive
> compared to thee.

Such bombast led one *Bristol Mercury* reader to wonder if '...ever the Thunder of the Vatican roared with half the violence of the *liberal* and *humane* Mr. Thorp'?[70]

Certainly local Catholics took care to present themselves as rational champions of fair play. Robert Plowden, in an otherwise conciliatory open letter to local anti-Emancipationists, reminded them that they did not see *Catholics* 'mount a tub in the streets to harangue the people and divert them from frequenting *your* places of worship'.[71] Both Plowden and his co-religionist Farrell argued that the bad old days of Catholic intolerance were past. The anonymous 'Catholicus' (possibly Plowden) assured Protestant readers of the *Bristol Mercury* that they did not have 'much to fear from the Pope especially in the abject and enslaved state he is now in'.[72] Ironically, Plowden was soon after forced to leave 'the Bristol Mission' after a breach with his superiors on doctrinal matters, having evidently departed, in the words of one Catholic source, 'from that spirit of submission to episcopal authority which is characteristic of the SJ'. [Society of Jesus, i.e. the Jesuits.][73]

The Catholic issue dominated the Bristol press and Protestant pulpits in the ensuing years. Time after time, the prospect of political rights for Catholics provoked an outraged response from the Bristol establishment. Resentment against those 'hundreds [of] ... half starved Irish labourers [who] daily throng our [Bristol] streets ...'[74] was a continuing theme. The press despised Ireland 'not only as an exporter of disreputable humanity' but as the dangerous 'claimant of political rights'.

It was the Irish Catholics in England, who according to a satirical ballad of 1828, '... gladden Shiel and O'Connell with cheering, And follow Jack Lawless wherever he goes ...'[75] To native English Protestants then, suspicions of 'disloyal and alien' Roman Catholics were exacerbated by a 'dislike and distaste, often amounting to racial prejudice' of the Irish immigrant.[76]

Evangelicalism, Catholic Emancipation and the Repeal of the Test and Corporation Acts

The second and third decades of the nineteenth century saw the birth of an extraordinary number of societies founded to promote – through education or missionary work – various forms of Protestantism.[77] Some of these movements were divided along Anglican/nonconformist lines, but others were coalitions of evangelically-minded individuals from both Church and chapel. These groups helped to overcome some of the sectarian feeling which had so divided Anglicans and non-Anglicans at the beginning of the period and some afforded female Bristolians an important entré into the civic arena. But a significant minority of these groups displayed a more aggressively proselytising attitude towards non-Protestants. In particular, the Bristol Auxiliary of the Missionary Society – an influential group where nonconformists such as William Thorp joined forces with the vicars of St Mary Redcliffe and St Philip and St Jacob's, M. R. Whish and William Day, to spread the Protestant word.[78] These individuals seem to have been particularly active not only in opposing Catholic claims – for virtually all the Bristol parishes put their efforts into that[79] – but in introducing a newly aggressive tone into the mainstream of public debate, or, in the words of one local Catholic, attempting to rekindle 'the fires of Smithfield'.[80]

Though mainstream Anglicans tended to hold aloof from the more extreme manifestations of evangelical anti-Catholicism, they tolerated them and the extent of ecclesiastical opposition to Russell's Emancipation Bill was immense, as evidenced by petitions, vestry meetings and sermons against both the Bill and 'that Hydra-headed Beast of the Seven Hills'.[81]

Compared to the furore over the Catholic question, the repeal of the Test and Corporation Acts, by the spring of 1828, proved far less controversial. Evangelical activity had proved a powerful bonding activity for Church and chapel in Bristol and to some extent at least, doctrinal differences between them seemed to matter less than they had done.[82] Even the Tory press was not adamant against Russell's Repeal Bill providing some sort of loyalty test to substitute for the sacramental test was implemented. However, both Tories and Whigs saw the repeal of disabilities against Dissenters as a precursor of Catholic Emancipation, with the Tories fearing that once these Bills were passed, the next 'inevitable step' would be the 'pulling down of the Establishment altogether'.[83]

The new style evangelicalism reached its apogee in 1827 with the founding in London of the Society for Promoting the Religious Principles of the Reformation. By August 1828 an attempt was made to establish a Bristol branch of the Society. This was indeed a 'controversial mission' whose 'avowed object' was 'proselytism' – particularly against the 'corrupt' Catholic Church. Such militant evangelicalism alarmed the traditional Tory Establishment in Bristol. The Anglican clergy generally absented themselves from its inaugural meeting at which Catholics present were hissed down and denied a hearing and where, after some Dissenters there began to attack the Catholic elements in the Established Church, the meeting dissolved into a sectarian melée.[84]

Catholic priests and their friends attempted to counter the work of evangelical anti-Catholics through letters and personal appearances at public debates. They emphasised the divisions within Protestantism and rightly took Protestants to task for ascribing to Catholics outdated beliefs no longer widely held or taught.[85] On the other hand disagreement between Catholics over certain doctrinal issues could 'unintentionally further the Protestant cause' as when, at a public meeting of the Bristol and Clifton Association, two priests contradicted each other over whether or not individual Catholics had the right to interpret the Bible for themselves.[86]

Perhaps the most influential local advocate of Emancipation came from the most unexpected quarter – the Church of England itself. Rev.

Sydney Smith, the newly appointed prebendary of Bristol Cathedral, in 1828, continued in the tradition of Josiah Tucker. Guy Fawkes Day was traditionally a time of anti-Catholic triumphalism in England and in 1828, Smith, a famous wit, pointedly chose that very day to give a sermon at Bristol Cathedral on the subject of toleration, a decision which occasioned apoplectic rage amongst members of the Corporation.[87] Soon after, the president of the Tory Dolphin Club took the opportunity of Colston's anniversary to 'indulge in a strain of invectives against his Catholic fellow subjects'.[88] During the course of the next months, handbills and newspapers opposing Emancipation reminded their readers of Catholic atrocities, dating back to the medieval period. At the beginning of 1829, a coalition of 200 of the city's 'most respectable citizens' including evangelical vicars Whish and Green, the Independent pastor William Thorp, *Felix Farley's* printer, John Gutch, the mayor Thomas Daniel and road maker extraordinaire J. Loudon MacAdam, met to call for yet another public meeting against the Bill for Catholic Emancipation.[89]

Both the Tory and Whig press played crucial roles in the agitation leading up to the passage of the Catholic Emancipation Act in April 1829. The *Bristol Mercury* had acted as headquarters for the pro-Emancipationist 'Friends of Religious Liberty' a largely Unitarian pressure group. The offices of *Felix Farley's Bristol Journal* had allegedly supplied 'the violent and treasonable placards' which 'roused the passions of the lower classes' and probably reprinted Thorp's 1813 sermon against Catholicism which was again 'in every booksellers in Bristol'.[90]

In February some 20,000 Bristolians converged on Queen Square for what was reportedly the nation's first great rally against Catholic Emancipation. The vivid descriptions of people thronging windows, housetops and trees to witness the event was celebrated by *Felix Farley's Bristol Journal*[91] and deplored by the *Bristol Mercury* which sourly complained that the 'uneducated and unenlightened class of the community ... the labourers, draymen and porters, ... constituted the great majority of the meeting'.[92]

Anglican involvement was evident. The ultra clergy and churchwardens had, according to the clearly hostile account of the *Bristol Mercury*, been canvassing their respective parishes all week and as the crowd slowly assembled, 'Every now and then the suspense of the meeting was relieved by the arrival of some parish procession, headed by their clergy.'

Felix Farley was quick to assert that Dissenters also opposed

Emancipation, but the *Mercury* pointed out that only one Dissenting minister (Thorp) had signed the requisition requesting the meeting. The truth so far as one can tell, was that Dissenters were split, with Unitarians and Parson Leifchild's Congregationalists supporting Emancipation and Baptists and Methodists tending to oppose it. Popular anxiety about Papal repression was expressed in graffiti attacks observed near the rally: 'Wanted a thousand gridirons for burning heretics – Apply to Parson Leifchild.'[93]

35,000 signatures opposing Emancipation were gathered as a direct result of the meeting, the largest number of signatures from any single city. Both men and women seemed to have signed some of the anti-Emancipation petitions issued by the parishes and patronage was an important factor in obtaining signatures. In Clifton, for example, it was alleged that, 'the usual modes of obtaining signatures have been resorted to, – gentlemen have taken their lackeys, and in some instances mistresses their maids, to sign it.'[94]

Church authorities were accused of virtually frog-marching children in their Diocesan school to sign the large petition.[95] Though this was strenuously denied, the *Mercury* later verified the signatures of Diocesan schoolboys whose ages ranged from nine to fourteen.[96]

Overall, the evidence strongly suggests that Catholic Emancipation was opposed by the vast majority of Bristolians and both the city's MPs. Magistrates were accused with siding with the three to four hundred youths who, under the leadership of a chimney sweep known as 'one eyed Dick' took to the streets

> with their blue flag and orange and after destroying the windows in Marsh Street and Host Street [went on] to insult the poor Irish who reside there and whose peaceable conduct has been most exemplary ... [and then] made an attack on the Catholic Chapel in Trenchard street, every window of which they demol- ished.[97]

The Bill however, had passed, and John Gutch bitterly called for the government's dissolution on the grounds that its '... liberalism in religion as well as in commerce' was bringing the country to the 'brink of ruin'.[98]

After Emancipation, anti-Catholic feeling seems to have deepened as evinced by the successful reinstatement of both the Protestant Association[99] and the Reformation Society with increased Anglican backing for its programme for 'the Conversion of the Roman Catholics and the Defence of the Protestant Church'. When its leading light, the Rev. M.R. Whish opened the new church at Bedminster of which he was pastor,[100] *thousands* were reported to have attended its opening, many carrying banners proclaiming such slogans as 'Church and King' and 'Protestant Ascendancy'.[101] When Father O'Farrell repeatedly offered to raise 250 Catholic men to help the Corporation restore law and order during the Bristol riots of 1831, he was curtly refused.[102]

At the same time Catholics were also increasing in numbers and confidence. In 1829 the Benedictine Peter Baines succeeded Peter Collingridge as Vicar Apostolic of the Western District, one of four such Vicars Apostolic in charge of English Catholics. A dynamic highly cultured individual, Baines was the friend of Pope Leo XII himself indicating the growing ascendancy of Papal control over English Catholicism.[103] Throwing aside the inhibitions of a pre-Emancipationist clergy, Baines was a good deal 'less timid; than his predecessors' in promoting the interests of English Catholics.

In 1830 he established Prior Park College in Bath, a development which occasioned a series of hostile pamphlets from the fictional 'Mr Job Nott of Bristol, the Labouring Man's Friend' deploring 'the construction of Jesuitical colleges ... and other monastic Institutions, thereby allowing a foreign jurisdiction in the State'.[104] Baines also encouraged the Rev. Francis Edgeworth to purchase land for a church in Clifton in 1834 to 'meet the rapid increase of Catholicity' in the city. According to Little, it was hoped, that 'this church should surpass any other contemporary Catholic place of worship in England' and form the core of a future cathedral. But although these ambitious plans ended embarrassingly with Edgeworth's bankruptcy and consequent flight to the Continent, the growth of the community continued apace. Edgeworth's successor at the Trenchard Street Chapel, Father O'Farrell, purchased the 'well built and graceful church of the Irvingites (that most anti-Catholic of Protestant off-shoots) which was consecrated by Baines in 1843 as St Mary's-on-the-Quay.[105] By then the Bristol Statistical Society calculated some 500 regular attenders at the city's three Catholic churches, and Oliver reported 2000 Roman Catholic communicants in the city by 1857.[106] Much, though not all, of this increase was due to Irish immigration to Bristol which reached high levels both locally and nationally as a result of general economic distress and the Great Famine of the later 1840s.

This increasing Catholic presence came at a time when the Anglican Diocese was under tremendous pressure. Not only had the

Bishop's Palace been burnt in the riots of 1831, but five years later this 'Cinderella of English Sees' was amalgamated with Gloucester. The independent Bishopric of Bristol existed no longer but became part of a dual diocese.[107] The Church, discredited for its stance against the 1832 Reform Act, had also to contend with a growing number of non-conformists empowered by the newly-widened franchise and emboldened by their growing restiveness over the imposition of church rates.[108]

It is in this context that one needs to consider the controversy over the Oxford Movement's attempts to reinvigorate Anglicanism by reinstating some aspects of Catholic ritual and organization. In Bristol, the Oxford or 'Tractarian' Movement was by the late 1840s particularly identified with Horfield parish church, and such new East Bristol churches as St Mark's in Easton, St Jude's, and St Simon's. In 1850 the Dean of Bristol attacked the Tractarians 'for doing the work of Rome', but the Movement excited interest beyond its immediate supporters. When Edward Pusey, a prominent Tractarian, was invited to preach at St James's, the church was packed and the audience included Quakers, Roman Catholics and the Jewish rabbi.[109]

In the same year, the Whigs allowed the re-establishment of an official Catholic hierarchy in Britain to replace the Vicars Apostolic. The installation of the Catholic Bishop of Clifton caused a furore in Bristol. Many sermons were preached against 'Papal intrusion' and a popular demonstration at Brandon Hill included the burning of guys, bonfires and crackers and 'a rude effigy of the Cardinal Archbishop of Westminster ...'[110] Whig and Tory councillors expressed their displeasure and even the Unitarians who had favoured Catholic Emancipation petitioned against the installation of a formal Catholic hierarchy in England.[111]

Jews, Evangelicals and Liberals

Once Catholic Emancipation was achieved, the Reformation Society turned their attention to proselytization of the Jews. Whilst evangelicals shared many of the older prejudices held against Jews and certainly condemned their rejection of Jesus as Christ, they would have rejected the cruder excesses of Jew-baiting on humanitarian grounds. More importantly, many evangelicals saw the conversion of the Jews as an essential pre-condition for the Second Coming. Working amongst the Jews for their conversion, some missionaries were favourably impressed by the Jewish stress on family life and self-sufficiency. Some evangelically-minded people became personally friendly with the Jews, but always with the hope of converting them. The approach of the Bristol branch of the Reformation Society and the Society for the Promotion of Christianity amongst the Jews was altogether more aggressive and caused resentment amongst Bristol's Jews.[112]

Despite this, relations between Jews and the wider Bristol community seem generally to have improved somewhat since 1753 as evidenced by the response of both the Radical and the Tory press to the Jewish Disability Relief Bill which came to Parliament in 1830 and would have lifted political restrictions on Jews. The debate it occasioned showed the *Bristol Mercury* in favour of the Bill, if implicitly somewhat disdainful of Judaism and Jewish traditions. Replicating without comment an anti-semitic legend from Turkey, the newspaper justified the Bill on the grounds that a man's religion, no matter how mistaken, was between him and the Deity alone.[113]

Felix Farley's Bristol Journal now found Jewish participation in public life palatable in most circumstances arguing that the Jews might be disbelievers but unlike those 'active scheming' Catholics, they were not active proselytizers or enemies of the Establishment. But there were still certain limits:

> Let them crowd into Corporations if they will. But to suffer a JEW TO BE A JUDGE would in a Christian court, be indeed a mockery of all religion. We may as well surrender at once our natural religion and let the SPIRIT OF LIBERALISM have its full play.[114]

The allusion to 'our' natural religion underlines the notion that only the ethnically English and religiously Protestant could be counted as full citizens. In a subsequent editorial, Gutch asserted the impossibility that a Jew could ever be considered an Englishman since Jews could not possibly 'love our native land as Thank God an Englishman was wont to do'.[115] And one Tory broadside held that a supporter of Jewish Emancipation could not possibly have been English but was a secretly circumcised 'Orange boy from Change-Alley' instead.[116] Yet two Bristol petitions for Jewish Emancipation were presented to Parliament in 1830, one being from Protestant Bristolians and the other from 'British-born Jews resident in Bristol'.[117] Jews it seems were now confident enough to put forward a petition but were seen, and saw themselves, as still 'in but not of' the city. Even so, each Sabbath, Jews would offer grateful prayers of obedience to a king and country which had afforded them safe haven.

In the case of the Jews, whilst religious liberalism and Christian charity certainly helped to foster their growing inclusion into Bristol's corporate life, the decisive factor seems to have been an economic one. By 1842 the Jewish community had prospered enough to open a handsome new synagogue in Temple Street. The opening ceremony was attended by a broad range of Christian clergy whose close physical proximity with each other and their hosts during the service was implicitly seen as of symbolic importance:

> On the same bench might be seen some of the strictest of communicants of the established church, with independents, Methodists, quakers and Baptists and all in immediate contact with the descendant of Abraham.[118]

Three years later the wealthy Jewish merchant and shipbroker Abraham Alexander was elected as a Conservative councillor on the reformed City Council. His younger brother William became an alderman in 1850.[119] Their party affiliation tells us more about their class position than their religion and was unlikely to have been representative of the majority of Bristol's Jews. But the entry of the Alexander brothers marks the beginning of the end of the Jews' pariah status in the city.

Conclusion

By 1851, nonconformists outnumbered Anglicans in Bristol, the 1851 Religious Census indicating that just over 44 per cent of those attending a religious service on a particular Sunday were Anglican whilst the rest were nonconformists or Catholics. Yet Anglicans constituted 80 per cent of City councillors and no Catholics sat on the Council in the years immediately after local government reform.[120] Nevertheless, sectarian divisions between Anglicans and nonconformists were beginning to fade significantly under the combined influence of evangelicalism, Church reform and liberal ideology.

The election of the two Jewish councillors by 1850 shows how far the Conservative Party and civic Anglicanism had been affected by religious as well as economic liberalism in the 1840s. Liberalism itself, with its emphasis on individualism and rationality was intertwined with its own particular notions of Protestantism and Englishness. One wonders, for example, why the Unitarians, who of all the nonconformists were the most liberal and consistent champions of both Catholic and Jewish Emancipation, had invited the Hindu reformer Raja Rammohan Roy to preach at Lewin's Mead in 1833. Did they do so not because he was Hindu, but because they saw in him a fellow reformer, advocating a rationalistic and monotheistic humanitarianism so very like their own?[121]

Only a minority in mid-Victorian Bristol had completely internalized a world view based on liberal individualism. Unitarians and other liberal Dissenters were attacked by one at least one clergyman for allegedly wishing to establish the

> liberty of Mahomedans, Hindoos and all sorts of Idolators, to set up in this land of Bibles their Mosques, Pagodas and other idolatrous Temples, *and even to legislate for the Christian Church* ...[122]

This telling phrase neatly encapsulates the fears of a traditional religious and political culture. Once Catholics and Jews were enfranchised, anything might happen. Religious liberalism betokened cultural dissolution, even political subjugation. And there was a sense in which the inclusion of those outside the Judeo-Christian tradition was particularly 'beyond the boundary'. Over a century later, local resistance to the erection of a Bristol mosque revealed the longevity of old anxieties. The cultural resonances of religious exclusion continue to echo long after the political Emancipation of Catholics and Jews.

Notes

1   See 'Letter to the Printer', *FFBJ*, 26 Sept. 1767.

2   H. J. Wilkins, *Edward Colston (1636-1721 A.D.) A Chronological Account of his Life and Work Together with an Account of the Colston Societies and Memorials in Bristol* (Bristol, 1920), 92.

3   B. Little, *The City and County of Bristol: a Study in Atlantic Civilisation* (1954); R. E. Davies, 'Religious Movements in Bristol since the Reformation', in C. M. MacInnes and W. F. Whittard, *Bristol and its Adjoining Counties* (Bristol, 1955); R. E. Davies, *The Church in Bristol: A Short History* (Bristol, 1960); J. Barry, 'The Cultural Life of Bristol, 1640-1775' (unpublished DPhil thesis, University of Oxford, 1985); id., 'The Parish in Civic Life: Bristol and its Churches 1640-1750', in S. J. Wright, ed., *Parish, Church and People: Local Studies in Lay Religion 1350-1750* (1988), 152-78 (thanks to J. Barry for lending me a copy of this chapter); J. Barry and K. Morgan, eds, *Reformation and Revival in Eighteenth-Century Bristol* (BRS, 45, 1994). Older histories of Bristol containing useful material on religion include: J. Latimer, *Annals of Bristol in the Seventeenth, Eighteenth and Nineteenth Centuries* (Bristol 1887-1902), II and III; J. Taylor, *Cursory Observations on the Churches of*

Bristol (Bristol, 1843); G. Pryce, *A Popular History of Bristol: Antiquarian, Topographical and Descriptive from the Earliest Period to the Present Time with Biographical Notices of Eminent Natives and Residents* (Bristol 1861); J. Taylor, *A Book about Bristol: Historical, Ecclesiastical and Biographical from Original Research* (1872); J. F. Nichols and J. Taylor, *Bristol Past and Present* (Bristol 1881-2), II; C. S. and H. Mowvley, *Tradition and Challenge: the Story of Broadmead Baptist Church, Bristol from 1685-1991* (Bristol, 1991); I. Jones, *Bristol Congregationalism* (Bristol, 1947); G. H. Wicks, *Free Church Life in Bristol* (Bristol, 1910); Rev. M. Caston, *Independency in Bristol: With Brief Memorials of its Church and Pastors* (1860); J. G. Fuller, *The Rise and Progress of Dissent in Bristol Chiefly in relation to the Broadmead Chapel* (1840); G. Oliver, *Collections Illustrating the History of the Catholic Religion in the Counties of Cornwall, Devon, Somerset, Wiltshire and Gloucestershire* (1857). There seem to be no historical treatments of Bristol Jewry published for this period.

4   H. Meller, *Leisure and the Changing City, 1870-1914* (1976), 79.

5   Barry, 'The Parish in Civic Life', 152-78.

6   For a general introduction to the various religious divisions within Protestantism see R. Brown, *Church and State in Modern Britain, 1700-1850* (1990), 92-129; H. Perkin, *The Origins of Modern English Society, 1780-1880* (1969), 196-208.

7   U. Henriques, *Religious Toleration in England 1787-1833* (1961), 13-15; R. Hall, 'Christianity Consistent with the Love of Freedom', in O. Gregory, ed., *The Miscellaneous Works and Remains of the Rev. Robert Hall, with a Memoir of his Life* (1846), 128, 212-3.

8   See D. Hempton, *Methodism and Politics in British Society, 1750-1850* (1987 ed.) for an excellent assessment of Methodism, esp. 20-55; also D. Hempton, 'Religion in British Society, 1740-1790', in J. Black, ed., *British Politics and Society from Walpole to Pitt* (1990), 214. For Bristol Methodism, see for example K. Morgan, *John Wesley and Bristol* (BHA, 75, 1990) and John Kent, ed., 'Wesleyan Membership in Bristol, 1783', in *An Ecclesiastical Miscellany* (Bristol and Gloucestershire Archaeological Society, Records Section, 1976) XI, 105-32; D. Raimo, 'Spiritual Harvest: The Anglo-American Revival in Boston, Massachusetts, and Bristol, England, 1738-1742' (unpublished PhD thesis, University of Wisconsin, 1974).

9   'Account of the Life of Thomas Newton Written by Himself', in *Lives of Pocock, Pearce and Newton*, I (1816), 126-8 for the reference to Methodism as a 'bastard kind of Popery'; D. Hempton, *Methodism and Politics*, 278-9.

10   *Gentleman's Magazine*, 21 (May 1751), 186; but Bristol's small Huguenot community soon assimilated, see R. Mayo, *The Huguenots in Bristol* (BHA, 61, 1985).

11   C. Roth, *A History of the Jews in England* (Oxford, 1941), 213-20; T. W. Perry, *Public Opinion, Propaganda and Politics in Eighteenth Century England: A Study of the Jew Bill of 1753* (Cambridge Mass., 1962); F. Felsenstein, *Anti-Semitic Sterotypes: A Paradigm of Otherness in English Popular Culture, 1660-1830* (1995), 187-244; T. Endelman, *The Jews of Georgian England: Tradition and Change in a Liberal Society* (Philadelphia, Pa., 1979), 86-117.

12   *The Parliamentary History of England from the Earliest Period to the Year 1803*, XIV (1747-53), 1384.

13   Rev. M. Adler, 'The Jew of Bristol in Pre-Expulsion Days' (paper delivered to Jewish Historical Society of England, 12 Nov. 1928); Roth, *A History of the Jews in England*, 3ff; H. G. Richardson, *The English Jewry under Angevin Kings* (1960); 'Worth a Jew's Eye', in I. Evans, ed., *Brewer's Dictionary of Phrase and Fable* (1990), 604-05 on penalty imposed on a Bristol Jew in this period.

14   H. Pollins, *An Economic History of the Jews in England* (Brunswick, N.J., 1982), 24.

15   *FFBJ*, 1 Dec. 1753; E. Ralph, ed., 'Bishop Secker's Diocese Book', in P. McGrath, ed., *A Bristol Miscellany* (BRS, 37, 1985), 47, 49.

I Bristol, by John Speed, 1610.

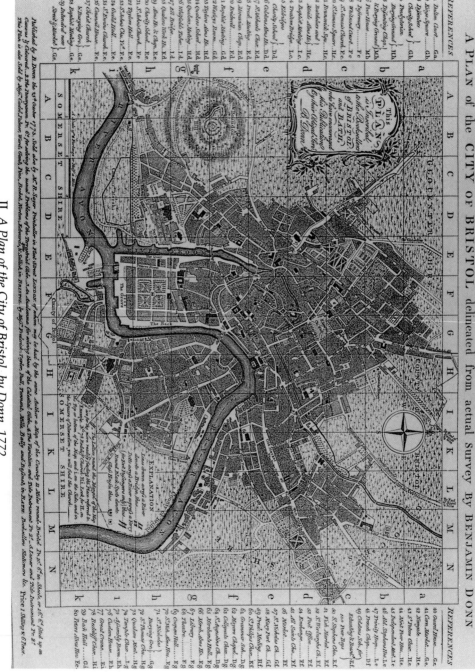

II A Plan of the City of Bristol, by Donn, 1772.

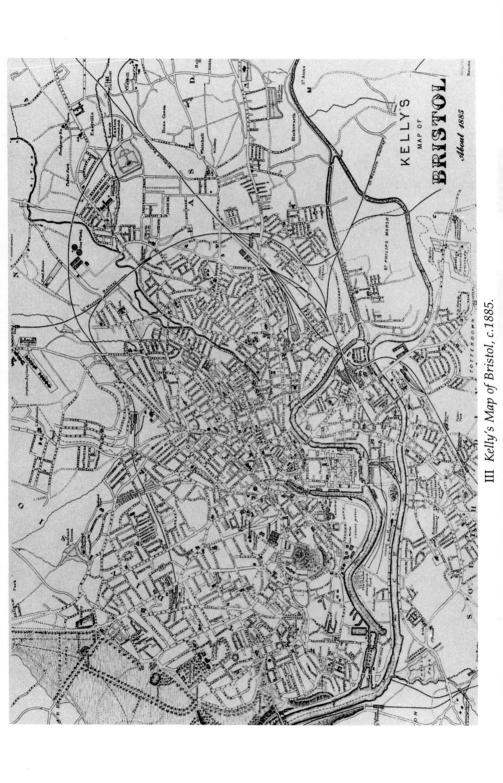

III *Kelly's Map of Bristol, c.1885.*

IVa (above), b, and c (opposite) The slave trade is literally and symbolically marginalized in Nicholas Pocock's celebratory portrayal of a Bristol privateer, c.1760. Arms, and other English goods were traded for slaves on the West African coast. Slave labour was central to the sugar industry on which so much of Bristol's prosperity once depended.

V North West Prospect of Bristol by Samuel and Nathaniel Buck, 1734. Bristolians exercise their rights on Brandon Hill above the symbolic geography of Queen Square. Surrounded on three sides by shipping, the elite houses of Queen Square frame the public sphere as well as the centrepiece statue of William III.

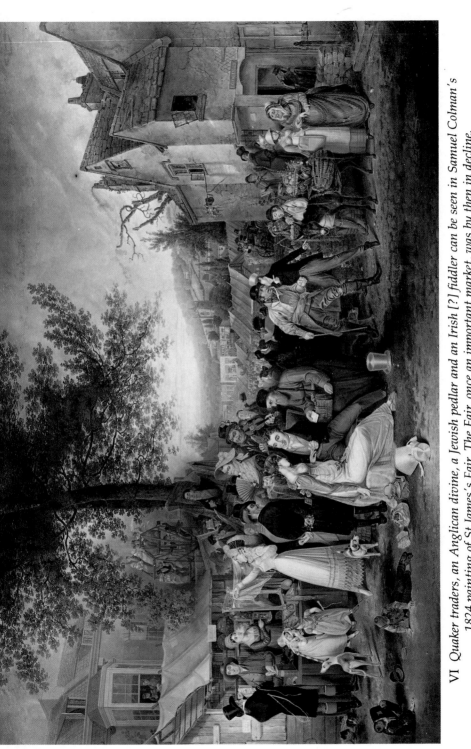

VI Quaker traders, an Anglican divine, a Jewish pedlar and an Irish [?] fiddler can be seen in Samuel Colman's 1824 painting of St James's Fair. The Fair, once an important market, was by then in decline.

VII Bristol Bridge by T.L.S. Rowbotham, c.1825. Horses and wagons, handcarts and porters bring goods over the Bristol Bridge.

VIII *The panic and impending ruin occasioned by an unstable banking system are evoked in*
The Stoppage of the Bank, *Rolinda Sharples' somewhat fictionalized Bristol streetscape of 1825.*

IX A peaceful day in Queen Square painted in 1827 by T.L.S. Rowbotham. Shortly thereafter, the Square was to serve as the site of one of England's largest rallies against Catholic emancipation.

X *This lithograph of the 1831 Bristol riots by W.J. Muller shows one rioter in Queen Square toasting William III, whose 'Glorious Revolution' in 1688 symbolized 'Protestant Liberty'.*

XI *Bristolians celebrate the passing of the Great Reform Act of 1832 in this detail from* The Grand Reform Dinner on Brandon Hill *by W.J. Muller and T.L.S. Roubotham.*

XII *Nonconformity in the ascendant. Zion Chapel Bedminster by Samuel Colman c.1832.*

XIII The SS Great Britain proved too large for the port of Bristol as Joseph Walter's 1845 potrayal of her, high in the water, shows.

XIV *A late Victorian photograph of Bristol's congested central area, taken from St Mary Redcliffe in 1872.*

XV *An architect's view of the late Victorian Bristol business community: 'Corn Exchange, Bristol; design for upper storey and glass roof', by E.M. Barry, 1872.*

XVI Woodwell Lane Buildings, designed by Elijah Hoole, from The Architect, 21 August 1875. The Winkworth sisters' pioneer model dwellings scheme for workers predated the first Council housing in Bristol by more than a quarter of a century. Insets: Catherine and Susanna Winkworth.

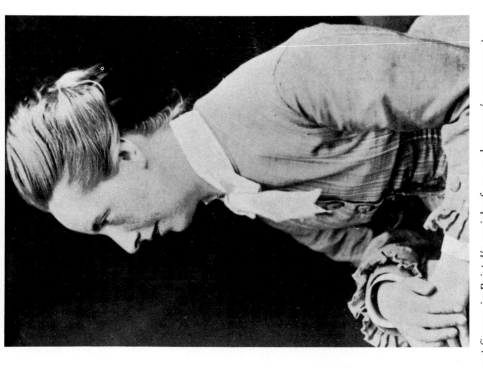

XVII *Mary Clifford* (left) *and Emily Sturge* (right) *were two important figures in Bristol's social reform and women's movements.*

XVIII *Workhouse as rural idyll. The Flax Bourton workhouse, depicted by William Curtin in 1855, served Bedminster as well as other parts of Bristol.*

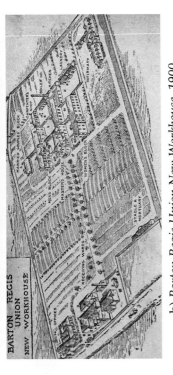

b) *Barton Regis Union New Workhouse, 1900.*

c) *Fishponds Workhouse.*

XIX *Bristol's other workhouses: a) St Peter's Hospital, Joseph Pike, 1914.*

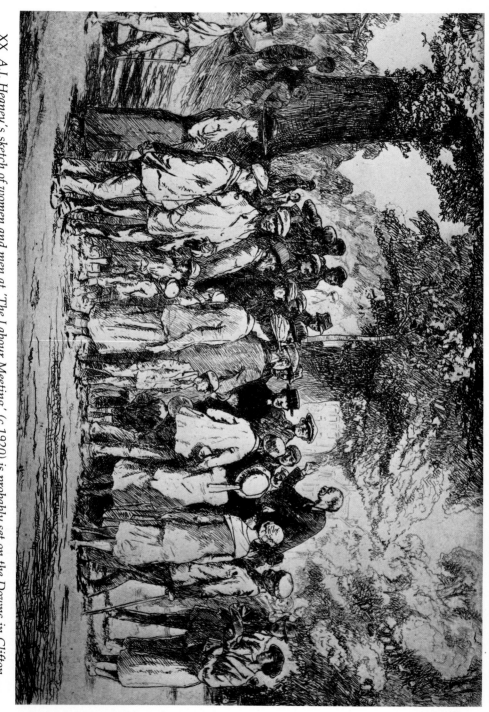

XX A.J. Heaney's sketch of women and men at 'The Labour Meeting' (c.1920) is probably set on the Downs in Clifton.

XXI Some Who Made Bristol Famous, *by Ernest Board, 1930. Bristol's civic pride is recast in the early twentieth century to include a select band of Bristol luminaries celebrated for their exploits in commerce and charity, the arts and sciences, religious reform and imperial rule.*

1. *General Sir William Draper 1721–1787.*
2. *Edmund Burke 1729–1797.*
3. *John Carr D. 1586.*
4. *Henry Overton Wills 1800–1871.*
5. *H.H. Wills 1856–1922.*
6. *Sir George Wills 1854–1928.*
7. *Robert Fitz Harding (Lord of Berkeley).*
8. *W.G. Grace 1848–1915.*
9. *Richard Renolds 1735–1816.*
10. *Joseph Fry 1728–1787.*
11. *Mary Carpenter 1807–1877.*
12. *George Muller 1806–1898.*
13. *Ald. John Whitson 1557–1629.*
14. *Edward Colston 1636–1721.*
15. *Lord Winterstoke 1830–1911.*
16. *John, Lord Lawrence 1811–1879.*
17. *Robert Southey 1774–1843.*
18. *Thomas Chatterton 1752–1770.*
19. *Martin Pring 1580–1626.*
20. *John Guy D. 1628.*
21. *Robert Thorne D. 1527.*
22. *Sir Ferdinando Gorges, 1566–1647.*
23. *and 24. John Cabot and Sebastian Cabot.*
25. *William Wyrcestre 1415–1482.*
26. *William Canynges 1399–1474.*
27. *W.J. Muller 1812–1845.*
28. *E.H. Baily 1788–1867.*
29. *Sir Thomas Lawrence 1769–1830.*
30. *Hannah More 1745–1833.*
31. *Sir Humphry Davy 1778–1829.*
32. *John Addington Symonds 1840–1893.*
33. *John Latimer 1824–1904.*
34. *Robert Lucas Pearsall 1795–1856.*
35. *Mary Robinson (Perdita) 1758–1800.*
36. *Sir Henry Irving 1838–1905.*
37. *Robert, Earl of Gloucester D. 1147.*
38. *John Wesley 1703–1791.*
39. *Admiral Sir William Penn 1621–1670.*

XXII *Men at work on the steam tug Bull Dog in the Bristol Docks c.1900.*

XXIII Women at work in the early twentieth century. a)(top left) Fry's [?] Chocolate Angels, n.d. b)(bottom left) Wills Tobacco worker, n.d. c)(right) Underglaze 'paintresses' in the Bristol Pottery, Fishponds, Pountney & Co. Ltd., c.1928. The 'scientific' ethos of the Fry's and Wills's factories contrasts with that of the Bristol Pottery, Fishponds, where underglaze 'paintresses' are pictured in a workshop setting.

XXIV *The printing industry and car manufacture came into their own in inter–war Bristol.*
(above) *Worker printing cigarette packages at Mardon, Son & Hall.*
(below) *The 'Bristol' car passing the Bristol City Docks.*

16 For blood libel see *FFBJ*, 16-23 June 1753, 7-14 July 1753; for usury see *FFBJ*, 2-9 June 1753.

17 See for example, *FFBJ*, 12-19 May 1753, 19-26 May 1753, 2-9 June 1753.

18 See *FFBJ*, 14-15 July 1753.

19 See for example *FFBJ*, 2-9 June 1753, 9-16 June 1753, 21-28 July 1753.

20 On circumcision see *FFBJ*, 2-9 June 1753, 30 June-7 July 1753, 14-21 July 1753, 10-17 Nov. 1753, 12-19 Jan. 1754. See also S. Gilman, *The Jew's Body* (New York, 1991).

21 See for example, *FFBJ*, 12-19 May 1753, 7-14 July 1753, 17 Nov. 1753.

22 *FFBJ*, 9-16 June 1753. See also 28 July-4 Aug. 1753.

23 *FFBJ*, 21-8 July 1753.

24 *FFBJ*, 10-17 Nov. 1753.

25 The absence of surviving Whig newspapers in Bristol prevents a definitive verdict on this point. But see Rev. Samuel Seyer, *Memoirs Historical and Topographical of Bristol and its Neighbourhood from the Earliest Period Down to the Present Time*, II (Bristol, 1823), 596; BRL, Jefferies Collection, XII, 'Anecdotes of Dean Tucker, Formerly a Canon of Bristol Cathedral', *Bristol Times* (undated extract) and Jefferies Collection, X, Anon. '"The Mountains in Labour" to the Worthy Electors of Bristol' (1754). See also BRL, B20095, William Dyer Diaries 1767, which offers a vivid description of a procession and effigy burning of Tucker in protest against the Bill for naturalizing the Jews, but dates it as 18 April 1751, the day the Bill to Naturalize Foreign Protestants was postponed; Roth, *A History of the Jews in England*, 218-19; H. Brown, 'The Life and Works of Josiah Tucker' (unpublished MA thesis, University of Bristol, 1928).

26 BRL, *The Bristol Contest: being a collection of all the Papers Published by Both Parties on the Election, 1754*, B10942, 16, 35-6, 50, 55; for Nugent's views see *The Parliamentary History of England from the Earliest Period to the Year 1803*, XIV (1747-53), 1383-4; and W. S. Lewis, ed., *The Yale Edition of Horace Walpole's Correspondence*, XXXV (1973), 179 (thanks to Steve Poole for this reference); see also *FFBJ*, 17 Nov. 1753.

27 See E. P. Thompson, *Customs in Common* (1993 ed.), 486.

28 Pollins, *Economic History of the Jews in England*, 78, 81, 101; also J. Samuel, 'The Jews of Bristol' (unpublished paper delivered to Bristol Jewish History Group, 1993).

29 *Sarah Farley's Bristol Journal*, 22 Sept. 1786. I am indebted to Judith Samuel for this reference.

30 Oliver, *Collections*, 108.

31 H. T. Buckle, *History of Civilisation in England* (1885), I, 401.

32 BRO, 09701 (14), Letter John Paston to Justice Haines 1719; see C. Haydon, *Anti-Catholicism in Eighteenth-Century England, c.1714-80: A Political and Social Study* (Manchester 1993), 142 who indicates Catholics were kept under close surveillance by Bristol authorities.

33 Haydon, *Anti-Catholicism in Eighteenth-Century England*, 46.

34 Oliver, *Collections*, 108.

35 Little, *City and County of Bristol*, 201; D. Osborne, 'The Catholic Community of Bristol in the Eighteenth Century: A Social Survey' (unpublished thesis for a Post-graduate Diploma in Local History, University of the West of England, 1993), 38, 45; see Latimer, *Annals of Bristol*, II, 115 and Nichols and Taylor, *Bristol Past and Present*, II, 273-5; B. Little 'Catholic Bristol: Some Eighteenth-century Facts', *South Western Catholic History*, 5 (1987), 47.

36 L. Colley, *Britons: Forging the Nation 1707-1837* (1992), 11-55.

37 *FFBJ*, 23 Dec. 1753.

38 Misses Leonore Knapp and Marianne Galton showed an early interest in

Catholicism, as is discussed in my unpublished paper 'The Religious Experience of Moravian Women in Bristol 1755-1833'. For references to anti-Catholic publications see Colley, *Britons*, 11-55; see letter from 'A Friend to Toleration', in *BMerc*, 21 Dec. 1812.

39 Oliver, *Collections*, 108.

40 Newton, *Lives*, 158-9; B. Little, 'Some Catholic Facts', 49; Ralph, 'Bishop Secker's Diocese Book', 27, gives a somewhat different interpretation of Newton's account from my own.

41 BRL, Jefferies Collection, X, Anon, 'To the Gentlemen Clergy, Freemen and Freeholders of the City of Bristol' (c.1780).

42 Osborne, 'The Catholic Community of Bristol', 40-9. For John Wesley's concern over the Catholic influence see Hempton, *Methodism and Politics in British Society*, 34-8.

43 *FFBJ*, 17 June 1780.

44 E. Black, *The Association: British Extraparliamentary Political Organization, 1769-1793* (Cambridge, Mass., 1963); Haydon, *Anti-Catholicism in Eighteenth-Century England*, 207.

45 *FFBJ*, 17 June 1780. See also BRO, undated anonymous journal, 11931 (1) which puts the threat at the 10 June.

46 UBL, Bristol Moravian Collection, Elders' Conference (26 June 1780).

47 Newton, *Lives*, 221, 218; see E. P. Thompson, *The Making of the English Working Class* (1963), 85.

48 M. Fedden, *Notes on the History of St Mary's-on-the-Quay* (Bristol, 1949), 12; P. Marshall, *Bristol and the American War of Independence* (BHA, 41, 1977), 19; W. and R. Chambers, *Chambers Biographical Dictionary* (1897), 154.

49 Oliver, *Collections*, 114.

50 Nichols and Taylor, *Bristol Past and Present*, II, 74.

51 Henriques, *Religious Toleration*, 138, Clark, *English Society*, 353.

52 J. Wolffe, *The Protestant Crusade in Great Britain, 1829-1860* (Oxford, 1991), 26.

53 Unitarians, according to Clark, *English Society*, 281-3 tended to be Socinian, i.e. deny Christ's divinity and by implication the whole need for divine redemption; BRO, O. Griffiths, 'Sidelights on the History of Presbyterian-Unitarianism from the Records of Lewin's Mead Chapel, Bristol', n.d., A3. The congregation did not call itself Unitarian until 1813 probably because Unitarianism, as it denied the existence of the Trinity, was not legally tolerated until 1812.

54 BRO, 39399 CD/A/3/(a), Minutes of the Bristol Dissenters Committee (1790-5); BRO, Jefferies Collection, XIII, The Bristol Dissenters Committee (1790), 121.

55 BRO, 5, Roger Angerson, 'Descriptive list of the records of the Bristol and Frenchay Monthly meetings of the Society of Friends 1667-1946' (unpublished typescript, Jan 1963).

56 R. Hole, *Pulpits, Politics and Public Order in England 1760-1832* (Cambridge, 1989), 123.

57 BRL, Jefferies Collection, XIV, 69, 'Old Mother Church'.

58 G. M. Ditchfield, 'The Parliamentary Struggle over the Repeal of the Test and Corporation Acts, 1787-1790', *EHR*, 89 (1974) 551-77 for an analysis of the Parliamentary response to repeal; W. Gibson, *Church, State and Society, 1760-1850* (1994), 68; James Bradley, *Religion, Revolution and English Radicalism: Nonconformity in Eighteenth Century Politics and Society* (Cambridge, 1990), 195-223.

59 *BMerc*, 6 April 1812.

60 *BMerc*, 6 July 1812. For a wider discussion of the political implications of Dissent and Methodism in Bristol see Steve Poole, 'Popular Politics in Bristol, Somerset and Wiltshire, 1791-1805' (unpublished PhD thesis, University of Bristol, 1993).

61 *BMerc*, 3 Feb. 1812.

62 I. Sellers, *Nineteenth-Century Nonconformity* (1977), 65.

63 See Jones, *Bristol Congregationalism*, 14. For the Baptists see O. Gregory and J. Foster, eds, *The Miscellaneous Works and Remains of the Rev. Robert Hall, with a Memoir of his Life* (1846), 16-17, 48-53. Robert Hall left Bristol in 1791 as a religious radical, veering on the edges of Socinian materialism and came back in 1826 to be Minister to the Broadmead Baptists a pious evangelical.

64 Hempton, *Methodism and Politics*, 141-2.

65 Bodleian Library, Oxford, John Johnson Collection, Religion, *Petition of members and friends of the Wesleyan Methodists Society of the City of Bristol*, (c.1812).

66 *BMerc*, 28 Dec. 1812.

67 Hempton, *Methodism and Politics*, 116.

68 *BMerc*, 28 Dec. 1828.

69 The Rev. William Thorp (1771-1815) Born in Yorkshire, his father was a Congregationalist pastor. In 1806 he served as a pastor at Bristol and was a very popular preacher. Evangelical Anglican divines such as Biddulph and Day attended his funeral. Price, *A Popular History*, 212. The sermon discussed is W. Thorp, *Catholic Emancipation* (Bristol, 1813) and was kindly lent to me by Dr Martin Crossley Evans.

70 *BMerc*, 8 Feb. 1813.

71 Bodleian Library, John Johnson Collection, Religion, J. Plowden, *To Samuel Birch, Esq. and Others* (emphasis added).

72 *BMerc*, 21 Dec. 1812.

73 Nichols and Taylor, *Bristol Past and Present*, II, 274; Oliver, *Collections*, 110-12, Feyden, *St Mary's-on-the-Quay*, 10.

74 *BMerc*, 18 Feb. 1828; *FFBJ*, 14 Jan. 1829.

75 See 'I'd Be a Catholic' printed in the *BG*, 30 Oct. 1828

76 G. Parsons, 'Victorian Roman Catholicism: Emancipation, Expansion and Achievement', in G. Parsons, ed., *Religion in Victorian Britain*, I (Manchester, 1988), 150.

77 The Bristol Auxiliary of the British and Foreign Bible Society (1810), The Church of England Tract Society (1811), Bristol Auxilliary of Missionary Society (1812), the Church of England Missionary Society for Africa and the East (1813), The Bristol Auxilliary Society for Promoting Christianity Amongst Jews, the City Mission, the Seaman's Mission, the Bristol and Clifton Association for Promoting the Moral and Religious Improvement of Ireland are all mentioned in the local press.

78 G. Wicks, *Free Church Life in Bristol* (Bristol 1910); BRL B17074, 141; *Seyer's Calendar*, 7 Feb. 1820.

79 *BMerc*, 14 Dec. 1812.

80 *BMerc*, 28 Dec. 1812; 4 Jan. 1813.

81 Rev. J. East, *The Death of a Protestant Prince Improved by a Reconsideration of Protestant Principles in Contrast with those of the Church of Rome in a Discourse Delivered in the Parish Church of St Philip and St Jacob on Sunday evening, January 21, 1827* (Bristol, 1827), 28. Thanks to Dr Martin Crossley Evans for the loan of this sermon.

82 *BMerc*, 24 March 1828.

83 *FFBJ*, 15 March 1828.

84 *FFBJ*, 9 Aug. 1828; *BMerc*, 12 Aug. 1828.

85 *BMerc*, 7 April 1828; Letter to Editor from 'G.C.', *BG*, 23 Oct. 1828.

86 See letter 'From a Sincere Lover of Truth', *FFBJ*, 19 July 1828.

87 Latimer, *Annals*, III, 127.

88 *BG*, 20 Nov. 1828.

89 *FFBJ*, 7 Feb. 1829; for Robert Southey's opposition see R. Hole, *Pulpits, Politics and Public Order*, 234.

90 *BMerc*, 3 March 1829. J. M. Gutch, *FFBJ*'s printer had originally published Thorp's pamphlet.

91 *FFBJ*, 14 Jan. 1829.

92 *BMerc*, 17 Feb. 1829.

93 Nichols and Taylor, *Bristol Past and Present*, II, 295. I am indebted to Dr Crossley Evans for drawing my attention to this reference.

94 *BMerc*, 17 Feb. 1829.

95 *BMerc*, 17 Feb. 1829.

96 *BMerc*, 24 Feb. 1829; *FFBJ*, 21 Jan. 1829.

97 *BMerc*, 24 March 1829.

98 *FFBJ*, 4 April 1829.

99 See BRL, 28605-09, *Memoir of the Late Rev. T. T. Biddulph*, 11.

100 The Rev. Martin Richard Whish was also Prebendary of Sarum and Perpetual Curate and Lecturer of St Thomas in Bristol.

101 *BMerc*, 15 Sept. 1829.

102 Fedden, *St Mary-on-the-Quay*, 13.

103 Little, *The City and County of Bristol*, 271-2; Parsons, 'Victorian Roman Catholicism', 153.

104 BRL, Weare Collection of Broadsides, I; B22361; The Rev. J. S. Roche, *A History of Prior Park College and its founder Bishop Baines* (1931), 32, 107ff. Thanks to Dr Crossley Evans for the loan of this volume.

105 Oliver, *Collections*, 112-13; Little, *City and County*, 271-2.

106 BRO 4596, *Proceedings of the Bristol Statistical Society, 1841*. Thanks to Matthew Woollard for this information; Oliver, *Collections*, 112 ff.

107 Little, *City and County of Bristol*, 270.

108 E. R. Norman, *Church and Society in England 1770-1970* (Oxford, 1976), 105ff; see Fuller, *Dissent in Bristol*, chap. 9 for an example of nonconformist contempt for Anglicanism.

109 P. G. Cobb, *The Oxford Movement in Nineteenth Century Bristol* (BHA, 68, 1988), 6-15; see Arnold's comment quoted in R. Brown, *Church and State in Modern Britain, 1700-1850* (1991), 540.

110 *BMerc*, 9 Nov. 1850. See also *FFBJ*, 26 Oct. 1850. 2 Nov. 1850, 9 Nov. 1850.

111 *BMerc*, 9 Nov. 1850; G. Bush, *Bristol and its Municipal Government 1820-1851* (BRS, 29, 1976), 211; O. Griffiths, 'Sidelights on the History of Presbyterian-Unitarianism...', 23-4.

112 Letter to Rev. Mr Whish from 'Cosmopolite', in *BM*, 22 Sept. 1829 and editorial *BM*, 29 Sept. 1829; Letter from Mr Whish, *FFBJ*, 26 Sept. 1829; 22 Nov. 1845; Henriques, *Religious Toleration*, 175-205.

113 *BM*, 20 April 1830; for anti-Jewish legend see *BM*, 1 June 1830. See A. Gillam *The Emancipation of the Jews in England 1830-1860* (1982), 17-31.

114 *FFBJ*, 24 April 1830.

115 *FFBJ*, 22 May 1830.

116 BRL, B22361, Weare Collection of Broadsides, 'Replication to the Parsons and Quakers' (c.1830).

117 *BG*, 11 May 1830.

118 *BMerc*, 20 Aug. 1842; thanks to Judith Samuel for references regarding Bristol's support for Jew's right to hold municipal office, *BMerc*, 27 Mar. 1841, and William Gladstone's opposition to it, *BMerc*, 3 Apr. 1841.

119 Bush, *Bristol and its Municipal Government*, 131, 238.
120 Bush, *Bristol and its Municipal Government*, 130.
121 R. Barot, *Bristol and the Indian Independence Movement* (BHA, 70, 1988), 6 and V. Ware, *Beyond the Pale: White Women, Racism and History* (1992), 123-5.
122 *BM*, 3 March 1829.

ECONOMIC GROWTH AND THE BUSINESS COMMUNITY IN BRISTOL SINCE 1840

Philip Ollerenshaw and Peter Wardley

Introduction

Bristol entered the nineteenth century a prosperous large urban centre with a diversified economy. Its population derived income from a wide variety of activities including mining, agriculture, commerce, manufacturing and personal services.[1] Although Bristol's economic development at this time has been compared, not always favourably, with the rapidly growing industrial cities of Lancashire and Yorkshire, its history and fortunes are perhaps distorted by such comparisons.[2] By contrast with the new centres of textile production of Yorkshire and Lancashire, which exhibited rapid population growth and experienced both the benefits and costs associated with a high degree of dependence upon a narrow range of industrial activities, Bristol's economic growth throughout the nineteenth and twentieth centuries appeared more sedate, though always persistent, and encompassed a broad range of economic occupations.

Although Bristol exhibited a relatively stable and predictable economic growth over the long run, substantial changes occurred in its economic structure as the relative size of industries changed within the city, occupations were created in new industries, and some previously prosperous industries, including brass and glass manufacture, first declined and then vanished. This pattern of undramatic but sustained economic growth, rising incomes, industrial innovation and structural change over the long run is also a reasonably accurate description of the experience of the United Kingdom as a whole.[3] To that extent, Bristol could be viewed as a microcosm of recent British economic experience.

As the unofficial regional capital of the south west, Bristol, like York,[4] was a centre of secular and ecclesiastical administration and a focus of judicial, military, social and cultural activities. The income derived from occupations associated with these activities sustained demand within the city for goods and services and stimulated the growth of commerce and industry. However, the relative success of Bristol's manufacturing and commercial businesses depended upon the ability of producers to provide goods and services demanded in

124

regional, national and international markets. Although some producers, including those of perishables, construction, transport and personal services and, after 1900, the tobacco industry, often faced little effective competition until recently, other sectors of the Bristol economy, including shipping services, textile manufacture, iron and steel production and marine engineering, usually operated in a highly competitive environment.

Bristol's Economic Growth in the Long Run

Although evidence can be produced which illustrates Bristol's economic development since 1841, it is difficult to provide a comprehensive picture of long-run economic growth in the absence of data which capture changes in income and productivity. The four indices employed here to provide this outline are population growth, employment patterns, a volume measure of trade through the port of Bristol and a measure of financial activity, inter-bank clearing.[5]

Comparisons of the decadal censuses of population provide information on the growth of population and changes in the economic structure of the city as reflected in the distribution of the labour force by economic sector and by industry. The size and growth of Bristol's total and economically active population is presented in Table 3, which enumerates the effects of the major boundary changes and indicates a watershed in the city's development after 1961. In part this more recent change reflects changing patterns of residence and work, with an increasing number of those employed within the city's boundaries choosing to live outside Bristol. Changes in Bristol's economic structure over the period are indicated by Table 4 which records the sectoral composition of the city's labour force. Economic development in Bristol was associated with a relative shift of employment from personal services to manufacturing and, over the last thirty years, a shift from manufacturing into commercial, financial and government services. The two major changes in industrial employment during this period have both been associated with changes in defence spending that had direct effects on the local manufacturing sector. The first, a major increase in the 1930s, was a result of rearmament which caused a rapid expansion of the aircraft and motor vehicle industries.[6] The second, a drastic decrease in the 1980s, was associated with a national decline in industrial production, but Bristol firms which depended to a large extent on defence contracts were hit particularly hard.[7]

Trade through the Port of Bristol offers another opportunity to assess the long-run trends of economic growth but the shortcomings of the statistics preclude an assessment of the whole period. The net registered tonnage of vessels entering Bristol between 1850 and 1939, presented in Figure 2, provides an indicator of the volume of traffic; here 'total tonnage' is the sum of its two components, tonnage reported as either 'coastal' or 'foreign' trade with countries outside the UK.[8]

TABLE 3: The Population and Employment Structure of Bristol, 1841-1991.

	Boundaries of 1835	City of 1935	Post 1941 Census	All Economically Active	Minimum age of those Active
1841	125146	n.a.		47590	Unspecified
1851	137328	n.a.		55650	Over 20 years old
1861	154093	179000		74451	Unspecified
1871	182696	219000		99110	Over 20 years old
1881	206874	263500		117508	Over 5 years old
1891	221578	299500		101769	Over 10 years old
1901	224013	342500		145474	Over 10 years old
1911	357114	362000		163612	Over 10 years old
1921	376975	382436		174103	Over 12 years old
1931	397012	403948		188461	Over 14 years old
1941	n.a.	355408*		169977**	Over 14 years old
1951			442994	199201	Over 14 years old
1961			436520	200600	Over 15 years old
1971			425203	188000	
1981			384875	166470	
1991			376146	159830	

Source: *Population Census of the England and Wales*, 1841 et seq.; H. A. Shannon and E. Grebenik, *The Population of Bristol* (Cambridge, 1943), 6; W.H. Whyte, Nuffield College Social Reconstruction Survey [NCRS] (unpublished, 1941; copy held in Nuffield College Library, NCRS/C1); Bristol City Council, *Bristol: An Employment Profile* (Bristol, 1987); C.H. Lee, *British Regional Employment Statistics, 1841-1971* (Cambridge, 1979).

*   National Registration Statistics. (415,500 in mid-1938.)

**   Exchange of Uninsurance Books at five Bristol Exchanges. NCSRS, Changes in Occupied Population in Bristol, 1938-41.

While the volume and value of goods flowing into Bristol by ship has always greatly exceeded the outflow, the relative contribution of shipping received by trade from sources outside the UK can be all too easily overstated. One of the striking features of Figure 2 is the very different growth paths reported under the these two headings, 'coastal' and 'foreign'. At the beginning of the period coastal tonnage outweighed foreign but the latter experienced higher rates of growth for most of the subsequent period. In 1851 the balance between the two classes was of the ratio 1:4 in favour of tonnage arriving from other ports in the UK. By 1860 the ratio was 1:2.4; parity was achieved by 1892 and by 1910 tonnage recorded as foreign was double that of the coastal trade. After the First World War the ratio of 2:1 was re-established and by 1939 recorded foreign exceeded coastal tonnage by 3:1.[9]

TABLE 4: Occupational Structure of Bristol, 1841-1961.
Per cent of total employment by industrial order.

	1841	1871	1901	1931	1961
Agriculture, forestry and fishing	2.6	1.9	0.8	0.8	0.7
Mining and quarrying	1.3	0.5	1.3	0.4	0.0
Food, drink and tobacco	3.9	4.5	6.2	4.1	3.3
Coal and petroleum products	0.0	0.1	0.0	0.0	0.0
Chemical and allied industries	0.8	1.0	1.2	0.3	0.4
Metal manufacture	3.3	2.2	0.1	0.8	0.4
Mechanical engineering	2.1	1.8	3.0	5.8	10.7
Instrument engineering	0.4	0.3	0.1	0.1	0.0
Electrical engineering	0.0	0.0	0.2	0.9	2.3
Shipbuilding and marine engineering	0.7	0.9	0.2	0.0	0.0
Vehicles	0.8	0.7	0.9	0.2	0.0
Metal goods not elsewhere specified	1.2	0.7	1.7	0.0	0.0
Textiles	2.9	2.3	1.3	0.2	0.0
Leather, leather goods and fur	1.1	1.2	1.1	0.4	0.5
Clothing and footwear	14.3	16.9	14.0	5.1	1.5
Brick, pottery, glass, cement, etc.	1.3	1.5	0.8	0.3	0.2
Timber, furniture, etc.	6.5	3.2	2.8	3.3	1.6
Paper, printing and publishing	1.0	1.5	4.1	4.1	3.5
Other manufacturing industries	0.3	0.6	0.0	0.0	0.6
Construction	4.9	8.1	7.8	4.0	4.0
Gas, electricity and water	0.0	0.7	1.0	0.0	0.0
Transport and communications	3.8	6.6	11.0	11.7	13.5
Distributive trades	3.7	7.3	8.3	13.6	10.7
Insurance, banking, finance & business services	0.3	2.2	5.8	13.6	15.0
Professional and scientific services	5.4	4.3	4.9	4.3	9.3
Miscellaneous services	23.8	19.3	14.9	13.0	11.1
Public administration and defence	1.4	1.4	1.7	0.9	2.3
Not Classified	12.1	8.5	4.9	12.1	8.3
	100.0	100.0	100.0	100.0	100.0

Source: *Population Census of England and Wales.*

Apart from the marked hiatus during and immediately after the First World War these data show a steady growth of trade volume throughout the period. Given the contemporary political debates

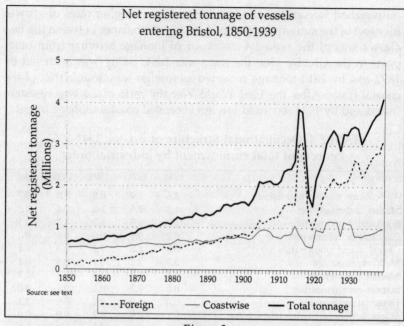

Figure 2

which focused on the dock facilities, and the importance attached to them subsequently by historians,[10] it is perhaps worth noting that none of the new major docking facilities was associated, either immediately or after a short time-lag, with a marked increase in traffic recorded for the customs area covered by the Bristol office.[11] It is probable, however, that the improved access for larger ships secured traffic which might otherwise have been diverted to other ports. This factor certainly encouraged those who sponsored the construction of Avonmouth Docks (opened in February 1877), the Portishead Docks (April 1880) and, after the City's Docks Committee had taken over the management of the Severn Estuary facilities in September 1884, the Royal Edward Docks (July 1908).[12]

The development of these new facilities soon proved to be of strategic as well as commercial importance. By contrast with the Boer War, Bristol played a significant role in the prosecution of the First World War and, as Figure 2 shows, a marked increase of incoming tonnage from foreign countries occurred. Bristol in war, as in peace, was an important point of entry to the UK, particularly for imports from North America, but it also played a significant role in the despatch of the Gallipoli expedition of 1915.[13]

Figure 2 suggests a story for Bristol which differs from the standard narrative of the British economy between the wars. After the precipitous decline of trade in the period between 1916 and 1919, tonnage levels recovered steadily through the 1920s. After this recovery, with expansion of trade stimulated by imported goods, tonnage levels exceeded significantly those achieved in the Edwardian period.

Despite the labour disputes of 1926 the dramatic events of the General Strike appear to have had relatively little impact on the port's trade performance that year. The 'blip' which appears in Figure 2 records data for 1927; this apparent downturn is partially the result of a change in accounting practice, which required only eleven months data to be recorded, rather than a direct consequence of the General Strike. There is, however, a potentially paradoxical aspect to Bristol's trading pattern in the inter-war period which contrasts with the national experience of economic growth. In the 1930s, and particularly at the end of the decade under the stimulus of rearmament, domestic sources of demand appear to prompt national economic recovery which contrasts with diminished activity in the world economy after 1929. Bristol's coastwise traffic, however, held up well until 1931 when it fell sharply to 1933; thereafter there was a steady expansion to 1939. By contrast, foreign tonnage increased in 1930 and 1931 and remained stable at a peace-time maximum of 2.6 million tons and, although there was a 13 per cent fall in 1933, these high levels were recovered as growth continued, reaching three million in 1939. Overall, the shipping data for Bristol reveal at least some of the positive achievements of the inter-war period.

One feature of the Bristol's inter-war trade was its emergence as a major tobacco importing port. Whereas Bristol had imported 349 tons of tobacco in 1880 and 2278 tons in 1910, rapid expansion took place between 1919 and 1923, a year when an exceptional 32,275 tons were imported. For the following decade tobacco imports averaged 24,000 tons; thereafter the trend was for imports to increase again, exceeding 45,000 tons in 1939.[14] This level was only surpassed in 1947, a highly exceptional year when 50,598 tons were imported, and tobacco imports to Bristol resumed levels typical of the inter-war period until the trade diminished significantly after 1969. More recent decline is indicated by the disappearance of the trade as a separate category in the 1982 edition of the *Port of Bristol Handbook*.[15] Tobacco, it should be noted, was not typical and the pattern of imports varied substantially by commodity. Other products, for instance, wood, petroleum and wheat exhibited quite different trends.[16]

After the Second World War total tonnage imported into Bristol returned to the high levels recorded at the end of the 1930s and continued to grow until the early 1960s when annual arrivals averaged over 6 million tons. Although this period saw a downward trend, total tonnage in the late 1960s and early 1970s remained above the levels achieved between 1925 and 1939. Another feature of this period was a change in the balance of the components of shipping traffic identified above; the loss of tonnage was principally in foreign trade with coastal arrivals showing rapid growth in the early 1970s.[17] By this time annual tonnage levels recorded in the *Port of Bristol Handbook* show a rough parity between the two classes, with arrivals from within the UK boosted by petroleum products, which comprised two thirds of coastal tonnage.[18] Following the reorganisation of the port in 1991, which is discussed below, recorded tonnage leapt from 4 million to 6.6 million tons within two years, a performance which equalled previous high levels.[19]

Turning from trade to finance, the evolution of banking in Bristol from the late eighteenth to the early twentieth centuries was similar to many other provincial cities. A number of small privately owned banks either converted to joint-stock concerns following the enabling legislation of 1826 or disappeared through failure or amalgamation. Joint-stock banks with branch systems gradually eclipsed private banks but were themselves taken over in increasing numbers in the forty years or so from the 1870s onwards. This amalgamation movement resulted in a loss of local ownership and control with the emergence of the 'Big Five' banks which dominated English banking by 1918.[20]

Another indicator of economic growth in Bristol is provided by an index which represents settlements of cheque payments between the large commercial banks for transfers within the city which appear in Figure 3. This, it should be noted, provides only a partial indicator of local financial activity because it excludes clearings within a particular bank, or its own branches, and interbank clearings with other cities and regions, which were undertaken at the Clearing House in London. However, despite these shortcomings, clearings within Bristol do shed some light on the nature of the city as a provincial financial centre. Provincial clearance was introduced at Bristol in 1898 and terminated when the banks abolished the Provincial Clearing system in 1967.

Annual clearings recorded in current prices show stability and slow growth before 1914 but a marked increase in the First World War and for the next two years. The sharp fall in the value of local clearings

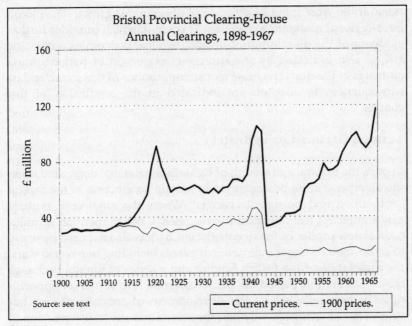

Figure 3

in the three years after 1921 coincided, paradoxically, with some restoration of Bristol's share of total provincial clearing which reached 4 per cent in 1921 and 1922, fell back to around 3.5 per cent through the 1920s, before rising to 5 at the end of the 1930s. The first two years of the Second World War saw a sharp increase in local clearings but this fell off even more precipitously in 1943. Thereafter local clearings, in current prices, grew steadily through the post war years apart from a minor fall between 1956 and 1959 and a more major fall between in 1963 and 1965.[21]

If, however, the changing value of money is accounted for by using constant price data, here based on 1900, a very different story emerges from Figure 3.[22] The constant price series indicates two distinct periods broken by a major fall in 1943. The first period, 1898 to 1942, shows remarkable stability though the rise in the 1930s and the onset of the Second World War can still be discerned. The second period, 1943 to 1967, shows an almost constant level of local clearings in real terms. Given the national economy was experiencing relatively high rates of economic growth in historic terms, and Bristol shared in this growth, this data on local clearings suggests that inter-regional and international trade were more likely sources of economic growth than local, intra-regional economic expansion. This trend, which provides further evidence of the dissolution of distinct regional economies within the UK, is also indicated by the enormous expansion of national bank clearings in London. The more recent implications of this trend, and its consequences for Bristol, are indicated in the conclusion of this chapter.

Business Organisation in Bristol

In part, the income and wealth of Bristol's inhabitants depended upon the enterprise of its businessmen to sustain production in the face of competition and persistent change.[23] Where the nineteenth century saw significant technological developments, not to mention a multitude of new products, the twentieth century has also required business to accommodate major international events including two world wars, the dissolution of the British Empire and a series of foreign exchange crises. During this period the perpetual unfolding of market opportunities is best reflected by the development of communications but technological change is only half the story since the transformation of markets achieved by the associated rapid flows of information and long distance commodity trade was of at least equal importance.

However, although enterprise and business acumen were necessary they were not sufficient in themselves to secure income in local, national and international markets. Responses from the state, in the form of both the national government and the local authorities, were also essential to secure the provision of communally provided services essential to the functioning of a modern society, including education, health and social security, and the development of a transport infrastructure which would support economic growth. Moreover, Bristol's business community required other responses additional to individualistic enterprise to secure its place in the sun. Collective and institutional responses were required to mobilize support for many innovations essential to the maintenance of competitiveness in the region.

The role of the Chamber of Commerce is an excellent example here. Its history, discussed later, demonstrates not only the nature of collective action in operation but also the ability of organizations which were created in the early nineteenth century to survive and adapt while retaining their essential functions until the end of the twentieth century. In the Chamber of Commerce members of the Bristol business community generated an organization which functioned as a pressure group to represent their interests *vis-à-vis* the railway companies, the organised labour movement and the state.

Even in the face of evidence which affirms the existence of a Bristol business community, it is clear that the 'Bristolness' of local enterprises has diminished during the last hundred years. In 1841 the predominant form of business organization was the firm run either by owner-manager or a partnership, though Bristol's water and gas supplies were provided by joint stock limited companies.[24] Increasing perceptions on the part of businessmen of the benefits of larger scale units of organization and production, accommodated by legislation which permitted the development of joint stock companies, fostered the establishment and growth of limited liability companies which became increasingly important towards the end of the nineteenth century. Family firms often adopted limited liability but retained a majority, and sometimes all, of the ordinary shares, issuing debenture stocks to raise the required additional capital. In the longer run, though, continued growth of a firm led to increased capital requirements and shares, which had voting or participating rights, were issued to the general public. While share ownership was often confined to a region initially, inheritance and the purchase of shares on the stock exchanges led to a national, and then international, pattern of share ownership. In this way the very success of a family firm could lead, eventually, to a loss of control and a change in ownership.[25]

Over the last hundred years many changes occurred which have diluted the regional identity of economic enterprises; among these can be included those which have fostered the development of large scale enterprises. Although large factories and offices were the obvious manifestations of this trend, its consequences were much more far reaching than just the concentration of labour in larger buildings and organizations. For example, corporate growth, if it was to continue, often required the development of management tools which facilitated the management and supervision of a complex industrial organization. A pioneering example of such a management system devised by W. D. & H. O. Wills in 1886, and subsequently improved through the 1890s, used 'dissection sheets' to provide a comparative view of the company's production expenses and sales. In 1903, within two years of the creation of the Imperial Tobacco Company (of Great Britain and Ireland) Ltd, twenty previously independent companies were overseen by a unified Executive Committee which extended this system to all its branches.[26]

133

Bristol, like all the major provincial centres in Britain, has seen a major change in the nature of its largest employers. At the end of the nineteenth century almost all the region's employers of labour, including companies with a large work force, were based in Bristol; the sole exception was the Great Western Railway Company which had its head offices at Paddington in London. After 1900 three trends associated with corporate growth reduced the regional affinity of large companies.

The first was the result of decisions taken by Bristol firms to locate production outside the city, either through the purchase of existing facilities or the construction of new production sites. This trend had two facets: on the one hand, Bristol-based companies obtained production sites outside the city and, on the other, companies located in other regions acquired production units within Bristol. The second was the tendency for big businesses to relocate their head offices to London to take advantage of a location at the heart of the British economic and political system.[27] The third, and most recent, is a consequence of 'short-termism' endemic in the British economy, and a direct consequence of the volatile shareholding behaviour of financial institutions. Senior managers tend no longer to identify their companies with a particular region and respond to demands for high and immediate returns from shareholders. As these are usually large financial institutions, and distant from the locality, a desire to play a major role in the region is, at best, of secondary importance. The historic role a company may have played in a region, or even its own corporate culture, may count for little in the search for performance indicators approved of by the 'City'.

A brief resumé of one local company's history, E. S & A. Robinson, from its early days of growth through internal accumulation to its recent dissolution, will illustrate and exemplify the two routes to corporate growth – internal accumulation and merger. The company was founded in 1844 by Elisha Robinson, the son of a Tewkesbury paper-mill owner, and an apprenticeship-served paper maker. Originally the business concentrated on wrapping paper production but by 1850 he and his brother Alfred were the owners of a thriving paper-bag making business. Profits were 'ploughed back' to finance investment which not only expanded bag production but also allowed diversification into lithographic printing and, later, colour printing and packaging. New technology played an important role, being adopted to expand output and extend the range of products. In 1873 Elisha Robinson, while on a visit to the United States, acquired for

£1000 the patent for a machine which made gusseted paper bags.[28] This crucial acquisition proved highly profitable and provided an impressive demonstration of technology transfer across the Atlantic which was to be followed a decade later with even greater success by another Bristol family, the Wills, who purchased the exclusive British rights to use the Bonsack cigarette-making machine in 1883.[29]

After Elisha Robinson's death in 1885 control of the company passed to his sons, Edward and Arthur, who reorganized the family firm as a limited liability company when their uncle Alfred retired in 1893. Over the next twenty years expansion and innovation continued and new processes were developed, including a process for the continuous production of pre-printed bags. This proved a highly lucrative venture; first, because the bags could be printed with advertisements for the products they contained, which secured commercial customers eager to promote their products and, second, because the patent was sold to the Union Bag Company of New York, a reversal of the technological transfer which had proved so important for the company thirty years before.

The third generation of Robinsons, Foster G., Harold and Percy, made their mark in the period during and immediately after the First World War when the company, while continuing its traditional policy of internally financed growth, adopted a different strategy: the acquisition of subsidiary companies. Between 1917 and the 1932, Robinsons purchased a number of companies which manufactured paper and paper-related products in Devon, Scotland and the east of England.

Diversification, though in a related field, was also achieved in 1920 through the acquisition of Strachan & Henshaw Ltd., a local engineering firm, which had produced bag-manufacturing machines for Robinsons. Overseas markets became more important as output expanded and new forms of corporate organization were required. Until the end of the First World War representatives and agents arranged overseas sales but subsidiary manufacturing companies were established in South Africa (1921) and Canada (1932) to circumvent tariffs. Closely associated with these developments were the establishment of subsidiary companies, established to exploit licences held on specific patents in Britain and South Africa.[30] Thus Robinsons achieved growth in the inter-war years by a variety of means which used established techniques and new productive processes and included the development of existing plant, the creation of new subsidiary companies, such as the Keynsham Paper Mills Ltd., and the acquisition of limited companies.

With this strategy in place, E. S. & A. Robinson prospered after the Second World War, developing new packaging products which included such specialist lines as sterile packs for medicine and surgical supplies and foil packets for Polaroid film cassettes. In 1960 reorganization saw the creation of E. S. & A. Robinson (Holdings) Ltd. to co-ordinate corporate assets in excess of £40 million.[31] By the 1960s no member of the Robinson family was engaged in senior management of the company and the shareholders opted in 1966 for a merger with John Dickinson & Co. Ltd. of Hemel Hempstead to produce the Dickinson, Robinson Group (DRG), a union of the two largest printing and stationery companies in the UK.[32]

Although the company remained loyal to Bristol for the location of its head offices, and despite its status as Bristol's largest business after the transfer of the Imperial Group headquarters to London in the mid-1970s, the extent to which it could be regarded as a 'Bristol' company was diluted to some extent by the Dickinson connection and the internationally diverse location of its factories.

By the 1980s DRG faced several difficulties, only some of which were caused the national economic climate. One major problem arose because the expiry of a number of patents prompted new entrants into previously secure markets and profits were undercut by the competition. In 1989 the Pembridge Group, later Redcliffe Investments, acquired a majority shareholding with a view to realizing the asset value of the company through restructuring and sale. Work continued at many of the local factories, as sections of DRG were disbursed to a number of companies, including Bowater Industries, Weir Group and Credit Lyonnais, but this significant local firm, with its notably Bristol character, was lost.

Although the specific circumstances differ, the history of many of Bristol's longer lived companies, including, for example, those of J. S. Fry & Sons, Georges, G. B. Britton, Mardon, Son & Hall, Avonside Engineering Company, W. D. & H. O. Wills, and John Lysaght can be told by reference to some, if not all, of these themes.[33] As this cast of firms suggests, the story also fits a range of industrial activities, including confectionery and chocolate, beer, footwear, printing, locomotive building, tobacco and iron and steel.

At present, there is insufficient information on Bristol's small firms, the sole proprietors and the partnerships, those more recent and less celebrated business successes, which have provided the 'seed corn' for subsequent generations of firms which have or are undergoing the process described above. A prosopographical approach, based on a collective biography of Bristol's elite has shed some light on this,[34] but recent research has already identified individuals who made important but rather less conspicuous contributions to Bristol's economy.[35]

In addition to the private concern and the joint stock company, there have been at least three major alternative forms of organization which have co-existed alongside the limited liability corporation: the municipal enterprise, the nationalized industry, and the co-operative enterprise. The economic significance of these alternative forms of ownership and organization has changed significantly over the last fifty years for a variety of often interrelated reasons. Bristol's utilities, both the municipally-owned electricity and the privately-owned gas supply industries were absorbed into large state-owned industries under the nationalization programme enacted by the first majority Labour government in 1948.[36] After 1984, Conservative governments privatized the public corporations which provided telecommunications, gas, and electricity distribution and generation to create large national and regional corporations in the private sector.[37] Nationalization in the 1970s, under Labour and Conservative governments, also proved essential for the restructuring of the aircraft industry at Filton which resulted in the creation of British Aerospace and Rolls-Royce's Bristol Engine Division. British Aerospace was the corporate descendant of the British Aircraft Corporation which, in turn, had been created in 1959 by a merger that absorbed the Bristol Aeroplane Company originally founded in 1910 by Sir George White.[38]

Municipal enterprise has always played an important role in the local economy as an employer of labour and capital, a supplier of services, including market facilities, and a provider of infrastructure. In 1906, for example, Bristol County Borough employed 5,963 people, and its municipal trading departments employed 782 at the docks and 174 in the city's electricity supply industry.[39] The electoral implications of large numbers of municipal employees led to expressions of concern by some contemporary political commentators,[40] but in Bristol this was potentially less contentious than in cities where water, gas, and tramways were also owned by the local authority.[41]

The role of the Docks Committee has loomed large in debates concerning Bristol's economic development in the nineteenth century.[42] Once control and management of the city's docks had been achieved the question of municipal ownership remained largely unproblematic until the 1970s. Clapham provided a positive assessment of the Port's performance in the late nineteenth century:

> Altogether the state of the port was creditable to the Corporation of Bristol, which alone among the Corporations of the major ports had retained that complete control of shipping and harbour which at one time had been normal.[43]

A recent study of the Port of Bristol in the inter-war period suggests that the managers of the port were relatively successful and faced little or no political opposition.[44]

However, this state of affairs did not survive the stringent financial controls imposed on local authorities by successive Conservative governments after 1979 which intended their consequent fundamental reassessment of all municipally provided services. For the Port of Bristol, changing economic circumstances, including entry into the EEC, technical change associated with containerization, perceived national dock labour relations problems, and continuing locational difficulties of the city-centre docks, conspired against the continuation of the *status quo*. Although the Council responded, notably with the closure of the City Docks in 1969, the development of new industrial estates and the completion of the Royal Portbury Dock in 1978,[45] it became increasingly clear that only a private company could secure the required capital investment. In 1991 municipal management was terminated when the Port of Bristol was leased to First Corporate Shipping, owned by Terence Mordaunt and David Orr;[46] ironically, the 150 year lease was almost identical to the period of municipal control.

Finally, it should be noted that the co-operative movement was engaged in both manufacturing and distributive activities in Bristol; these were owned by both the Co-operative Wholesale Society (CWS) and the local co-operative societies.[47] By 1939 the CWS owned an extensive range of factories in Bristol, including the Avonmouth Flour Mill, the Penner Cattle Cake Mills, Brislington Butter Blending Factory, and factories producing furniture, clothing, and corsetry.[48]

The Business Community

This section focuses on a previously neglected organization, the Bristol Chamber of Commerce and examines aspects of its growth and role from the 1820s to the 1960s. Although the Chamber has been overshadowed by the Society of Merchant Venturers, not least because the latter has been the subject of a full-scale history[49], it played a much more active part in Bristol's industry and trade during this period. Founded in 1823, the Bristol Chamber of Commerce, Trade and Manufactures aimed 'to protect and promote' local business interests.[50]

Chambers of Commerce began to be established in the British Isles during the later eighteenth century in both new and older centres of industry and trade, for example Glasgow and Belfast (1783), Edinburgh (1785) and Manchester (1794). Bristol was the first in the south west of England and other towns in the region followed only after many years, for example Gloucester (1839), Exeter (1867) and Bath (1902).[51] In new centres of industry Chambers tended to be the first representative bodies organized to speak on behalf of local business communities. In Bristol, however, the Society of Merchant Venturers had since the later sixteenth century been closely identified with business interests, though at least from the early nineteenth century it tended to concentrate on retaining its privileges as well as on a rather more successful strategy of developing its extensive property interests and on educational and charity work. As Patrick McGrath has argued, the formation of the local Chamber of Commerce was 'but one indication that the business community was looking elsewhere for leadership'.[52] Uppermost in the minds of the promoters of the Bristol Chamber was the relatively slow growth of the local economy compared to many other towns and cities including those that had a Chamber of Commerce.[53]

In its early years the Bristol Chamber was largely protectionist and did not move to a free trade position until the middle of the nineteenth century. During this same period its membership fluctuated, but was generally static (see Table 5). In the later 1840s, however, the Chamber, together with the Free Port Association led the campaign for a takeover of the City Docks and it effectively ceased to have an independent existence, but once the docks question was settled the need for such a body became even more urgent than before. Between 1850 and 1853 the modern Bristol Chamber of Commerce took shape. The first step was a petition from 108 individuals and firms, headed by local Bank of England Agent Joshua Saunders, which invited support from the Master of the Merchant Venturers and proposed the Merchant Venturers fill all the Chamber's senior posts. Though generally supportive, the Merchant Venturers did not accept such close links and judged it preferable that the Chamber was completely independent.[54]

However, the Merchant Venturers agreed to support the Chamber to the extent of £100 per year, and agreed that the Master and two senior wardens of the former should be President and Vice-Presidents of the latter and also provided use of the Merchants' Hall for their general meetings. To some extent the three years it took to re-establish the Chamber was due to the intervention of both local and general elections, and it was felt desirable to 'allow the ascerbities of feeling which these proceedings always create before commencing to subside'.[55]

TABLE 5: Bristol Chamber of Commerce:
Membership for selected years, 1824-1953.

Year	Membership	Year	Membership
1824	230	1933	415
1833	146	1943	433
1843	106	1944	460
1853	194	1945	460
1863	161	1946	549
1873	220	1947	602
1883	275	1948	863
1893	288	1949	1097
1903	350	1950	1194
1913	465	1951	1234
1923	415	1952	1278
		1953	1316

Source: BRO, BCCP, 38605/PV/18, *Bristol Chamber of Commerce Journal*, 28 (1953), 49.

The aims of the new Chamber were similar to those of the old, but were extended to include the settlement of trade questions or disputes through arbitration. On incorporation in 1874, the Chamber's remit was widened again.[56] As befitted a city such as Bristol, promotion of trade, commerce and manufactures were all represented in the aims and from its inception membership was drawn from across the spectrum of local economic interests. Regular, active participation in the Chamber's affairs was, however, confined to a small minority of men especially the office holders and Committee. As the Chamber became more established and its workload increased, the original committee was abolished and its place taken by a number of sub-committees each of which dealt with a specific area. The number and size of these committees changed from time to time, but in general this organizational structure was an accurate reflection of the work of the Chamber in the twentieth century. Table 6 provides two examples to illustrate this.

It is important to stress that the business community in Bristol, through the Chamber, became connected to the wider world through membership of national and international bodies whose aims were consistent with its own. The first of these was the Association of British Chambers of Commerce, established in 1860, to represent the diverse interests of individual Chambers and provide a forum in which issues of national significance might be debated. The Association, moreover, placed great emphasis on parliamentary lobbying and its Presidents between 1860 and 1896 were, without exception, MPs.[57] Bristol, along with fifteen other Chambers (including Gloucester) was a founder member of this Association, as it was of the Federation of Chambers of Commerce of the British Empire whose first congress took place in London in 1886.[58]

TABLE 6: Bristol Chamber of Commerce: Standing Committee Structure, 1916 and 1957.

1916*		1957†	
Docks and Shipping	16	Civil Air Transport	15
Railways and Canals	10	Education Advisory	15
Finance	8	Finance and General Purposes	11
Parliamentary	6	Overseas	30
Commercial and Technical Education	6	Property, Planning & Rating	20
General Purposes	9	Publicity	12
		Taxation and Public Finance	12
		Transport	34

Sources: BRO, BCCP, 38605/M/14, Monthly Meeting of the Council, 21 June 1916; 38605/M/51, Nominations for Membership 1957/8, 143-5.

Notes: Figures indicate maximum membership.

* President, Vice-President and Past Presidents were ex-officio on all standing committees.
† President, Vice-President and Immediate Past President were ex-officio on all standing committees.

As Helen Meller has shown, while the Merchant Venturers tended to be Anglican and Conservative, the success of both the Free Port Association and the Chamber owed a great deal to the influence of Liberal nonconformists, a group that helped to transform the nature of municipal politics from the late 1860s. It was this group above all that brought a new style to local politics 'compounded largely from their experience in socio-religious work and philanthropy on the one hand, and politics on the other', leading to a 'civilising mission' in the final quarter of the nineteenth century.[59] Recent comparative research into business communities in England and Germany before 1914 has suggested that businessmen in the former were far more active at local level in charitable, educational, cultural and religious work, and there is substantial evidence from Bristol to support this argument.[60] Moreover, the relatively slow growth of Bristol for much of the nineteenth century, together with its limited involvement in export markets, combined to limit the opportunities for, and significance of, immigrant businessmen in the city compared to other centres such as Birmingham and Manchester.[61]

Bristol's highly diversified economy meant that, unlike many other towns in the nineteenth century, no single interest dominated the local Chamber of Commerce. Furthermore, unanimity was rare in the City Council where Conservatives outnumbered Liberal businessmen. Reference to port management demonstrates this point. Between 1848 and 1884, 73 councillors and aldermen served on the Docks Committee, many of whom were leading figures in the local business community. Of this number 43 were Conservatives, the remainder Liberal; wholesalers and manufacturers together provided easily the largest two groups, but shipping interests, warehousemen, merchants, stockbrokers and even two surgeons also served.[62] Disputes over port management did not conform to party lines. Moreover, its controversial decision not to develop rivermouth docks provided an incentive for individual committee members to form groups to promote major dock development at Avonmouth and Portishead.[63]

If there was no unanimity about the pace and direction of port development, there was rather more agreement, at least within the Chamber, about the way in which Bristol was treated by its main railway company, the Great Western. In the later nineteenth and early twentieth century, the Chamber directed a major campaign to obtain improved passenger and freight services. This was an issue which touched virtually all members of the Bristol business community, and it was driven by a conviction that this community was not merely ill-served in absolute terms, but also that it was discriminated against relative to other towns within the GWR network and in comparison with the services received by several other major cities outside the south-west of England. Criticism of the GWR gathered pace from the 1870s, and may be illustrated by the decision of the company to construct the Severn Tunnel. When the Bill for this was placed before Parliament in 1872 the Bristol Chamber petitioned the Commons to support it and at the AGM of that year C. J. Thomas, moving the adoption of the petition, judged that the scheme would have 'incalculable advantages' for Bristol. However, his subsequent comments were indicative of the strength of feeling against the GWR within the Bristol business community and the way in which the scheme was seen as an act of atonement for that company's previous behaviour:

> Since the formation of the GWR it had often been a reproach to that railway that although it had its origin in Bristol it had neglected the interests of the city; but ... when the GWR should have completed that grand and noble project it would have in large measure redeemed its character in this respect.[64]

Redemption of the GWR's reputation did not, however, materialize and the company's image became increasingly tarnished. The campaign against the GWR was led by Charles Wills, a leading member of the Chamber and a warehouseman in Bristol. Among others, he employed the useful tactic of canvassing the growing number of commercial travellers whose business was crucially dependent on the railway and who demonstrated deep dissatisfaction with the GWR. In 1882 two petitions, one signed by 260 commercial travellers in the south-west, the other by 45 travellers representing firms in the Bristol area, confirmed the GWR's poor reputation. The latter argued that GWR policy damaged the trade of Bristol 'to an alarming extent'.[65] These criticisms continued into the twentieth century, and increasingly focused on the fact that Bristol was the only major city in England with only one line to London and, further, that because the GWR were dock owners, they competed with local business interests. The company's dock interests at Fishguard, Newport and Plymouth were held to be one reason why trade was being diverted from Bristol, not least because the company could arrange through rates with the steamship companies.[66]

In addition to local and regional issues, the Bristol business community became involved in a range of questions which were of national importance, including some that historians have highlighted in their search for the origins of the relative economic decline of the British economy. Outside the UK during the late nineteenth century more countries industrialized, free trade crumbled, protection of domestic markets became commonplace and, coupled with the related rise in international competition, the 'new' imperialism gathered pace. Within the UK, reactions to these developments depended on their impact on local economies, but all regions were affected to a greater or lesser extent and business interests called for action at national level.

Historians have sometimes suggested that it took the humiliations of the Boer War (1899-1902) for UK business leaders to call for changes in the way government and businessmen related to one another, more especially for the latter to play a much more active role in combating the attitudes of the British political Establishment. It has also been suggested that until the early twentieth century only outsiders perceived the failures of government as far as industry and trade were concerned.[67] Certainly the Business Leagues set up in different areas after 1910 (Bristol's Business League was established in 1912) lobbied for major changes, but it is usually forgotten that chambers of commerce had been calling for a reconsideration of government attitudes to business since at least the 1860s. In 1864 the Association of Chambers of Commerce judged that neither the Board of Trade nor the Foreign Office, as then constituted, were suited to the task of protecting and promoting the interests of business. Ten years later the Association was calling for the creation of a Ministry of Commerce which would be 'the official guardian of the mighty and ever-widening interests of the industry of this great Empire'.[68] The Bristol business community consistently supported this potentially important move but despite years of intermittent lobbying until well into the twentieth century, nothing came of it.[69]

The need to promote industrial and commercial interests also generated a debate on free trade versus protectionism as well as a related discussion on the desirability of imperial preference. As protectionist foreign powers engaged in empire building, so the Bristol Chamber lobbied Parliament to protect traditional markets and sources of raw materials from this threat. Their efforts, and their mixed success, have been documented elsewhere, but it is worth noting here that within Bristol itself there was no immediate desire to abandon the national policy of free trade.[70] However, as the international economy became ever more competitive, more businessmen began to reconsider their position and moved to support imperial preference. One of the most vocal exponents of a far-reaching scheme of imperial preference was the *Bristol Times and Mirror* which, in a leading article on 30 July 1906 criticized those whom it considered too lukewarm to the idea of imperial preference, mainly because they found it difficult to abandon free trade as an ideal. The electorate, and indeed much business opinion, remained generally unimpressed about the need for any protectionism, and the UK remained basically a free-trading nation until 1932. However, the Bristol Chamber (through its representation on the Association of Chambers of Commerce) continued to press for anything that would improve the city's trading prospects with the Empire, and this can be illustrated by its support for the work of the Imperial Institute (formed in 1887), upon whose Executive Committee the Bristol Chamber, together with the Chambers of London, Manchester, Hull, Glasgow, Liverpool and Middlesbrough were represented by 1916.[71]

Another area of national significance with which the Bristol business community became involved from the later nineteenth century was education. Commentators on relative economic decline have long discussed the extent to which technical and higher education met business needs, and the debate has continued for over a century. Indeed, it was real cuts in the funding of leading civic universities such as Bristol, Leeds and Manchester during the 1980s that helped to shift the emphasis of historical research away from Oxford and Cambridge towards the role played by provincial universities especially from the 1870s.[72] In Bristol there is little evidence that the business community felt badly served by Bristol University College, established in 1876; on the contrary within a few years the Chamber of Commerce judged that it had been 'successful beyond all expectation' in its provision of high quality education to some 5000 students. A meeting of Bristol citizens in 1887 called on the state to improve the financial position 'of colleges for higher adult education in great centres of population like Bristol, with such a scale of fees as will place higher education within the reach of students of all classes'.[73]

In addition to its support for state-aided higher education with entry on merit, the Bristol Chamber was a firm advocate of technical and commercial education at school and college level. It particularly deplored the paucity of schools of commerce and the 'almost total absence' of commercial education in the world's leading commercial nation. It did, however, pay tribute to the efforts made by Bristol Grammar School and above all to the Merchant Venturers' College in serving the needs of local economy. The latter had Art, Chemistry, Mining & Technical Departments and provided evening classes for men and women 'in a range of practical and technological skills'. This kind of education, the Chamber argued, was similar to that in the German Schools of Commerce and it provided the skills necessary for manufacturing and commercial employment, construction trades and for the English Civil Service.[74] In Bristol before 1914 the evidence points less to a lack of provision of commercial and technical education, but rather to a disappointing demand for it. Lamenting the 'still unsatisfactory' attendance in classes on business methods and modern languages at the Merchant Venturers' Technical College, the Chamber concluded in 1907 that 'employers might do much more to extend the interest in these classes amongst their employees and would appeal to them to use their influence in this direction'.[75]

The relatively peaceful economic conditions characteristic of most of the century before 1914 were shattered by the First World War. Unprecedented state intervention in economic affairs during the war, severe post-war dislocation, and generally depressed trading conditions for much of the 1920s and 1930s, affected businessmen in all parts of the UK. The blend of envy and admiration that had characterized businessmen's attitudes towards Germany before 1914 tended quickly to change to a more aggressive stance after war had broken out, and increased as the war went on. Bristol, in common with other commercial towns such as Manchester took a hard line towards the treatment of Germany and argued as early as 1916 that the British government should not leave German ships free to increase their share of world trade and that no peace terms should be concluded until Germany had replaced all Allied ships lost as a result of her 'piratical methods'.[76] Apprehension about how British trade and industry would fare after the war was amply confirmed by the economic problems and labour unrest that followed the Armistice in 1918.

The first problem was demobilization, more especially how best to accelerate the rate at which directors and managers could be demobilized and reinstalled in their companies so that the loss of expertise caused by the war could be repaired with minimum delay. Such demobilisation of 'Pivotal men' would help to rebuild industry and trade and make a crucial contribution to employment in the private sector. The Bristol Chamber was closely involved in this process and it also encouraged ex-servicemen, both fit and disabled, to enrol in a range of educational courses designed to prepare them for civilian life.[77] The second big problem was the dislocation that inevitably accompanied the winding-down of the war economy, and in no sphere was this more serious than congestion on the railways and at the docks which in October 1919 (almost a year after the Armistice) 'was worse than it had been even at the most acute period of the war'.[78] The Chamber was so concerned at the situation that it took the unusual step of inviting Sir Eric Geddes, then Minister of Transport, to Bristol to discuss the problems faced by the city's business community.[79]

During the inter-war period as a whole, Bristol's diversified economic structure, and the relative unimportance of heavy, export-dependent, 'staple' industries meant that it was spared the worst excesses of depression. Partly as a result of this, the 1926 General Strike, though undoubtedly a major event in Bristol, was of less consequence for the business community than it was in many other cities. The Chamber of Commerce, especially through its Railway Committee, tried to minimize disruption caused by the strike and was in 'innumerable ways' able to 'render useful and material assistance to members and to the community at large'.[80] Unemployment was a problem in inter-war Bristol, but it tended to be at, or slightly below the national average in the twenty years to 1935. From then until the end of the Second World War, thanks largely to rearmament, job creation in Bristol increased at faster than the national average rate, and between 1938 and 1943 employment in engineering and aircraft manufacture doubled to reach 60,000, which represented some 36 per cent of the insured workforce.[81]

The world in which the Bristol Chamber operated after 1945 was in key respects very different from that which had preceded it. Full employment and the election of a Labour Government, governing in its own right for the first time and committed to an extensive programme of nationalization and extension of social welfare provision, had major implications for businessmen throughout Britain and to a large extent determined the agendas of their representative organizations. At local and regional level, business communities had to come to terms with new Town and Country Planning legislation as well as with the Distribution of Industry Act of 1945 which inaugurated a new phase of regional planning.

The landslide electoral victory of Labour in 1945 was probably the main reason why membership of the Bristol Chamber increased so dramatically in the six years of that government. Membership stood at 460 in 1945, less than it had been in 1913; within four years it had more than doubled and by the time Labour left office in 1951 it had risen still further to 1234. It is likely that small and medium size firms in all sectors felt threatened by Big Government to an unprecedented extent and felt a correspondingly urgent need to join an organization that would protect their interests. At local level, the evidence suggests that the Chamber increasingly saw itself as the only organization that could stand between the local authorities and the ratepayers. Although the Federation of British Industries had a Regional Council and a Regional Office in Bristol its membership was 'exceedingly small' compared to the Chamber and in any case it tended to cater for large firms.[82]

The Chamber was resolutely opposed to nationalization and, though it remained overtly apolitical, it did encourage its members to join the right-wing Aims of Industry organisation even if it felt unable to join in its own name.[83] However, the realities of post-war politics meant that it had no choice but to work with the more interventionist state at both local and national level, and this did much to cement a close and constructive relationship with the City Council. This was symbolized by the formation of an Industrial Development Consultative Committee in 1949.[84] A key part of this included the development of the Broadmead Shopping Centre, the proposals for business within the City centre and those for overspill industrial estates and associated infrastructural requirements. As early as 1945 the Chamber, together with other interested parties such as the local Rotary Club, voiced its concerns at the City Council's plans to force firms to relocate 'to more distant premises', not least because it feared that such moves would cause firms to lose their skilled labour. Bristol, it declared, 'was primarily a manufacturing city and unless greater consideration is given to the position of industrialists there appears to be a serious danger of industry leaving the city'.[85] Moreover, the Chamber led the campaign to secure better compensation for firms whose premises were compulsorily purchased, and this was a good example of the way in which it championed the cause of small business in its dealings with Council planners. Later, and significantly just after Labour's victory in the general election of 1964, the Chamber considered various ways in which businessmen could play an increasingly active role in local government, arguing that their expertise would be invaluable in this sphere. Amongst other things, it recommended there was some scope for both an increase in the size of local councils and for more frequent co-option of businessmen to local authority committees.[86]

We noted earlier that the Bristol Chamber had always concerned itself with improvements in dock facilities and railway services, and this continued after the Second World War. In addition another question familiar to Bristolians in the 1990s occupied an increasing amount of the Chamber's time: the relative merits of Lulsgate and Filton as airports for the city. From the start, the Chamber worked to secure improved air services, and liaised with several companies including Aer Lingus, British European Airways, and Cambrian, and was keen to ensure that Bristol did not lose out to competitor cities such as Cardiff.[87]

Throughout the post-war period the Chamber continued its role as a major exponent of commercial education, and it showed increasing interest in the question of training industrial labour, youth employment and the place of graduates in business. Though it bemoaned the lack of interest sometimes shown by local employers in educational issues,[88] the Chamber sustained its efforts in this area, especially through its Educational Advisory Committee. It commented on all aspects of the 1944 Education Act and continued to press for better facilities for vocational education, drawing attention to the shortage of properly-equipped classrooms at the College of Technology and College of Commerce, and the often 'insufficient and inadequate staff'. Another debate which took considerable time was the value of Arts graduates in industry, and the salaries which such graduates could expect.[89] Above all it was impressed by business education provision in leading competitor countries. In the later nineteenth century the German example was much admired, but by the mid-twentieth century attention turned to the United States. In 1955 the Principal of Bristol College of Commerce was part of a 23-strong team from ten European countries which visited the United States as members of a European Productivity Agency project on the development of advanced management facilities in Europe. His report was given wide publicity by the Bristol Chamber and it highlighted key differences between the USA and the UK.[90] Its conclusion, that managerial education and training in the UK was deficient, was probably instrumental in the Chamber's decision in 1963 to declare its qualified support for the creation of business schools in Britain along similar lines to those already well-established at Harvard and the Massachusetts Institute of Technology.[91]

Finally, because Bristol did not have Development Area status, it could not expect much in the way of preferential treatment from government. The difficulty of obtaining Industrial Development Certificates from the Board of Trade was seen as a major obstacle in Bristol's ability to attract new industry.[92] In 1957, the Chamber undertook a self-critical review of its structure and functions and from this emerged reorganization with an increased emphasis on promoting Bristol through a Special Development Committee working more closely with other bodies in the city and region. Part of this drive was the compilation and publication of 10,000 copies of a Classified Trade Index of members of the Chamber of Commerce for worldwide circulation.[93] This important initiative was an acknowledgement that the Bristol business community was broadening its horizons and a reflection of the fact that other English cities including Manchester, Birmingham and Leeds had already distributed similar publicity.[94]

These initiatives and policies underline the fact that almost a century and a half after the formation of the Bristol Chamber of Commerce in 1823, though its structure and the world in which it operated had changed beyond recognition, the original aims of the Provisional Committee were still in evidence: a watchful eye on the activities of business organizations in other cities and the promotion of local business interests in the city, the region and beyond.

Conclusion

Throughout the past century and a half most of the inhabitants of Bristol and its region have enjoyed the benefits of sustained economic growth. Although the region has experienced some of the dysfunctional aspects of modern economic growth, including unemployment, economic uncertainty, overcrowding and pollution, it has suffered relatively little in comparison with some of the more peripheral regions of the British Isles. If the standard of comparison is extended to the rest of the world then the enduring relative prosperity of the Bristol region is obvious with few regional economies having experienced a more peaceful, prosperous and secure record of economic development in this period. Bristol's long-run economic performance does not appear paradoxical though a focus on shorter sub-periods might highlight particular aspects which indicate more problematic aspects of this process. Unsurprisingly, the relative success of the region's entrepreneurs and managers, in the both private and public sector, suggests they cannot be condemned as failures. No evidence of an appropriate nature has been proposed which would vindicate such a view and the performance of the economic actors who took the major decisions determining Bristol's economic trajectory have, at least by a national standard, a respectable record.

The most recent development in this evolutionary process in business structure and organization has seen the relocation of economic activities to the Bristol area, particularly service-sector jobs. Large multinational corporations and major government agencies, often reacting to both the high direct costs of functioning in the capital and the external diseconomies associated with its overcrowded and polluted environment have viewed Bristol as an attractive alternative location. One of the most important relocations was completed in 1989 when Lloyds Bank moved many of its head office functions to a purpose-built dockside complex in the city centre at Canon's Marsh.

The rationale which justified this move by Lloyds Bank is highly revealing. The expansion and diversification of the bank's financial activities, partially under the stimulus of the deregulation of capital markets, the 'Big Bang' of 1986, had resulted in severe pressure on the office space available for the conduct of central operations. The move to Bristol concentrated activities previously undertaken in more than twenty office buildings in and around the City of London at a single, relatively less expensive site which offered scope for further expansion. Furthermore, Bristol, which had emerged in the early 1980s as one of Britain's most important financial centres and a centre of recent economic expansion, was viewed not only as a location likely to be attractive to existing staff faced with relocation because of its road and rail links to London but also because the skills of the local labour force provided a seed-bed for future recruitment.[95]

Similar motives have prompted a decision to relocate on the part of public sector agencies such as the Higher Education Funding Council (HEFC) and the Ministry of Defence Procurement Agency, both of which are currently housed in north Bristol. This expansion of service sector employment has, to some extent, offset the loss of 'high-tech' manufacturing jobs in the defence sector as cuts in military spending followed 'Détente' and the 'Peace Dividend'. These developments not only reveal Bristol's recent locational advantage but also demonstrate that future prosperity in the region will depend upon the development of human capital and access to modern technological processes and infrastructure. The geographical factors which generated Bristol's economic comparative advantages in the past, including the proximity of locally mined coal and a relatively secure local market, have long since passed into history. Future prospects, as in past, will depend on competitiveness and a crucial role will be played by economic agencies in the region, including businesses, local authorities, trade unions,[96] and the Chamber of Commerce, which voice the opinions and aspirations of various sections of Bristol's community.[97]

Notes
1. K. Morgan, 'The Economic Development of Bristol, 1700-1850', chap. 3 above.

2 .A qualified but pessimistic view was propounded by B. W. E. Alford, 'The Economic Development of Bristol in the 19th Century: An Enigma?', in P. McGrath and J. Cannon, eds, *Essays in Bristol and Gloucestershire History* (Bristol, 1976), 252-83. B. J. Atkinson, 'An Early Example of the Decline of Industrial Spirit? Bristol Enterprise in the First Half of the Nineteenth Century', *Southern History*, 9 (1987), 71-89 held that Bristol's businessmen were not early representatives of a class of nineteenth-century entrepreneurial failures who haunt the literature of economic history. More positive assessments of nineteenth century entrepreneurship in Bristol appear in H. Reid, *Bristol & Co.: The Story of Bristol's Longest Running Businesses, 1710 to the Present Day* (Bristol, 1987), 104-16 and Harvey and

Press, 'Industrial Change and Economic Life in Bristol since 1800' in C. E. Harvey and J. Press, eds, *Studies in the Business History of Bristol* (Bristol, 1988), 1-32.

3   C. H. Lee, *The British Economy Since 1700: A Macroeconomic Perspective* (1986).

4   C. H. Feinstein, 'Population, Occupations and Economic Development, 1831-1981', in id., ed., *York 1831-1981: 150 Years of Scientific Endeavour and Social Change* (York, 1981), 109. In some respects York, always a smaller urban centre but nevertheless the historic capital of the north of England, provides a more appropriate comparator for Bristol than, say, Manchester or Leeds.

5   Other indices could be adopted to supplement the illustrative material used here: for example, statistical series on house completions, the housing stock, the construction of business premises and the stocks of commercial premises provide useful supplementary information: see, for example, R. Jevons and J. Madge, *Housing Estates* (Bristol, 1946) and M. Dresser, 'Housing Policy in Bristol, 1919-30', in M. J. Daunton, ed., *Councillors and Tenants: Local Authority Housing in English Cities, 1919-1939* (Leicester, 1984), 156-216.

6   G. Stone, 'Rearmament, War and the Performance of the Bristol Aeroplance Company, 1935-45', in Harvey and Press, eds, *Studies*, 187-212.

7   Anon, *Bristol: an Employment Profile*, (Bristol, 1987).

8   BRO, 08929, (21) *City and County of Bristol – Abstract of Accounts, 1914-15*, Statistics of the Port, 10; BRO, 16198/11a, *Annual Reports, Epitomes and General Statements of City Accounts*, 1939, 34.

9   *City and County of Bristol – Abstract of Accounts*, 1914-15; *Annual Reports, Epitomes and General Statements of City Accounts*, 1939.

10   C. Wells, *A Short History of the Port of Bristol* (Bristol, 1909); D. Large, ed., *The Port of Bristol 1848-1884* (BRS, 36, 1984).

11   *Statistical Abstract for the United Kingdom for each of the fifteen years 1871 to 1885, et seq.* These data on the volume of incoming shipping suggest that none of the three expansion schemes was directly associated with either an instantaneous increase in volume tonnage or an increase in its rate of growth; similar conclusions can be drawn from the statistics of Port of Bristol cited above.

12   Wells, *Short History of the Port of Bristol*, 162, 207, 320-21, 337.

13   W. G. Neale, *The Tides of War and the Port of Bristol, 1914-18* (Bristol, 1976), chap. 8.

14   *City and County of Bristol – Abstract of Accounts*, 1914-15, Statistics of the Port, 12; *Annual Reports, Epitomes and General Statements of City Accounts*, 1939, 35.

15   *The Port of Bristol*, 1945-1982.

16   See fn. 12.

17   *Abstract of Regional Statistics*, 1, et seq., (1960-).

18   *The Port of Bristol Handbook*, 1965-1984.

19   'The Bristol Port Company', promotional literature and brochure (Bristol, 1995).

20   P. Ollerenshaw, 'The Development of Banking in the Bristol Region, 1750-1914', in Harvey and Press, eds, *Studies*, 55-82.

21   *The Banker's Magazine*, 1901-1967.

22   The constant price series is derived from C. H. Feinstein, *National Income, Expenditure and Output of the United Kingdom, 1855-1965* (Cambridge, 1972), T132-3, and D. Jackson, *Introduction to Economics* (1982), 166.

23   Businessmen should be read to include businesswomen, although females can always be identified as organizers of economic activity, there were significantly fewer businesswomen throughout the period under investigation.

24   F. C. Jones, *Bristol's Water Supply and Its Story* (Bristol, 1946); H. Nabb, *The Bristol Gas Industry 1815-1949* (BHA, 67, 1987).

25 P. L. Payne, 'The Emergence of the Large Scale Company in Great Britain', *EcHR* (1967), 20, 519-42.

26 B. W. E. Alford, 'Strategy and Structure in the UK Tobacco Industry', in L. Hannah, ed., *Management Strategy and Business Development* (1976), 74.

27 Of the largest 50 British companies, by estimated market value, in 1904 and 1934 there was only one with head offices in Bristol, Imperial Tobacco; by 1985 Imperial had moved to London; see P. Wardley, 'The Anatomy of Britain's Largest Fifty Companies in 1904, 1934 and 1985', *Bristol Polytechnic Research Paper in Business History*, 1, 1990. In 1995 only two of the largest 500 British companies had their corporate headquarters in Bristol; *Financial Times: FT 500*, 20 Jan. 1995, 27.

28 B. Darwin, *Robinsons of Bristol, 1844-1944* (Bristol, 1945), 19; D. Bateman, 'The Growth of the Printing and Packaging Industry', in Harvey and Press, eds, *Studies*, 83-107, at 96-8.

29 B. W. E. Alford, 'Penny Cigarettes, Oligopoly and Entrepreneurship in the U.K. Tobacco Industry in the Late Nineteenth Century', in B. Supple, ed., *Essays in British Business History* (Oxford, 1977), 57.

30 Darwin, *Robinsons of Bristol*, 38-52, 58-66.

31 *Illustrated Bristol News*, Nov. 1964.

32 *Stock Exchange Official Year-Book*, 1974-5 (1975), 1496-7.

33 S. Diaper, 'J. S. Fry & Sons: Growth and Decline in the Chocolate Industry', 33-54; G. Channon, 'Georges and Brewing in Bristol', 165-86; J. Press, 'G. B. Britton and Footwear Manufacturing in Bristol and Kingswood, 1870-1973', 213-37; D. Bateman, 'The Growth of the Printing and Packaging Industry', 83-107; P. Davis, C. E. Harvey and J. Press, 'Locomotive Building in Bristol in the Age of Steam, 1837-1958', 109-36, all in Harvey and Press, eds, *Studies*; B. W. E. Alford, *W. D. & H. O. Wills and the Development of the U.K. Tobacco Industry, 1786-1965* (1973); E. Jones, *A History of GKN. Volume Two: The Growth of a Business 1918-1945* (1990), chap. 2.

34 H. Berghoff, 'Regional Variations in Provincial Business Biography: The Case of Birmingham, Bristol, and Manchester, 1870-1914', *Business History*, 37 (1995), 64-85.

35 S. Jordan, 'Regional Newspapers and Prosopography: A Neglected Source for Business History', *Business Archives*, 69 (1995), 13-26.

36 Nabb, *Bristol Gas Industry*; P.G. Lamb, *Electricity in Bristol, 1863-1948* (BHA, 48, Bristol, 1981).

37 L. Hannah, 'The Economic Consequences of the State Ownership of Industry, 1945-1990' in R. Floud and D. McCloskey, eds, *The Economic History of Britain since 1700. Vol. 3. 1939-1992*, (Cambridge. 1994), 171.

38 J. Lovering, *The Development of the Aerospace Industry in Bristol, 1910-1984* (Bristol, 1984).

39 D. Knoop, *Principles and Methods of Municipal Trading* (1912), 278.

40 Knoop, *Principles and Methods*, 366-87, 389-91, 393.

41 Knoop, *Principles and Methods*, 278.

42 More recently, the development of air traffic facilities at Lulsgate has been linked to its status as a local authority owned and controlled venture.

43 J. H. Clapham, *An Economic History of Modern Britain, III*(Cambridge, 1938), 386.

44 K. P. Kelly, 'Public Agencies and Private Interests: The Port Transport Industry in Bristol, 1918-1939', in I. Blanchard, ed., *New Directions in Economic & Social History* (Avonbridge, 1995), 143-9.

45 J. Gough, 'A Brief History of the Port of Bristol' (Bristol, 1995).

46 'The Bristol Port Company'. See fn. 19.

47   E. Jackson, *Industrial Co-Operation in Bristol* (Manchester, 1911).
48   P. Redfern, *The New History of the C.W.S.* (Manchester, 1938) 44, 52, 188, 223-4, 171, 318, 345, 347, 349, 360, 372, 374, 387-9.
49   P. McGrath, *The Merchant Venturers of Bristol* (Bristol, 1975).
50   *Rules, Regulations & Bye-Laws of the Bristol Chamber of Commerce: Also Copies of Memorials, Correspondence Etc. Relating to its Establishment; and a Report of the Proceedings of the First General Meeting, Held on the 5th January 1853, in the Merchants' Hall, King-Street* (Bristol, 1853), 4.
51   A. R. Ilseric, *Parliament of Commerce: The Story of the Association of British Chambers of Commerce, 1860-1960* (1961), 246-8.
52   McGrath, *Merchant Venturers*, 543.
53   BRO, Bristol Chamber of Commerce Papers (hereafter BCCP), 38605/A/2, Report to the Provisional Committee, 13 Feb. 1823, 15.
54   *Rules, Regulations & Bye-Laws*, 14.
55   *Rules, Regulations & Bye-Laws*, 19.
56   BRO, BCCP, 38605/A/10, Incorporation of the Bristol Chamber of Commerce, Memorandum of Association, 16 Sept. 1874, 3-4.
57   Ilseric, *Parliament of Commerce*, 243.
58   The Federation of Chambers of Commerce of the British Empire held its sixth congress in Bristol in 1906.
59   H. Meller, *Leisure and the Changing City, 1870-1914* (1976), 90
60   H. Berghoff and R. Moller, 'Tired Pioneers and Dynamic Newcomers? A Comparative Essay on English and German Entrepreneurial History, 1870-1914', *EcHR*, 47 (1994), 278-9.
61   H. Berghoff, 'Regional Variations in Provincial Business Biography', 65, 70.
62   Large, ed., *The Port of Bristol*, xx-xxviii.
63   Wells, *Short History of the Port of Bristol*, 164-208.
64   BRO, BCCP, 38605/A/10, Annual General Meeting, 10 April 1872, 18.
65   BRO, BCCP, 38605/A/13, Annual Report, 1882, 91-2.
66   BRO, BCCP, 38605/A/25, Annual Report, 1907, 60-1.
67   R. P. T. Davenport-Hines, *Dudley Docker: The Life and Times of a Trade Warrior* (Cambridge, 1984), 69-70.
68   BRO, BCCP, 38605/A/10, The Memorial of the Association of Chambers of Commerce of the United Kingdom, to the Rt. Hon. Benjamin Disraeli, M.P., First Lord of the Treasury, in Favour of the Appointment of a Minister of Commerce, 20 March 1874.
69   See for example, BRO, BCCP, 38606/A/23, Annual Report, 1905, 16.
70   BRO, BCCP, 38605/A/14, Address of the President, Mr J. Colthurst Godwin at the Annual General Meeting, 1886, 49. For the Chamber's efforts in this area see C. M. MacInnes, *Bristol: A Gateway of Empire* (Newton Abbot, 1968), 376, 378, 382ff, 395-8, 403-6, 408ff.
71   BRO, BCCP, 38605/M/14, Monthly Meeting of the Council, 15 Nov. 1916.
72   M. Sanderson, 'The English Civic Universities and the "Industrial Spirit", 1870-1914', *Historical Research*, 41 (1988), 104.
73   BRO, BCCP, 38605/A/14, Annual Report, 1887, 15.
74   BRO, BCCP, 38605/A/14, Annual Report, 1887, 13-14.
75   BRO, BCCP, 38605/A/25, Annual Report, 1907, 90.
76   BRO, BCCP, 38605/M/14, Monthly Meeting of the Council, 18 Oct. 1916.
77   BRO, BCCP, 38605/M/14, Monthly Meetings of the Council, 27 Nov. 1918; 22 Jan. 1919; 19 Feb. 1919.

78 BRO, BCCP, 38605/M/14, Railways and Canals Sub-Committee, 31 Oct. 1919.
79 BRO, BCCP, 38605/M/14, Monthly Meetings of the Council, 19 Nov. 1919, 17 Dec. 1919, 18 Feb. 1920. K. Jeffery and P. Hennessy, *States of Emergency: British Governments and Strikebreaking Since 1919* (1983), 15-16, 20-1, 23, 27-30, 36-8.
80 BRO, BCCP, 38605/M/20, Monthly Meeting of the Council, 19 May 1926.
81 BRO, 40426S(16), City and County of Bristol Town and Country Planning Act 1947, Report of the Survey and Analysis (Development Plan), 70.
82 BRO, BCCP, 38605/M/51, Some Notes for the information of the Ad Hoc Committee (1957), 327.
83 BRO, BCCP, 38605/M/43, Publicity Committee, 31 Oct. 1949; 38605/M/44, Publicity Committee 30 Dec. 1950; Finance and General Purposes Committee, 19 Mar. 1951.
84 BRO, BCCP, 38605/M/44, Report on Industrial Development Joint Consultative Committee, 4 Dec. 1950.
85 BRO, BCCP, 38605/M/39, Joint Meeting of Representatives of the Bristol Incorporated Chamber of Commerce and Shipping, the Bristol Replanning Association, and the Rotary Club of Bristol to consider the question of Bristol Replanning, 12 Dec. 1945.
86 BRO, BCCP, 38605/M/57, Special Meeting of the General Purposes Committee to consider People in Local Government, 2 Oct. 1964.
87 BRO, BCCP, 38605/M/43, Civil Air Transport Committee, 4 Aug. 1945; 38605/M/50. Civil Air Transport Committee, 20 June 1956.
88 Note the comments on the lack of interest shown in a talk on 'University graduates in industry and commerce' by Professor N. F. Mott of Bristol University in BRO, BCCP, 38605/M/43, Finance and General Purposes Committee, 17 April 1950.
89 See in particular the General Report on Educational Matters Which Have Been of Concern to the Chamber. BRO, BCCP, 38605/M/43, Education Advisory Committee, 20 Mar. 1951.
90 BRO, BCCP, 38605/PU/20, *Bristol Chamber of Commerce Journal*, 30 (1955-6), 14, 21.
91 BRO, BCCP, 38605/M/57, Monthly Meeting of the Council, 1 Nov. 1963.
92 BRO, BCCP, 38605/M/52, Special Development Committee, 9 March 1959.
93 BRO, BCCP, 38605/M/52, Meeting of the Special Development Committee, 11 Dec. 1958.
94 BRO, BCCP, 38605/M/52, Publicity Committee Report on Classified Trade Index of Members, 8 Jan. 1959.
95 Lloyds Bank Archive, B. I. Pitman, 'Why are we moving to Bristol?', Staff Memorandum, June 1987.
96 B. Atkinson, *Trade Unions in Bristol c.1860-1914* (BHA, 51, 1982); K. Kelly and M. Richardson, 'The Shaping of the Bristol Labour Movement', chap. 9 below.
97 The statistical series which inform this chapter will be made available in a machine-readable format under the auspices of the Bristol Historical Databases Project located at the University of the West of England and, subsequently, at the ESRC History Data Archive. Thanks to Dr John Williams and the staff at the Bristol Record Office; Dr John Booker at Lloyds Bank; and, Dr Donald Bateman, Geoffrey Collard, Julie Gough, William Lovett, Dr Mike Richardson, Linda Taylor and Matthew Woollard. UWE provided financial assistance for Drs Ollerenshaw and Wardley; Peter Wardley was also the recipient of a Nuffield Social Science Fellowship during the period in which this chapter was written.

MANAGING THE POOR:
THE ADMINISTRATION OF POOR RELIEF IN BRISTOL IN THE NINETEENTH AND TWENTIETH CENTURIES

Moira Martin

The history of Poor Law administration in Bristol is a neglected area, and with good reason. The administrative headquarters of the former Bristol Poor Law Union, St Peter's Hospital, was hit by a bomb in 1940 and much of the archive relating to the administration of Poor Relief in Bristol was 'destroyed by enemy action'. The Poor Law itself proved somewhat more resilient, for while it was finally replaced in 1948 by the introduction of the National Assistance Act, its legacy, in terms of both buildings and attitudes, remained part of the social fabric of Bristol for decades after the creation of the 'welfare state'.

Butcher's study of the Bristol Corporation of the Poor remains one of the few published texts to examine the development of the Poor Law in Bristol.[1] It is, however, principally concerned with the period before the Poor Law Amendment Act of 1834 and does not examine the work of the two new Boards of Guardians which were set up in the nineteenth century. One of the aims of this chapter is to encourage further research in this area, though inevitably the content is determined both by personal interest and availability of evidence. Thus, the chapter examines the policies and practices of the local organizations officially responsible for assisting the poor. The changing profile of these boards and committees will be considered and the particular role of women members assessed. The official discourse on poverty and pauperism needs to be explored in a national as well as a local context and the relationship between the central and local state examined. The definition of social problems and the development of new systems of classification and treatment are central themes of this chapter. However, it may be useful to begin by providing some background information on the development of Poor Law structures in Bristol in the nineteenth century.

The Administrative Structures in the Nineteenth Century

For most of the nineteenth century Bristol had three separate bodies responsible for the administration of Poor Relief in different parts of the city. The oldest was the Bristol Corporation of the Poor, established in 1696 by the Bristol Poor Act, which constituted the first Board of Guardians in England. In 1698 the old mint was purchased as a workhouse and administrative centre and was named St Peter's Hospital. In a retrospective examination of the Corporation of the Poor in 1894, the *Bristol Mercury* noted that:

> In addition to providing for the care of the destitute, the Corporation performed duties of a semi-magisterial nature and had strangers and disorderly persons apprehended and brought before them and committed to the Bridewell for various periods.[2]

Eighteen parishes contributed to the maintenance of the workhouse and poor rates were collected by churchwardens. In 1714 senior churchwardens were made members of the Corporation and in 1822 they were allowed to maintain their status as *ex officio* Guardians, despite the fact that they were no longer responsible for collecting the poor rates. At various points in the nineteenth century there was tension between the 48 elected Guardians and the churchwardens.[3]

By the late eighteenth century St Peter's Hospital was overcrowded and it was proposed in 1822 that a new workhouse should be built. However, opposition from ratepayers meant that no new accommodation was provided until the 1830s.[4] The power of the ratepayers to oppose increased expenditure is one aspect of the political struggle over the provision of poor relief, another is the action taken by the poor themselves to resist or demand change. As Steve Poole's chapter suggests, the early 1830s constitutes a significant period in Bristol's history, not least in the history of the Poor Law.

The trade depression of 1830-32 resulted in increased pauperism and, in order to deter people from applying for outdoor relief, the Guardians decided that the task of work should be made more arduous. Thus, instead of breaking stone for eight hours a day, four days a week, able-bodied paupers were required to undertake this work for ten and a half hours a day, five days a week. Latimer records that the poor 'rose in revolt when this announcement was made, and for some time St Peter's Hospital was in great peril'[5] The mayor and aldermen responded by having the Riot Act read, troops brought in and ringleaders imprisoned. Eventually the paupers submitted to the new scales.

If conditions were made harsher for the outdoor poor, they were even worse for those in the workhouse, which by 1831 contained 600 inmates, many of whom were elderly, sick, infirm, or too young to care for themselves. Conditions were unhealthy and overcrowding severe, with 58 girls sharing ten beds and 78 boys sharing 17 beds. Unsurprisingly, the cholera epidemic of the early 1830s affected workhouse inmates to a much greater extent than the general population. Thus, of the first 261 cases reported, 168 were at St Peter's.[6] Latimer provides a vivid account of the impact these deaths, and the numerous burials in St Peter's churchyard, had on the local population. They

> appear to have driven many of the poor of the locality out of their senses. A delusion became prevalent that the authorities were burying people alive; and on one occasion a mob broke into the burial ground, and tore up some of the recently interred bodies.[7]

After a similar occurrence at Temple churchyard, corpses were buried at the Cattle Market, having been removed there by water, 'so that interments might escape public notice'. [8]

The delay in making additional provision for the indoor poor and the consequent overcrowding at St Peter's exposed a large number of less able-bodied paupers to cholera. It was difficult for opposition to a new workhouse to be sustained in the aftermath of this epidemic and in 1833 the Corporation hired and later purchased the former French Prison in Stapleton, to provide additional accommodation. This allowed for improvements to be made at St Peter's, such that when it was inspected by a member of the Poor Law Commission, C. Mott, in 1835, it was described as 'one of the most cleanly and well-ventilated establishments in England'.[9]

With the introduction of the Poor Law Amendment Act of 1834 and the Municipal Corporations Act of 1835, two new Poor Law Unions were created in Bristol. The municipal borough of Clifton constituted the Clifton Union, later to change its name to Barton Regis Union and, to the south of the city, Bedminster Union was created. The Bristol Corporation of the Poor remained responsible for the same area as before and continued to function in much the same way, but increasingly efforts were made by the central authority to force it to comply with the district scale of relief. The Corporation insisted that it should administer relief according to local bye-laws. In 1857, however, the Poor Law Board threatened the Guardians with legal proceedings for the recovery of £23,157 surcharge for improper expenditure (Bristol Corporation's scale of relief being considered too generous) and reluctantly the Guardians submitted to the central authority of the Poor Law.[10]

Clifton Poor Law Union, set up in 1836, was responsible for the poor of St Philip and St Jacob's parish, St James and St Paul's parish, the developing area of St George's, as well as for residential and rural parishes such as Clifton, Westbury-on-Trym, Horfield, Stapleton, Henbury, Filton, Stoke Gifford and Winterbourne. By 1844 the Union maintained three separate workhouses, one in Pennywell Road for able-bodied inmates, another in St George's for children and a third in Clifton for the aged and infirm. Conditions at the Pennywell Road workhouse were particularly bad. When the Assistant Poor Law Commissioner inspected the workhouse in 1835 he found it a

> disgraceful instance of neglect and mismanagement. The state of the workhouse was filthy in the extreme; the appearance of the inmates was filthy and wretched. There was no classification, men, women and children being indiscriminately herded together.[11]

Conditions did not improve much in the next ten years and in 1844 the Guardians proposed that a new workhouse be built for all the indoor poor of this Union. As in the case of the Bristol Corporation, ratepayers expressed strong opposition to plans which would incur further expenditure and increase poor rates. Most strident in their opposition were the ratepayers of Clifton parish, who agitated for the withdrawal of Clifton from the Union if plans went ahead. Despite this campaign, the Board of Guardians decided that a new workhouse was needed and they agreed to purchase 17 acres of land near Stapleton, to accommodate over 1000 inmates. The workhouse opened in 1847, but almost immediately proved inadequate to meet the increased demand for workhouse accommodation resulting from the economic depression of 1847-48. In 1848 a further £25,000 was spent on extensions to the building so that it could house 1161 inmates.[12] Additional buildings were erected on the site later in the nineteenth century, when it was known as Eastville workhouse; a fever hospital was built in 1868, extra lunatic wards in 1867, a tramp ward in 1873 and new pavilions for sick and lying-in cases in 1879 and 1880. The older workhouses were closed, though in 1880 a Vestry Hall and Parochial Offices were built on part of the Pennywell Road site and the premises at Clifton became Clifton Wood Industrial School.[13]

One of the intentions of the 1834 Poor Law Amendment Act was to create a more uniform administrative system and redistribute the cost of caring for the poor, but this was only partially achieved. Until 1865, parishes were largely responsible for the cost of their own outdoor poor, so that wealthy areas such as Clifton and Westbury-on-Trym had the lowest Poor Rates.[14] In Bedminster, which had a small number of ratepayers and a heavy burden in terms of poor relief, the annual charge in 1849 was five shillings in the pound on rental, whereas Clifton rates were 7d. in the pound.[15] The Union Chargeability Act of 1865 removed these inequalities in local taxation by making the cost of outdoor relief the responsibility of the union rather than the parish.

Another example of how the politics of poor relief exemplified divisions according to social class was the way in which the parish of Clifton sought to divest itself of the taint of poverty. As a fashionable health resort the reputation of Clifton was being tarnished by the high mortality statistics in Clifton Union. It was, therefore, agreed in 1877 that the Poor Law Union should be renamed Barton Regis, in order to avoid any association between Clifton and poverty and ill health.[16]

The three separate Poor Law Unions of Bedminster, Barton Regis and Bristol Corporation of the Poor continued to administer poor relief in their own districts until 1898. Each union had its own workhouse; Bedminster had a workhouse at Flax Bourton, Barton Regis was responsible for the workhouse at Eastville and in 1859 Bristol Corporation added to the accommodation in the converted French Prison by building a new workhouse on the Stapleton site.[17]

This duplication of provision, with three workhouses for one city, gave rise in the 1880s to discussions about the possibility of amalgamation. Bedminster Guardians were keen that the urban part of their union should be joined to Bristol. Some Bristol Guardians shared this view, but it was strongly opposed by the churchwarden Guardians and the proposal defeated. Barton Regis Board was also opposed to amalgamation and despite the intervention of the central Poor Law body, the Local Government Board (LGB), in 1882, no agreement was reached.[18]

By the late nineteenth century the growth and distribution of the population of Bristol and, in particular, the expansion of suburban areas, had resulted in considerable change in the composition of the three unions. In Barton Regis there was an increase in population between 1881 and 1891 of 26,978 and in Bedminster an increase of 10,170. In the Bristol Corporation area, by contrast, there was a decrease in population of 1938. As the Regional Inspector for LGB commented in 1892, this was partly a result of 'well-to-do members of the working class' leaving the city for residences in Barton Regis and Bedminster Unions.[19]

With the movement of younger and more skilled workers out of the city, Bristol Corporation was left with a smaller, older and poorer population. Thus, when Charles Booth undertook his research into the condition of the aged poor in the early 1890s, he found that Bristol Corporation had a population of 55,549, of whom 12.7 per cent were paupers and Barton Regis had a population of 193,094, of whom 5.7 per cent were paupers. Bristol Corporation's level of pauperism was above average for an urban area, but more striking was the proportion of old people in the population and the very high level of pauperism in old age. Of the population over the age of sixty-five, 54 per cent were paupers; in neighbouring Barton Regis the degree of aged pauperism was 21 per cent.[20]

Changing Composition of Boards of Guardians

Until the 1880s Poor Law Guardians in Bristol were exclusively male and predominantly middle class. This urban elite gradually changed as the qualification for membership of the Board of Guardians altered. The first major change came in 1882 with the election of four women Guardians, Miss Mary Clifford, Miss Alice Winkworth, Miss Catherine Woollam and Mrs Prentice Hall. Locally and nationally the support for women Guardians had been growing from the 1870s. The Society for Promoting the Return of Women as Guardians argued in 1881 that women had the leisure to visit the poor, were experienced in this work and were accustomed to household management. Moreover, since many paupers were women and children, it was appropriate that these cases should be dealt with by women Guardians.[21] Many of Bristol's leading citizens, including Lewis Fry MP, the Bishop of Bristol and several clergymen supported the campaign to have women elected,[22] though opponents argued that it would not be proper to discuss cases of vice with ladies present. Moreover, they considered that work of this nature made women mannish and 'nothing is more repulsive to a man than a mannish, strong-minded woman'.[23] Undeterred, the women stood and in two cases headed the poll.

This victory for women was facilitated by the relatively large number of female ratepayers in areas such as Clifton and Westbury-on-Trym. In the former there were nearly 830 women ratepayers. Support came from men too, including some of the wealthier ratepayers who each had 12 votes to cast. One male candidate complained that his name had been omitted from the voting papers of many Liberal voters who had awarded all their votes to Mary Clifford.[24]

The class composition of the Board changed somewhat after the property qualification for Guardians was reduced from £30 to £5 per annum in 1892 and abolished, along with plural voting, in 1894. Working-class Guardians were no more welcome at first than middle-class women Guardians. After some years as a Guardian, Frank Sheppard was nominated in 1901 for the position of Vice Chairman, but opposed by some members of the Board on the grounds that a working man should not hold such a position.[25] Despite this opposition Sheppard was elected by a small majority. Though gender and class inequalities continued into the twentieth century, by 1908 a working-class, socialist woman, Mrs Jane Tillett, was elected Guardian for Bedminster East. Helen Meller has examined the composition of the governing elite in Bristol, but further research is required on the political composition of Bristol Board of Guardians.[26]

The 1894 Local Government Act initiated a series of changes in local politics. Senior churchwardens and Justices of the Peace were no longer entitled to become *ex officio* Guardians, the property qualification for Guardians was abolished and Guardians were to be elected by a ballot of electors on the parliamentary and municipal registers.[27] The proposal to create a single Union with responsibility for poor relief in the enlarged municipal borough created by the Bristol Corporation Act of 1897 generated considerable debate in the local press. Even after the necessity for amalgamation had been accepted, debate continued as to the most appropriate system of representation. George Pearson, a staunch Conservative, argued that a system of representation based on rateable value would be preferable, since it would acknowledge the 'claims of property'. However, in March 1898 the Council rejected this method of determining the number of Guardians in each ward.[28]

The new Union for the borough of Bristol came into being in April 1898. The Bristol Corporation of the Poor and Bedminster Union were dissolved. Barton Regis continued to exist until 1904, but was much reduced in size, being made up of those parishes outside the municipal boundary. Three Guardians were elected for each of the municipal wards in the city, with the exception of Clifton, Redcliff and Bristol wards, which were allowed to have six Guardians each. At a Council meeting held in December 1899 a Labour member, John Curle, complained that the system of representation was still not equitable, since Clifton's 1904 burgesses elected six representatives, whereas the two Bedminster wards with a total of 7924 electors shared six representatives. Another Council member put the point rather differently, stating that in favoured wards 23,597 burgesses elected 42 councillors, while in the remaining wards 28,268 ratepayers elected 21 representatives.[29]

Defining Poverty

In the last decades of the nineteenth century increasing concern was expressed, both locally and nationally, about the problem of poverty. One feature of this new discourse on poverty was the demand for scientific principles to be applied to the measurement, analysis and treatment of the problem. For some people, including members of the Charity Organisation Society (COS), set up in 1869, this required thorough investigation into the circumstances of applicants for Poor Relief or charitable assistance, in order to ascertain whether their poverty resulted from individual moral failure or not. Key members of the LGB also shared this approach in the 1870s. By the 1880s and 1890s, however, further examination of the extent and causes of poverty identified the role of structural or environmental factors. Surveys, especially those of Booth and Rowntree, indicated that low wages, under-employment, old age and sickness all contributed to poverty and were beyond the control of the poor themselves.[30] Such surveys were complemented by examinations of the condition of the urban poor undertaken by journalists, clergy, Guardians and other 'social explorers'.[31] The investigation and exposure of poor social conditions did not result in a consensus regarding the causes and treatment of poverty and in the early twentieth century some people remained convinced that state help would undermine thrift and family responsibility.

The discourse and practice of Poor Relief in Bristol reflected these national trends, but few Bristol Guardians sought to withdraw out-relief and there was little formal co-operation between the Boards of Guardians and the COS. In the early 1870s the former were reluctant to provide the COS with lists of people relieved,[32] though there may have been some co-operation later in the decade.[33] In 1910, however, the LGB strongly advocated co-operation. The result was that Bristol Guardians agreed to exchange information with charitable agencies and to appoint four Guardians to the Council of the Civic League, which was then responsible for co-ordinating local charities.[34]

In the late nineteenth and early twentieth centuries there were several investigations into the social and economic circumstances of the poor in Bristol. A committee appointed by the Bishop of Gloucester and Bristol examined housing, health, labour and education, as well as the operation of charity and the Poor Law. The Committee concluded in 1884 that the local administration of Poor Relief was lax and advocated that the 'laws of philanthropic science must be studied ... in the same way as the laws of physical science'.[35] The recommendation that charity would be better than the Poor Law, since it would 'link the classes together in friendliness', echoed the approach of the COS to poverty.[36]

In the same year the *Bristol Mercury* published an article on the 'Homes of the Bristol Poor'.[37] The article brought to public attention the circumstances in which many of Bristol's working class lived, describing the housing, work and living conditions in different parts of the city. A more dramatic account of the contrast between poverty and wealth in Bristol appeared in the *New Penny Magazine* in 1903. The article, entitled 'Wealth and Want: Glitter and Grime' examined the contrast between 'Bristol's Outcast-land' and the 'Sunny Scenes of Fashionable Clifton'.[38] The journalist took the reader on a tour of St Jude's, Bristol's principal slum. The hostility of this environment is emphasized by the language of social exploration, which is more commonly associated with studies of the East End of London. Thus, the journalist invited the reader to 'penetrate into one of the smaller yards' and to 'explore' West Street. Again the dramatic conclusion emphasized the 'otherness' of the inhabitants:

> Such is the environment of Bristol's poor – squalid,
> despair-engineering, a morass in which men and
> women sink until they become parasitic animals ...
> What would become of us if Fate ordained that we
> should spend our days in Darkest Bristol?[39]

Concern about the effects of bad housing on the health and morality of the poor was shared by individuals and groups representing different political perspectives. In 1903 The Bristol Committee for the Better Housing of the Poor was established, with Lewis Fry as its President. The first report highlighted the problems associated with house clearance when no replacement housing was provided.[40]

A more radical examination of the housing problems in the city was undertaken in 1907 by Bristol Housing Reform Committee, whose remit was to examine the housing problem and press for change. The initiative came from Labour Party members of Bristol Council, such as F. Sheppard and J. Curle, who were concerned about overcrowding and ill health. The report of 1907 pointed to the major inequalities in health in different wards. Bristol Central, for example, had an infant mortality rate of 155 per 1000, while Clifton's was only 98 per 1000. The study showed that more than 20 per cent of deaths took place in public institutions. In the six districts investigated the researchers found overcrowded and unhealthy housing conditions, with poor sanitary arrangements and shared water taps. The report deplored the non-implementation of the 1890 Housing of the Working Classes Act and argued that, unless wages improved, it was the responsibility of the community to provide adequate housing as a 'safeguard against disease and crime'.[41]

Madge Dresser has examined the nature of Bristol's housing in some detail;[42] it is discussed here as an example of public concern about the plight of the poor and to highlight the circumstances in which many of them lived. A less sympathetic picture of life in Bristol's inner city is offered by the LGB inspector, E. B. Wethered. He commented in 1907:

> In Bristol there are an unusual number of the unskilled labouring classes, men who rely on casual labour, which dependence is itself demoralising. They reside in the poorest parts of the city in neighbour-hoods infested with public-houses, of one sort or other, and the men seem to spend their earnings as fast as they get them. In the matter of drinking the women are frequently as bad as the men.[43]

It would seem that Wethered considered drink to be a major cause of poverty, yet the previous year he acknowledged the difficulty in making the workhouse 'less eligible' than life outside:

> this difficulty arises from the fact that there are such a variety of circumstances regulating the lives of poor people who are not actually paupers. Naturally the food in the workhouse is more substantial than would be the fare of many poor persons who have a hard struggle to exist on the very verge of destitution, and are badly in want of food and clothing.[44]

The administration of the Poor Law was guided by the need to encourage the struggle for existence on the part of the poor. Independence and family responsibility were reinforced by systems of deterrence and the workhouse had a key symbolic and practical role in this regard. By the late nineteenth century, however, the system of deterrence was being refined in a number of ways.

The Classification and Treatment of those on Poor Relief

The scientific treatment of poverty demanded that the poor be dealt with on an individual basis and that the deserving be protected from association with those of dirty, vicious or immoral habits. Increasingly, different groups of paupers were removed from the workhouse through the provision of alternative institutions, such as mental asylums, separate infirmaries and children's homes. A relaxation in the rules of outdoor relief allowed some to remain in their own homes rather than enter the 'House', but age, gender and family circumstances were often as important as 'character' in determining how and where a person was relieved.

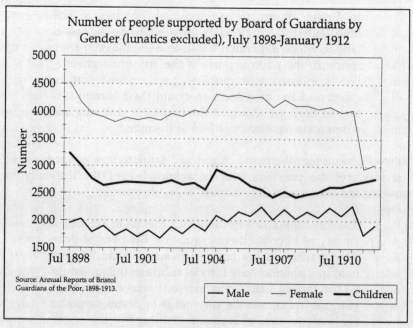

Figure 4

166

The Aged and Infirm

Although the new Poor Law was intended to deal with the problem of able-bodied pauperism, for much of the nineteenth century it was the old and infirm who constituted the largest class of paupers and even those who were classified as able-bodied were in many cases disabled in some way.[45] The classification 'aged and infirm' was also one which had changed since the early years of the nineteenth century. As the *Minority Report* of the Royal Commission of 1909 noted, there had been

> since 1834 a silent gradual shifting of the classifica-
> tion, the temporarily sick and acutely sick of whatever
> age being more or less taken out of the class of aged
> and infirm and all persons over sixty, however able-
> bodied, being more or less admitted to it.[46]

Although no standard definition of old age existed prior to the Old Age Pensions Act of 1908, in practice the majority of Poor Law Unions defined 'the aged' as those over sixty years. The agitation for old age pensions gave rise in the 1890s to a series of public enquiries to consider whether assistance other than the Poor Law should be available to the 'aged poor'. In the process of enquiry, the concept of 'desert' became central to the debate on old age and by the end of the decade the main policy recommendation to come from the LGB was that the 'deserving aged' should have preferential treatment in terms of Poor Relief. Circular letters from the LGB suggested that the 'deserving aged' should not have to enter the workhouse, unless infirmity or lack of a suitable home made this necessary. Rather they should receive adequate outdoor relief, while the deserving aged in the workhouse should enjoy certain privileges, which would minimize the deterrent nature of the workhouse regime.

In Bristol in the 1870s outdoor relief was given to elderly applicants, unless they were known to be drunkards or of idle habits.[47] Relief in aid of earnings was frequently given, but the level of relief was far from generous. In Bristol Corporation it varied from 2s. to 3s. 6d. a week, while in Clifton the upper limit was 2s. 6d., with the addition of a loaf of bread. Despite a fairly 'lax' attitude towards outdoor relief in the Bristol Unions, substantial numbers of elderly people entered the workhouse. Women who visited Bristol's workhouses in the 1860s and 1870s, such as Mary Elliot, Frances Power Cobbe and Mary Clifford, were dismayed at the treatment of the old and sick and did what they could to improve conditions.[48] Clifford was later to explain that her reason for becoming a Guardian was 'to protect old women who seemed oppressed'.[49]

Despite this sympathy for old people, Mary Clifford shared the view that desert should be the guiding principle in the administration of poor relief. Giving evidence before the Royal Commission on the Aged Poor in 1895 she deplored the lax system of outdoor relief which operated in Barton Regis Union, where she was one of the Guardians. Barton Regis had rules governing the grant of such relief, but according to Clifford they were frequently disregarded.[50] Clifford was also critical of the operation of some of Bristol's charities and the

> wasteful, even injurious way in which bequests were being used, and the appalling proportion of people dependent on the Guardians, in spite of the £5000 income of the ancient charities.[51]

She was opposed to the introduction of state pensions, as she later wrote, 'my evidence was intended to show that pensions are not needed *here*, if our charities were better managed'.[52]

By the first decade of the twentieth century the amalgamation of the three Unions allowed Bristol Guardians to make more progress on the moral classification of the Aged and Infirm and to implement the recommendations of the LGB circular regarding the creation of a special class of Deserving Aged. In 1898, when the new union was created, there were 2357 people in the various workhouses; 932 at Stapleton, 1124 at Eastville, 285 at Bedminster and 16 at St Peter's Hospital. When planning the changing use of workhouse space the Bristol Board of Guardians considered that accommodation was needed for up to 700 Aged and Infirm cases.[53] What proportion of these cases might constitute a separate class of Deserving Aged is not clear, but it was agreed in 1900 that the Deserving Aged on indoor relief should be allowed some small privileges and be placed in better accommodation when this became available.[54]

The majority of the Deserving Aged were expected to be eligible for outdoor relief and a special committee was set up in 1900 to deal with these cases. Those considered deserving were old people of good character, whose destitution was not their fault and whose homes were clean. Rather than having their cases reviewed at frequent intervals, the Deserving Aged were granted relief for a year at a time and were paid their allowance at a different time from ordinary paupers.[55]

By 1902 the moral economy of desert had been so refined that the amount of relief given was in part determined by the character of the applicant. For Class A applicants amounts varied from under 3s. to 6s. per person.[56]

In 1904 the extension of Bristol to include that part of Barton Regis which had hitherto remained outside the Bristol Union provided the latter with yet another workhouse. Barton Regis had built a new Workhouse in 1902 at Southmead, since the LGB would not permit it to make use of the workhouses controlled by Bristol Union. With the dissolution of Barton Regis, this new workhouse was now available to the Bristol Union and in 1904 it was agreed that Southmead should be used for 'aged inmates of good character, who do not need nursing'.[57] It was considered that accommodation could thereby be provided for 142 old people, 62 men and 74 women and three married couples.

An interesting development in this attempt to provide better accommodation for the Deserving Aged was the role adopted by the LGB Inspector in 1907. Concerned about the national demand for old-age pensions and the possibility that special accommodation for the Deserving Aged would incur unnecessary expense, Wethered asked the Clerk and Relieving Officers in Bristol to compile lists of the aged inmates in the Bristol workhouses. His aim appears to have been to prove that there were few, if any, Deserving Aged in the workhouse, apart from those in the infirmary blocks.

At Stapleton workhouse there were 156 men over the age of sixty. 'In some instances nothing was known about them, but only 19 cases, so far as information could be obtained, could come under the head of deserving poor'.[58] The first 12 cases on the list were reported in the *LGB Annual Report* for 1907-8:

No.1, 64 years of age. Addicted to drink.

No.2, 64 years of age. Addicted to drink.

No.3, 64 years of age. Worthless character.

No.4, 64 years of age. Drunken and improvident.

No.5, 65 years of age. Formerly a good tradesman,
but settled down to workhouse life. Addicted to drink.

No.6, 63 years of age. Married a widow with children,
disagreed with his wife, now an idle fellow; said by the
master of the workhouse to be simple-minded.

No.7, 63 years of age. Poverty caused by drink.

No.8, 54 (sic) years of age. Poverty caused by
improvidence and drink.

No.9, 65 years of age. Ticket of leave man.
No.10, 62 years of age. Ticket of leave man. Admitted to
the workhouse on discharge from prison.
No.11, 68 years of age. Heavy drinker.
No.12, 66 years of age. Addicted to drink, wastrel,
and improvident.[59]

At Eastville workhouse there were 158 men over the age of sixty, of whom only two were known to be of good character. No mention was made of the removal of more deserving cases to Southmead. If institutional relief was to lose its deterrent character then, argued the Assistant Secretary to the LGB, W. E. Knollys, that would remove 'one by one all the incentives to thrift in the working classes'.[60] Concern about family responsibility and the need to encourage thrift in the working class still acted as barriers to improved care for elderly people in the twentieth century. Thus, after Bristol Guardians had transferred their aged inmates of good character to Southmead they asked the LGB if they could rename the workhouse 'Southmead Home for the Aged Poor'. The LGB refused this change of title on the grounds that it would disguise the fact that the inmates were recipients of Poor Relief.[61]

The issue of old-age pensions was one which divided those involved in the administration of Poor Relief. Elderly workers were increasingly being pushed to the margins of employment and, both locally and nationally, unemployment and poverty in old age were rising at the end of the nineteenth century. Nonetheless some opposed the introduction of state pensions as unnecessary and counterproductive. Mary Clifford's views on the subject have already been mentioned, but it is interesting to note that her opposition arose from the belief that pensions would undermine the independence of the working class. As she wrote to a friend:

> I am very strongly of the opinion that State aid will be
> a serious national mistake, a blow to our national self-
> reliance. This is the unpopular side and my
> amendment was not seconded.[62]

Clifford's views on old-age pensions won little support on the Board of Guardians or amongst the local working class.[63]

Despite opposition from the COS and some within the Poor Law system, the Old Age Pensions Act was introduced in 1908, though it disqualified those who had been in receipt of Poor Relief during the previous year. Most Bristol Guardians considered this indiscriminate disqualification unfair and after some dispute it was agreed in 1909 that paupers over the age of seventy, who were disallowed pensions and were receiving less than 5s. a week in poor relief should have their cases reviewed.[64] After the review the number of single aged receiving five shillings or more in poor relief increased from 171 to 319. The impact of the Old Age Pensions Act on outrelief was most apparent in 1911 when disqualifications were removed. On 24 February 1911 there was a total of 3120 outdoor cases of all types, by the same date in 1912 the figure was 1844, a reduction due mainly to the wider availability of pensions.[65]

The impact of pensions on the workhouse was less dramatic. It was not easy for those who had lost everything to return to the local community, though in 1911 36 men and 18 women left the workhouse when they qualified for pensions.[66] The fact that 'old age' for pension purposes was defined as seventy years did little to help those in their sixties who were in poverty, but it did enable many of the very old to remain independent of the Poor Law.

Children

As Wethered wrote in 1908, 'poor law children are a class of inmates who always evoke sympathy from the fact that they are under the care of guardians from no fault of their own.'[67] For those children who could not be cared for in their own homes, separate accommodation was considered to be preferable to the workhouse. From the 1880s onwards, three main forms of care, other than the workhouse, were provided for these children: boarding out, emigration, and care in scattered or group homes for children.

Boarding out, or fostering, was intended for those children who were orphans or whom the Board of Guardians had adopted and its success depended on the quality of the foster home. Wethered was sceptical of the motives families had for accepting foster children. He considered financial gain, not love of children, was the main inducement and he insisted on the need for thorough enquiry into the suitability of such homes.[68] In 1911 the Bristol Board of Guardians endorsed this concern about the families with whom pauper children were placed and recommended that foster parents should be chosen with great care and that fostering should not be seen simply a business arrangement.[69]

Mary Clifford was one of the Guardians who took a particular interest in the welfare of pauper children and she and Miss Mason of the LGB were at one time responsible for finding suitable foster homes. Patricia Hollis suggests that in her concern to protect children from bad influences, Clifford refused to give parents any information about where their children were.[70] Miss Mason was also more concerned with the morality than the happiness of these children and would remove them from foster homes where they were loved, because the foster parents failed to instil character and backbone in their charges.[71] In 1898, when the new Union was set up, there were 163 children boarded out, two-thirds of them outside the Poor Law Union. No explanation was offered for the high number of children boarded out beyond Bristol's boundaries and it may be that there was more demand for children in rural areas.

In 1909 Poor Law children's homes accommodated 496 children in Bristol, but homes were overcrowded and the following year it was suggested by the Board of Guardians that emigration was the best way of 'extricating children from pauperism and evil surroundings' and that more use should be made of it.[72] Emigration of pauper children had been discontinued in 1874, but Mary Clifford seems to have been instrumental in persuading Barton Regis Board of Guardians to resume the practice in 1883. Mark Whitwill, Chairman of Bristol Education Committee undertook to help finance the venture and five boys were sent to Canada in June of that year. The emigration of a small number of children each year continued for the rest of the century. The Chairman of Barton Regis Board of Guardians, Major G. F. Rumsey, stated in 1898 that between 1883 and 1898 his Union had arranged for 136 children to emigrate.[73] Children selected for emigration were usually orphans or those adopted by the Board of Guardians, but other children could emigrate if their parents gave their consent. The Minutes of the Bristol Board of Guardians for 1901 give a list of the boys and girls, between the ages of seven and seventeen, who had emigrated to New Brunswick.[74]

Some care was taken to keep in touch with these children, both officially and on an individual basis. Mary Clifford sent letters and cards to those children she helped to emigrate, but further research is needed into the nature of the placements in Canada, not all of which were satisfactory. It should also be noted that whilst many of the children may have been willing to go to Canada, they had little knowledge of the circumstances in which they would live and the decision to remove these children to a foreign country was made for them by the Guardians.

While boarding out and emigration provided for some pauper children, most of those who were not relieved in their own homes were cared for in the workhouse or in special children's homes. By the end of the nineteenth century the workhouse was only considered appropriate for very young children, who needed to be with their mothers. In 1899 it was agreed by Bristol Guardians that all school age children should be removed from Stapleton workhouse to Scattered Homes or to Temporary Homes.[75] It was assumed that accommodation would be needed for 600 children in total.[76]

Scattered Homes were ordinary houses able to accommodate between eight and 16 children. There were four such homes in Bristol in 1895, ten years later there were 16, providing care for 198 children. While the process of moving children out of the workhouse was already under way in Bristol in 1900, an LGB circular of that year made it clear that this had become official policy. It may have been this which prompted the Guardians to buy 20 acres of land in Downend and erect a group of cottage homes on the site. Fourteen semi-detached homes, each capable of accommodating 12 children, as well as a small convalescent home and meeting hall were built by 1904. Much of the land was used for agriculture and market gardening, but 204 children were accommodated in the new homes. In line with the policy of encouraging children to integrate with the local community, the children attended the local elementary school, which Bristol Education Committee had recently opened. In addition to this scheme a Receiving Home was opened in Snowdon Road, Fishponds, which was able to accommodate 24 children and which could be used for classification purposes as well as for cases requiring special observation and supervision.

Mothers and Children

The number of children requiring residential care was to a large extent determined by the policy on outdoor relief. Rules governing outdoor relief tended to discriminate against women caring for children on their own. Thus the rules agreed by Bristol Board in 1898 stated that no outdoor relief should be given to married women whose husbands were in prison or whose husbands had deserted them, nor to women with illegitimate children. Widows might be eligible for outdoor relief, but were normally expected to support themselves and at least one of their children. However, widows receiving money from insurance societies were ineligible for outdoor relief, as was any widow who had spent lavishly on her husband's funeral. In addition there were general disqualifications affecting all who might be supported by their families, lived in filthy or overcrowded conditions, were of intemperate habits or bad character, had been seen frequenting public houses, were of dirty habits or lived in furnished rooms.[77]

Where relief was given to women and children it was dependent on investigation into the applicant's circumstances and a degree of supervision and periodic review. This supervision became more systematic in the early twentieth century and in 1910 the LGB recommended the appointment of female relieving officers to visit women on outdoor relief and see if 'they are living under proper circumstances; also to see if proper care is exercised in the bringing up of children'.[78] Bristol was one of the first Unions to appoint a female relieving officer and, though often unwelcome, increased supervision may have helped in those cases where 'insufficiency of bedding or want of clothes' was reported to the Relief Committee.[79]

Wethered argued that such supervision and advice was beneficial to the poor. However, there were penalties for those who did not conform to the expected norms. The new concern about the welfare of children, apparent in the 1908 Children Act, had an impact in terms of Poor Relief. Thus, mothers with illegitimate babies might be detained in the workhouse unless they could show that their child could be properly cared for. In order to satisfy themselves that this was the case, Guardians could arrange for the child to be visited once a month and removed to the workhouse if necessary.

For mothers with young children new regulations restricted their ability to work, since from 1911 they were not allowed to work unless the Guardians were satisfied that proper arrangements were made for 'the infant to be nursed during the mother's absence'.[80] Though such a ruling might increase the mother's dependence on the Poor Law, it also represented a relaxation in the expectation that it was the duty of the widowed or single mother to provide financially for her offspring.

A greater understanding of the difficult choices faced by widows is apparent in Wethered's analysis of the problem:

> sometimes it is not easy for the widow to find work and there is the family to be looked after while she is at work. The woman is very poor and the tendency is to resort to a cheap locality with doubtful surroundings for her children.[81]

It was recognised that she would either pay a neighbour to care for the children or leave them to their own devices and again the advice of a female relieving officer was considered to be an important safeguard. In 1910 Bristol Children's Committee recognized that widows might need extra relief if they were not working and it decided to judge every case on its merits.[82]

By the late nineteenth century the state was assuming greater responsibility for children's welfare and female Guardians and relieving officers were considered to be particularly suited to the supervision of mothers and children. The Infant Life Protection Act of 1897 was a measure intended to protect the welfare of children under the age of five who were in the paid care of people other than their parents. Its terms were extended by the 1908 Children Act, but the system of enquiry and supervision of a large number of cases continued as before.[83] Under the Poor Law Acts of 1889 and 1899 Guardians could assume control of children where there was evidence of neglect or cruelty. Between 1890 and 1898 Barton Regis Board adopted 77 children.[84] The 1894 Prevention of Cruelty to Children Act made illtreatment an offence punishable by imprisonment or a fine and Justices could send a child to the workhouse for safety. The 1908 Children Act expanded the role of the state with regard to children's welfare.

In the first few years of the twentieth century the extent and severity of child neglect was recorded in the Minutes of the Board of Guardians. Some examples for these reports might help to illustrate why some children found themselves in children's homes or being sent to Canada. The following cases were considered in 1901. Charlotte K. three years of age , weighed 12lbs. 8ozs., mother a prostitute, father in South Africa, mother imprisoned for six months for neglecting and starving her children. Florence T. ten years of age, found in a stinking room infested with vermin. Sister dead. Father in South Africa, but sending money home. Mother imprisoned one month for neglect. Emily H. both parents dead, admitted to Eastville Workhouse. George, James and Mary W. grossly neglected, despite several warnings. Father imprisoned for three weeks with hard labour. In all these cases the children were adopted by the Board.[85]

It is not certain to what extent the Boer War, and the disruption of family life and security, exacerbated the degree of neglect, but it appears that by the end of the decade the situation had improved. Certainly the women inspectors responsible for examining children under the provisions of the Infant Life Protection Act found in 1910 that the 'condition of homes has improved' and that children were cleaner and better cared for.[86]

It is impossible in a chapter of this length to examine the classification and treatment of all those on Poor Relief. The treatment of the sick poor was the subject of heated debate within the Bristol Board in the first decade of the twentieth century and divisions over whether or not to build a new infirmary, and on what site, delayed improvements for several years. Yet again ratepayers expressed opposition to proposed building schemes, but the Guardians themselves could not reach agreement on the best means to provide separate accommodation for the sick. It was not until 1912 that they finally agreed to develop the Southmead site by building an infirmary there for 550 patients.[87] Though completed in 1914, the outbreak of war resulted in requisition by military authorities and it was not occupied by the civilian sick until the 1920s.[88]

Little has been said about the able-bodied poor because, by the end of the nineteenth century, the Poor Law was principally concerned with relieving the sick, the old, children and women who were widowed or deserted by their husbands. During economic depressions, trade disputes and periods of severe weather, unemployed workers increased the numbers on outdoor relief, but these problems were considered to be temporary. With the increase in long-term unemployment in the inter-war period, however, able-bodied workers became once more the focus of attention at national and local level.

The Later History of the Poor Law in Bristol

The history of the Poor Law in Bristol after the First World War cannot be examined fully, but some consideration of the response to unemployment and poverty in the inter-war years is essential. Although Bristol's diversified economy protected it from the very high levels of unemployment experienced in the north of England, South Wales and parts of London, the city was nonetheless affected by unemployment and social deprivation in the inter-war years. The statistics of unemployment relief given by Poor Law agencies are not altogether reliable indicators of the total level of unemployment in Bristol, since Exchequer-funded Unemployment Benefit was also available to some of those out of work and various schemes to extend Unemployment Benefit enabled many who had exhausted their entitlement to remain independent of the Poor Law.

In 1922 the Guardians decided that men in receipt of Unemployment Relief should be employed in cultivating the land

owned by the Board at Downend.[89] The number of those in receipt of
Unemployment Relief in Bristol peaked in March 1927, with the after-
effects of the General Strike and the coal dispute exacerbating
unemployment. The cost of Unemployment Relief in the quarter year
to March 1927 was £38,592 compared with £29,162 in the same quarter
in 1926. (See Figure 5.)

Apart from the grant of Unemployment Relief, with or without the
work test, the other policy adopted by the Bristol Board of Guardians
with regard to the unemployed was to encourage emigration. In the
relief year 1926-27 the Guardians put 144 cases in touch with the
proper authorities and 59 of these emigrated to areas of white settlement in the colonies. In 1929 the Ministry of Health encouraged local
authorities to make arrangements for assisted passages to Canada and
Australia. Bristol Migration Committee initiated a training programme for young casual workers to fit them for life in the colonies.[90]

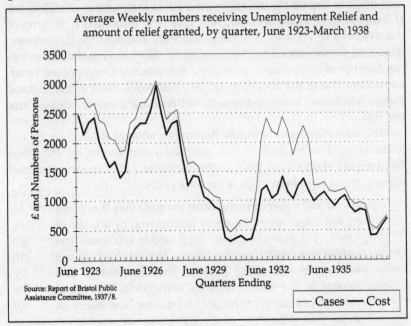

Figure 5

After 1918 those in receipt of Poor Relief were no longer disqualified from voting and this, in conjunction with the increasing strength
of the Labour Party and a rise in the number of left-wing Guardians
nationally, generated concern about the impact of the so-called

'pauper franchise'. The belief that locally elected Boards of Guardians might be too sympathetic to the plight of the unemployed, was one reason why central government was finally persuaded to abolish Boards of Guardians and transfer their powers and responsibilities to County and County Borough Councils.[91] Neville Chamberlain rejected the idea of District Councils being given these powers since he believed 'elections will be governed by one dominant consideration, namely those who promise the greatest amount of outrelief will be the ones returned to office'.[92]

The Local Government Act of 1929 transferred the functions of 625 Boards of Guardians to 145 County and County Borough Councils. Public Assistance Committees assumed responsibility for the poor and new categories of relief were introduced. It is difficult to assess the impact of this administrative change on Bristol, since the early 1930s were also associated with government demands for reduced local spending. In Bristol the dramatic increase in the number of claims for Unemployment Relief between 1931 and 1932 prompted L. N. Ure, of the Ministry of Health, to write to the Public Assistance Committee, demanding that something be done about the 'lax administration'.[93] If the number of cases rose dramatically, this was not accompanied by an equivalent rise in the cost of providing Unemployment Relief, indeed Figure 5 indicates a major disparity between the number of cases and the cost.

The administration of Public Assistance was considered lax by the Ministry of Health, but it was perceived differently by the poor themselves. Helen Reid quotes the views of one woman who had experience of state help in the inter-war years,

> if you had a pair of pictures on the wall they'd tell you to sell them – you couldn't own a rug, or a pack of cards, or a piano but they'd tell you to sell them first before you could have the tokens. If your child earned a few coppers doing errands, that counted. If one person in the family was in work, then they were expected to support the rest, no matter how many of them there were.[94]

The officials at the Ministry of Health considered that articles in *Bristol Labour Weekly* had affected the number of applications for relief by advising its readers how to claim.[95] Though not always effective, the political organization of the unemployed, both locally and nationally, made it possible for the poor to express their discontent and demand changes in the ways they were treated. For four weeks in 1928 the Committee Room at St Peter's Hospital was given a police guard and on at least one occasion there was a fierce struggle between protesters and the police.[96]

The rights of the unemployed in Bristol were promoted by the local Labour Party and by two radical pressure groups, the National Unemployed Workers' Movement (NUWM) and the Bristol Unemployed Association. In 1931 protests were organized against the Means Test and the proposed cuts in benefit and the NUWM staged demonstrations at St Peter's and outside the homes of relieving officers.[97]

The financial support of large numbers of unemployed was a considerable burden on local rates and by 1934 both central and local government were convinced that unemployment should be a national charge.[98] The Unemployment Assistance Act 1934 was intended to provide support for the able-bodied unemployed, but by the time it had become fully operative in April 1937, the number of unemployed in Bristol had declined from 17,561 to 12,815.[99]

By 1937 trade had improved and unemployment declined, but two studies undertaken in that year testify to the relatively high level of poverty in Bristol. Tout's study of the standard of living revealed a significant degree of child poverty, particularly in large families[100] and an official medical survey of malnutrition in Bristol schoolchildren indicated the ill-effects of economic hardship.[101] The *Annual Report of the Ministry of Health* for 1929-30 confirmed a connection between environmental factors and poverty and local authorities were recommended to 'make full use of public health and housing powers to attack the roots of pauperism'.[102] Though the council estates built in the 1920s, such as Hillfields, offered a high standard of housing to some members of the working class, by 1930 the 'slum areas of Bristol were almost as extensive as in 1919.'[103] The Housing Act of 1930 prioritized slum clearance and rehousing and in Bristol 3000 homes were identified as in need of demolition. Considerable efforts were made in the 1930s to eliminate the worst housing conditions, but studies of health, living standards and housing conditions suggest that it was not only those on Poor Relief (or Public Assistance as it was known after 1929) who experienced deprivation in the inter-war years.

Conclusion

Bristol Guardians varied in their response to poverty, but they rarely enforced the full rigour of the Poor Law and were castigated at different times by the central Poor Law authorities for being lax in their approach although in 1904 one Guardian thought that some members of the Board would like to 'do away with outrelief and put the poor in the workhouse'.[104] Who was offered the workhouse depended very much on assessments of desert and the associated moral classification of the poor. Those who failed to meet the standards of sexual propriety, thrift, sobriety, cleanliness and hard work might be excluded from their community and incarcerated in the workhouse or other institution. Similarly those granted outdoor relief could be placed on different relief scales according to their character. Thus, in 1929 the Home Allowance Committee operated two separate relief scales for Class A and Class B women.[105]

Looking at the history of the Poor Law in Bristol it is important to remember that although only a minority of the population had direct experience of the Poor Law, the lives of the majority of the working class were circumscribed by fear that unemployment, sickness, old age, death of a spouse or parent, could result in destitution and dependence on Poor Relief. The symbolic weight of workhouse structures was not lost on those who struggled to remain independent. If the workhouse, with its perimeter walls, railings and gatehouse represented the politics of exclusion in architectural form, the systems of segregation, of emigration and of pauper disenfranchisement were part of the same operation of power. The intention was not to punish, but to educate the poor, to encourage family responsibility and self-help. If poor people did not welcome enquiry into personal circumstances and the degree of supervision associated with Poor Relief and made alternative arrangements, then the system had succeeded in encouraging independence.

It has not been possible in this chapter to examine the ways in which poor Bristolians helped to modify the operation of the Poor Law. For much of the period studied they were denied the right to vote for those who would consider their applications for relief and could only express their views through organized protest. Nonetheless, the working class helped to shape the system of Poor Relief on an individual level, whether by making demands for assistance, by giving up their sick, insane or elderly to the care of the Guardians, or by refusing to accept poor relief, despite their need. The influence of the local community on the operation of the Poor Law needs to be explored further if we are to understand the dynamics of the relationship between Poor Law administrators and the poor. This chapter has examined the policies of the former, the voices of the poor and of the wider working class have yet to be heard.

Notes

1   E. E. Butcher, *Bristol Corporation of the Poor, 1696-1898* (BHA, 24, 1972).
2   *BMerc*, 11 Dec. 1894.
3   J. Latimer, *Annals of Bristol in the Nineteenth Century* (Bristol, 1887), 446, gives details of protest to Poor Law Board in 1869 regarding the ability of churchwarden Guardians to outvote ratepayers' Guardians; 518-9, division over amalgamation.
4   Butcher, *Bristol Corporation*, 22.
5   Latimer, *Annals*, 139.
6   Latimer, *Annals*, 139.
7   Latimer, *Annals*, 186-7.
8   Latimer, *Annals*, 186.
9   Latimer, *Annals*, 200.
10 *BMerc*, 11 Dec. 1894; Latimer, *Annals*, 351; Butcher, *Bristol Corporation*, 23.
11 Latimer, *Annals*, 200.
12 Latimer, *Annals*, 279.
13 BRL, B22122, G. F. Rumsey, *A Paper*, read by Major G. F. Rumsey to Barton Regis Board of Guardians, 18 March 1898.
14 Rumsey, *A Paper*; Latimer, *Annals*, 200-01.
15 Latimer, *Annals*, 201.
16 Rumsey, *A Paper*.
17 Latimer, *Annals*, 367. The workhouse buildings at Stapleton are now part of Blackberry Hill Hospital, Manor Road. Eastville workhouse has been demolished, but the entrance and perimeter wall still stand and homes for blind people have been built on the site.
18 Latimer, *Annals*, 518-19.
19 BPP C6745 XXXVIII, *21st Annual Report of the Local Government Board (LGB), 1891-2*, Appendix B, 163.
20 C. Booth, *The Aged Poor in England and Wales* (1894), 86.
21 *ER*, 15 March 1881, 123-4.
22 *ER*, 15 Feb. 1882.
23 *ER*, 15 May 1882.
24 G. M. Williams, *Mary Clifford* (Bristol, 1921), 106.
25 Williams, *Mary Clifford*, 198.
26 H. Meller, *Leisure and the Changing City, 1870-1914* (1976), 74-89.
27 *BMerc*, 11 Dec. 1894.
28 *BTM*, 3 Jan. 1898.
29 Latimer, *Annals*, 88-9.
30 Booth, *Aged Poor*; C. Booth, *Life and Labour of the People in London* (1889-1903); B. S. Rowntree, *Poverty: A Study of Town Life* (1901).
31 P. Keating, ed., *Into Unknown England, 1866-1913: Selections from Social Explorers* (Glasgow, 1976).
32 BPP C516 XXVIII.I, *1st Annual Report LGB, 1871-2*, App. B, 138-9; BRL, B20270, *Condition of the Bristol Poor* (Bristol, 1884), 164.
33 BRL, B12360, extract from *WDP*, 16 June 1883.
34 *Annual Report of Bristol Guardians of the Poor, 1910-11*, 14.
35 *Condition of Bristol Poor*, 169.
36 *Condition of Bristol Poor*, 714.
37 BRL, B14683, *BMerc*, 1884.
38 BRL, B12919, *New Penny Magazine*, 3 Jan. 1903.

39   *New Penny Magazine*, 3 Jan. 1903, 450.

40   BRL, B12941, Bristol Committee for the Better Housing of the Poor, *Report* (Bristol, 1903).

41   BRL, B13496, *Report of Bristol Housing Reform Committee, 1907*, 1-23.

42   M. Dresser, 'People's Housing in Bristol, 1870-1939', in I. Bild, ed., *Bristol's Other History* (Bristol, 1983), 129-60.

43   BPP Cd. 4347 XXX, *37th Annual Report LGB, 1907-8*, 322.

44   BPP Cd. 3665 XXVI, *36th Annual Report LGB, 1906-7*, 314.

45   BPP Cd. 746 XXV.I, *30th Annual Report LGB, 1900-1*, 129.

46   BPP Cd. 4499, XXXVII, 1909, *Royal Commission on the Poor Law and Relief of Distress: Minority Report*, 245.

47   BPP C516 XXVIII.I, *1st Annual Report LGB, 1871-2*, 137-8.

48   F. Power Cobbe, *Life of Frances Power Cobbe* (1904), 303-24. This gives an account of the visits made by Power Cobbe and Elliot to St Peter's Hospital.

49   Williams, *Mary Clifford*, 103.

50   BPP C7648 XVI.I, 1895, *Royal Commission on the Aged Poor*, II, 328.

51   Williams, *Mary Clifford*, 125.

52   Williams, *Mary Clifford*, 125.

53   *Annual Report of Proceedings of Bristol Guardians of the Poor, 1899-1900*, 5.

54   *Annual Report of Bristol Guardians, 1900-1*, 7-10.

55   *Annual Report of Bristol Guardians, 1900-1*, 9-10.

56   *Annual Report of Bristol Guardians, 1902-3*, 9.

57   *Annual Report of Bristol Guardians, 1904-5*, 6.

58   BPP Cd. 4347 XXX, *37th Annual Report LGB, 1907-8*, App. III, 324.

59   BPP Cd. 4347 XXX, *37th Annual Report LGB, 1907-8*, App. III, 324.

60   BPP H of C 271, *House of Commons Select Committee on Cottage Homes Bill: Report, 1899*, 37.

61   *Poor Law Annual 1908-9*, issued by Poor Law Officers' Journal (1908), 379.

62   Williams, *Mary Clifford*, 126.

63   Williams, *Mary Clifford*, 126.

64   *Annual Report of Bristol Guardians, 1908-9*, 10.

65   *Annual Report of Bristol Guardians, 1911-12*, 10.

66   *Annual Report of Bristol Guardians, 1910-11*, 13.

67   BPP Cd.4347 XXX, *37th Annual Report LGB, 1907-8*, App.III, 326.

68   BPP Cd.5865 XXXI, *40th Annual Report LGB, 1910-11*, App., 62.

69   *Annual Report of Bristol Guardians, 1910-11*, 16.

70   P. Hollis, *Ladies Elect*, 256-7.

71   Hollis, *Ladies Elect: Women in English Local Government, 1865-1914* (Oxford, 1987), 257.

72   *Annual Report of Bristol Guardians, 1909-10*, 11-12; *Annual Report of Bristol Guardians, 1911-12*, 16.

73   Rumsey, *A Paper*.

74   BRO, 10243, *Guardians of the Poor for the City and County of Bristol: Minutes of Board Meeting*, vol. vii, 1901, 28-29; 144-5.

75   *Annual Report of Bristol Guardians, 1898-99*, 10-12.

76   *Annual Report of Bristol Guardians, 1899-1900*, 4.

77   *Annual Report of Bristol Guardians, 1898-9*, 8.

78   BPP Cd. 6980 XXXI.I, *42nd Annual Report LGB, 1912-13*, 48.

79   BPP Cd. 6980 XXXI.I, *42nd Annual Report LGB, 1912-13*, 48.

80 BPP Cd. 6327 XXXV, *41st Annual Report LGB, 1911-12*, 96.
81 BPP Cd. 6980 XXXI.I, *42nd Annual Report LGB, 1912-13*, 46.
82 *Annual Report of Bristol Guardians, 1910-11*, 15.
83 *Annual Report of Bristol Guardians, 1909-10*, 14.
84 Rumsey, *A Paper*.
85 BRO, 10243, *Guardians of the City and County of Bristol, Minutes of Board Meeting*, vol vii, 1901, 123-325.
86 *Annual Report of Bristol Guardians, 1910-11*, 21.
87 *Annual Report of Bristol Guardians, 1911-12*, 8-9.
88 BPP Cmd. 932 XVII, *1st Annual Report of the Ministry of Health, 1919-20*, Pt. 3, 97.
89 *Annual Report of Bristol Guardians, 1929-30*, 28.
90 *Annual Report of Bristol Guardians, 1929-30*, 13.
91 PRO, MH/141 *Advantages of Poor Law Reform 1927*, see also MH57/138 and MH57/147.
92 PRO, MH57/153.
93 PRO, MH57/97E, *Poor Law Relief, Cause of increase 1931-33; City and County of Bristol Public Assistance Committee (PAC), Report of Proceedings, 1931-33*, 54.
94 H. Reid, 'They Were Terrible Years: Flappers, Women and Ladies' in D. Harrison, ed., *Bristol Between the Wars: A City and Its People, 1919-39* (Bristol, 1984), 70.
95 PRO, MH57/97E.
96 G. Huggins, 'As We Were: Memoirs of Local Government Service,1926-1972', *The Bridge*, Staff Newsletter of Avon Social Services Department, vol.1., No.9, 1975, 2.
97 *PAC Report, 1931-33*, 58-60.
98 N. Whiteside, *Bad Times: Unemployment in British Social and Political History* (1991), 76.
99 *PAC Report, 1935-7*, 70.
100 H. Tout, *The Standard of Living in Bristol* (Bristol, 1938).
101 *Annual Report of the Medical Officer of Health, Bristol, 1937*.
102 BPP Cmd. 3667 XIII, *11th Annual Report of the Ministry of Health 1929-30*, 185.
103 BRL, B14793, *City and County of Bristol, Local Government 1835-1935: A Century of Progress* (Bristol, 1935), 28.
104 *WDP*, 16 June 1904.
105 *Annual Report of Bristol Guardians, 1929-30*, 41.

'AN ENLARGED SPHERE OF USEFULNESS': THE BRISTOL WOMEN'S MOVEMENT, c.1860-1914[1]

June Hannam

When leading members of the nineteenth century women's movement came to write their memoirs they singled out Bristol as one of a small number of cities at the forefront of the development of feminist politics.[2] Josephine Butler, leader of the Ladies National Association for the Repeal of the Contagious Diseases Acts, described three Bristol women, Mary Priestman, Mary Estlin and Margaret Tanner as her 'body guard, a corps d'elite on whose prompt aid, singleness of purpose, prudence and unwearying industry ... I could rely upon at all times'.[3] Historians have also recognized Bristol's importance: Patricia Hollis, for example, in her study of women's participation in local government, claims that 'Bristol possessed one of the most impressive women's movements in the country.'[4]

Nonetheless, our understanding of feminist politics in the city remains fragmentary. With the exception of a pioneering article by Ellen Malos, which explores the relationship between women's suffrage and radical politics, there is no study which brings together the different strands of the Bristol movement.[5] This reflects a more general lack of attention in studies of the nineteenth century women's movement to the distinctive characteristics of provincial feminist groups and to their importance. And yet, as Jane Rendall suggests, networks of male and female supporters in provincial cities made up a key strand of the early women's movement. They had a 'grittier' style than their London counterparts and were more likely to be linked to the politics of popular liberalism and Radicalism.[6]

Most women were more comfortable, and found it easier, taking part in public life at a local level. Although they were denied the parliamentary franchise until 1918, women ratepayers and householders could vote in local elections after 1869 and could stand as candidates to School Boards and Boards of Guardians. In the 1860s and 1870s women took action locally to support a range of feminist campaigns, including access to education, women's property rights, female suffrage and the repeal of the Contagious Diseases Acts. Provincial branches could exercise considerable autonomy in terms of strategy, organization and finance, while initiatives taken locally often influenced national developments. It is the intention of this chapter to examine the women's movement in Bristol as a whole and to explore the relationship between the varied feminist campaigns in the period 1850-1914. This will not only reveal the specific features of feminist politics in Bristol, but will also add to our understanding of the women's movement more generally.

Feminist campaigners in the nineteenth century sought to challenge women's exclusion from public life and from participation in national politics. In doing so they had to confront the Victorian ideology of separate spheres which identified women with domesticity and the moral guardianship of the family. This role was thought to be biologically as well as socially determined and was underpinned by a series of legal, economic and social restrictions which reinforced women's dependence on, and subordination to, male relatives.[7] Although middle class women managed to carve out an increasingly active public role for themselves, their own arguments and demands were developed within, and to some extent shaped by, the separate spheres framework and its emphasis on what constituted appropriate masculine and feminine behaviour. The ideas and goals of the nineteenth-century women's movement, therefore, were complex: feminists took an interest in the conditions of family life and marriage, in sexual issues and morality as well as in education, employment and the suffrage, and saw all of these causes as interrelated.[8]

As a growing number of middle class women sought to enter public life, the opposite was the case for working class women. In the first half of the nineteenth century they had taken part in a variety of political movements, including Owenite socialism and Chartism.[9] By the 1850s, however, the decline of Chartism, the increasing separation of work, family and community life and the predominance of skilled male trade unions in the labour movement made it far more difficult for working class women to participate in politics.[10]

The most active members of the Bristol women's movement in the 1860s and 1870s, therefore, came largely from nonconformist professional and business families in the Clifton area who took an interest in political and social reform questions. They were linked by friendship and family ties, not only to each other, but also to families in other parts of Britain and in the United States.[11] These family and friendship networks helped to sustain women's commitment to challenging inequalities and contributed to the development of a woman-centred outlook which cut across differences based on class, religion and politics. On the other hand women did not necessarily share the same approach to feminist politics, which could make any emphasis on a common sisterhood difficult to achieve, and differences between them tended to surface in some periods more than in others.

Women who became active in the early Bristol women's movement had already gained experience of public life through their involvement in social work and in the campaign against slavery. The relationship between philanthropy, anti-slavery agitation and the development of an interest in women's rights was not, however, a straightforward one. Women's family, political and religious backgrounds, coupled with the local characteristics of particular movements, played a key role in explaining whether or not they would be drawn to feminist politics. Female critics of slavery, for example, tended to be concerned with the moral and religious questions which arose from the ownership of slaves and their evangelicalism legitimized, rather than challenged, existing gender relationships.[12]

Bristol was one of the few areas in which the anti-slavery cause did become linked with women's rights, although this connection took some time to develop. In 1840 a small group of Clifton women, predominantly from Quaker backgrounds, formed the Bristol and Clifton Ladies' Anti-Slavery Society (B&CLASS) as an auxiliary to the Quaker-run British and Foreign Anti-Slavery Society (B&FASS). B&CLASS held meetings in members' houses, raised funds for the parent Society, but were reluctant to hold public meetings.[13] In the same period Unitarian women, including Mary Estlin, Mary Carpenter and Anna Thomas, joined with male relatives in supporting the American abolitionist William Lloyd Garrison who championed women's right to take an active part in the anti-slavery campaign.[14]

Mary Estlin (c.1820-1902) was the only daughter of John Bishop Estlin, an ophthalmic surgeon who became a leading advocate of Garrison's views in England.[15] He was a personal friend of, and physician to, the family of Dr Lant Carpenter, Unitarian minister for Bristol, whose daughter Mary (1807-77) gained a national reputation for her work on behalf of destitute children and young offenders. Members of the Thomas family, who owned the Broad Plain Soap Works, were related to the Carpenters by marriage.[16] All of these Unitarian families took an active role in the social and political life of the city and encouraged their daughters, as well as their sons, to take an interest in events beyond the home. The girls all received a broad education, many of them in the school opened by Mary Carpenter and her mother in 1829.[17]

After a visit by William Garrison and the ex-slave Frederick Douglass to Bristol in 1846, members of B&CLASS began to show greater independence from their parent Society. It was not until two years later, however, when Mary Estlin became a member of the committee, that the Ladies' Society finally gave formal support to Garrison.[18] There is no suggestion in their minutes that B&CLASS at this stage considered women's rights to be an important issue. Indeed, Clare Midgley argues that a commitment to anti-slavery work may have delayed an involvement in feminist politics, although she notes that in the 1850s and 1860s the women's movement was able to make 'use of the network of female abolitionists in creating its own network and leadership'.[19] Female supporters of Garrison in Bristol certainly made contact with like-minded women in other cities, such as Edinburgh and Leeds, who later became active in the women's movement, as well as with American feminists. Mary Estlin's private correspondence was filled with references to women's unequal social position and, as the Civil War drew to a close, the topic of women's suffrage dominated the letters between herself and Sarah Pugh.[20]

An involvement in social work also encouraged many Bristol women to develop an interest in women's rights. Again, however, the relationship between the two was a complex one. Philanthropists who were largely concerned with moral issues and pauperism did not necessarily question their own social position, while their emphasis on individual rescue work could militate against an interest in political change.[21] In Bristol, however, a number of women sought to develop an 'informed scientific basis' for the exercise of their social responsibilities and aimed to explore the relationship between voluntary work and state provision.[22] They were able to develop and express their ideas through the National Association for the Promotion of Social Science (NAPSS), an organization in which Mary Carpenter played a leading role. She made clear that her priority was to change attitudes towards young criminals and to promote the establishment of ragged schools and reformatories, but was reluctant at first to speak at conferences on the subject in case she 'unsexed' herself. Nonetheless, her commitment to the needs of destitute children was so strong that by the late 1850s she was willing to read papers at NAPSS annual conferences and in 1861 she gave evidence to the Royal Commission on Poor Relief.[23]

In her very busy life Mary Carpenter did not have the time to take an active part in feminist campaigns, but she did give support publicly to the campaign to repeal the Contagious Diseases Acts and just before her death spoke at a large suffrage rally in Bristol.[24] This open support was seen as very important by the emerging women's movement, since Mary Carpenter's national reputation for her work on behalf of destitute children ensured that her views would be taken seriously by men as well as women. Reporting on the NAPSS Conference of 1857 the *Englishwomen's Journal* noted that:

> One whose name is sufficient to ensure respect for all that is dignified and delicate in her sex – Mary Carpenter – sat surrounded by the first men of England ... raised her own voice and was listened to with equal interest and veneration.[25]

Many of those who later became active in feminist politics were inspired by Mary Carpenter's work. Matthew Davenport Hill, a fellow Unitarian and founder member of the NAPSS, worked closely with Mary Carpenter after moving to Bristol in 1851 to become Commissioner for Bankruptcy. His daughters, Rosamund and Florence, helped in Mary Carpenter's reformatories and became part of her circle of friends. They were joined in 1862 by Catherine (d.1878) and Susannah (1820-84) Winkworth, who had already taken an interest in women's rights in Manchester; Susannah had a particular concern with the improvement of working-class housing and took a leading part in establishing the Jacob's Wells industrial dwellings.[26] Agnes Beddoe, the daughter of a clergyman, also worked in Mary Carpenter's ragged schools when she came to the city after her marriage to a Clifton physician. She assisted Mary in establishing the Indian Society, set up a home for working girls and in 1882 formed the Bristol Emigration Society to help women and pauper children to find new homes in the colonies.[27]

For some women it was their involvement with Mary Carpenter which formed the starting point for their interest in feminist causes. Frances Power Cobbe, for example, came to Bristol in 1858 especially to work with Mary Carpenter and became convinced that women needed the vote so that they could influence legislation which related to young criminals.[28] On leaving Bristol Frances Power Cobbe established a reputation as a feminist journalist, but she retained a close friendship with many Bristol women and corresponded with Mary Estlin throughout the 1860s.[29]

Women's concern with social questions increasingly raised issues about female education and employment opportunities. Mary Carpenter had a lifelong interest in promoting women's education and training. She accepted that men and women were destined for different social roles, but could not see why this should restrict women's intellectual development. Mary herself was taught physics, mathematics, natural science, physiology and history and she claimed that 'no part of that education have I felt to be superfluous to me'.[30] She was Vice President of the Girls' Public Day School Trust and emphasized the need to train teachers, both in England and in India. She also took an interest in Catherine Winkworth's work as secretary of the Clifton Association for the Higher Education of Women. Both Mary Carpenter and Florence Davenport Hill were honorary members of the Society for Promoting the Employment of Women.[31]

By the mid-1860s, therefore, a number of Bristol women already had shared interests in abolitionism, social work on behalf of women and children, female education and employment opportunities for women. From these interests they established new friendship networks as well as reinforcing existing ones which were based on family, religious and political connections. Given their own family backgrounds and the breadth of their education it is hardly surprising that they were receptive to women's rights and to the campaigns which developed around women's suffrage in the 1860s.

The first women's suffrage petition in 1866 was signed by several Bristol women, including Susannah Winkworth, Florence Davenport Hill and Agnes Beddoe. Three Quaker sisters, Margaret Tanner (1817-1905), Anna Maria (1829-1914) and Mary (1831-1914) Priestman, who were to play a significant role in the Bristol women's movement, were also signatories, although the Priestmans still gave their address as Newcastle.[32] The Priestman sisters were staunch radical liberals who had taken part in the anti-slavery campaign, in movements for peace and in the agitation against the Corn Laws. They were related to some of the leading feminist families of the day through the marriage of their eldest sister to John Bright, MP, whose brother Jacob and sisters Priscilla McLaren and Margaret Lucas were ardent feminists. John Bright's daughter Helen Bright Clark, who had married the shoe manufacturer William Clark of Street, and his niece Lilias Ashworth, who lived with her husband Professor Hallett in Bath, were both active in the Bristol women's movement.[33]

In the year following the petition women's suffrage committees were formed in Manchester, London, Edinburgh and Birmingham; the Bristol Society became the fifth when it was established in January 1868 following a meeting convened by Matthew Davenport Hill at his home. The Bristol Suffrage Society was affiliated to the National Society for Women's Suffrage and in 1870 was renamed the Bristol and

West of England Society for Women's Suffrage (BSWS); its aim was to spread suffrage propaganda throughout the region and to assist in the formation of local groups. Agnes Beddoe, Mary Estlin and Florence Davenport Hill were members of the committee from the start. Lilias Ashworth Hallett joined by the end of the first year and Anna Maria Priestman in 1870.[34]

Men were involved in the Society from the very beginning, including the Unitarians, Rev. J. Estlin Carpenter, Charles and Herbert Thomas, the Congregationalist minister Rev. U. R. Thomas, and Professor Newman, and they comprised almost half of all subscribers in the early years.[35] Increasingly, however, it was women who came forward to carry out day-to-day organization and to undertake public speaking. In the early 1870s Mary Estlin was treasurer of the Society and Elizabeth Ramsay and Lilias Ashworth were the honorary secretaries. Several women's suffrage Bills were put before Parliament in the 1870s and suffrage groups throughout the country tried to gain publicity for their cause. Bristol activists persuaded newspaper proprietors to report their meetings as fully as possible, sought the support of local MPs and gathered signatures for petitions to be presented to Parliament. In 1871 the Bristol Society joined with five others to organize a conference in London to help the progress of the latest Bill and to send a deputation to Gladstone.[36]

For the first time many middle-class women gained the courage to express their views in large public meetings rather than just in the comparative safety of the drawing room. Agnes Beddoe, Lilias Ashworth Hallett, Helen Bright Clark and Emily Sturge (1847-92), one of six daughters of a Quaker surveyor, were the main speakers for the Bristol Society.[37] Lilias Ashworth Hallett recalled that:

> the novelty of hearing women speakers brought crowds to the meetings ... It was evident that the audience always came expecting to see curious masculine objects walking onto the platform, and when we appeared with our quiet black dresses, the whole expression of the audience would instantly change.[38]

Speaking tours in the west country could mean seven meetings in a fortnight, which was a 'great nervous effort', especially when audiences were hostile. Before the Parliamentary debate of 1873 Lilias Ashworth Hallett spoke at 14 out of the 100 meetings held countrywide.[39]

Bristol suffragists were concerned to counter any arguments that implied their behaviour was 'unwomanly' and yet were prepared to make their demands as forcefully as possible. Emily Sturge argued that it would be pleasanter to wait for the vote to be granted without having to ask for it, but experience showed that all great measures had been obtained 'after much crying of "Give, Give" ... So that we hope that though we may not get it because it is just, yet we may prevail through our exceeding importunity'. The Priestman sisters felt so strongly that they refused to pay their rates and bailiffs seized some of their belongings.[40]

Jane Rendall argues that suffragists in this period were concerned to explore the meaning of citizenship for women and in doing so had to engage with contemporary liberal thought and traditions of radical popular politics. They not only demanded the vote as a right, but also because they wished to carry out their duties as socially responsible citizens and believed that women had a particular perspective to bring to politics.[41] The balance between these arguments, however, varied between individuals and also in different parts of the country.

In Bristol, Helen Bright Clark, Anna Maria Priestman and Emily Sturge saw their own demand for the vote as part of a broader democratic struggle. They referred in their speeches to earlier extensions of the franchise and expressed support for the agricultural labourers who were also seeking enfranchisement.[42] Although Bristol suffragists demanded the vote on the same terms as men, which would have enfranchised only unmarried female ratepayers and householders, property and marital status were not the main bases of their argument. As far as Emily Sturge was concerned 'there is nothing in the accident of sex which in any way disqualifies us.'[43] Helen Bright Clark concurred, and protested against 'the unjust exclusion which denies to my sex the rights, and I may say the sacred duties of citizenship'. She resented this exclusion even more now that 'every other great class' was enfranchised. Working-class men, by good luck or hard work, could at least aspire to become voters, whereas women, by virtue of their sex, were denied such a possibility.[44]

To strengthen their position suffragists challenged the liberal argument that private and public questions could be separated. Addressing a drawing-room meeting in Clifton in 1883 Mrs Downing Shearer noted the intimate relationship between private and public duty and morality. Legislation such as the Married Women's Property Act showed the necessity of consulting women: 'Political and social life were so intermixed that they could not be separated and much depended on women being represented in Parliament whether those questions were decided rightly or wrongly.'[45] The suggestion that women had a special point of view, in particular on moral questions, was also expressed by Florence and Rosamund Davenport Hill, who saw women's difference from men as 'the strongest argument in favour of their joint exercise of the franchise'.[46] Emily Sturge, however, was less interested in sexual difference. She thought, as a point of principle, that women should have a say in things which concerned them, including the so-called higher interests of the country, even if it made very little difference to the laws which were passed. If they were not able to exercise such responsibility women would remain as 'half developed creatures' in a state of 'mental childhood'.[47]

For Bristol suffragists the need for the vote was highlighted by the other main campaign in which they became involved in the period, the repeal of the Contagious Diseases Acts. The Acts had been introduced in the 1860s to control the spread of venereal disease among members of the armed forces in garrison towns. They gave the police wide powers to arrest any woman suspected of being a prostitute and to force her to undergo an internal medical examination. If found to have a sexual disease she was detained in a Lock hospital for nine months.[48] In 1869 a National Association was formed to seek their repeal and this was quickly followed by a Ladies' National Association (LNA) under the leadership of Josephine Butler.[49]

The LNA published its own protest against the Acts in December 1869 which raised issues of special concern to women, including the injustice of punishing those who were the 'victims of vice' and the cruelty of the measures taken against prostitutes. Mary Estlin, the Priestman sisters, Lilias Ashworth Hallett, Lucy, Anna and Eliza Thomas, Hannah and Mary Price and several members of the Leonard family signed the protest and in the following year an LNA branch was formed in Bristol.[50] Helen Bright Clark found that at first 'everyone spoke about it in whispers, but now women saw that they must not fear to speak out upon it,' and Bristol became one of the ten branches with the highest number of individual subscribers.[51]

Some Bristol members were active at a national level. Mary Estlin, Mary Priestman and Mrs Charles Thomas were members of the national executive and Margaret Tanner was treasurer. Along with Anna Maria Priestman, who was particularly active in the suffrage campaign, they became close friends with Josephine Butler who looked to them for support and advice. Mary Estlin, for example, worked hard from behind the scenes. She was described by Josephine

Butler as 'one of the silent workers. She never made speeches, never took outwardly a prominent part; but she was always at her post as a quiet and constant seconder of our every effort.'[52] Josephine Butler's role as an inspiring speaker and leader meant that she rarely had time to engage in detailed organising work which was left to her 'strong phalanx' of Bristol supporters. In a letter to Anna Maria Priestman she exclaimed:

> What good work you have done in forming a commit-
> tee at Plymouth before leaving! Perhaps it may turn
> out the best thing that was done in the whole of the
> Social Science week. I am glad you three stayed
> behind to do it.[53]

Mary Priestman in particular worked hard for the national organization; she sent the annual report to all subscribers, wrote a new handbill for use in municipal elections and, when Josephine Butler was ill, helped Margaret Tanner to sort out problems with the paid agents.[54] The Bristol group often came up with new initiatives. In 1877, for example, members undertook a mission week of propaganda in surrounding towns and persuaded the Trades Council to pass a resolution of support. Similar actions were then carried out by other branches.[55]

Bristol had a flourishing LNA group, not simply because national leaders lived there, but also because of the depth of interest already shown in women's rights in the city. The independence and feminism of the Bristol LNA can be contrasted with the conservatism of many other groups who discouraged single women from membership and preferred sex-segregated meetings. In Bristol over 40 per cent of LNA members were single and large public meetings were held for mixed-sex audiences.[56] Mary Priestman, who was a practising Quaker, saw the value of holding meetings in places of religious worship in order to overcome 'that natural shrinking from a painful subject', which held women back from joining the campaign. Nonetheless, she and other Bristol activists were tolerant and non-sectarian in their outlook and their religious beliefs never obscured their 'feminist and libertarian objectives'.[57]

Unlike many groups the Bristol LNA had strong links with the suffrage movement. Lilias Ashworth Hallett, Mary Estlin, Mary Priestman and Helen Bright Clark were speakers and office holders in both movements and in 1877 just over half of the subscribers to the

Bristol LNA were known suffrage supporters.[58] Some women, however, such as the Quakers Margaret Fry and Susan Pease, were drawn into political activity for the first time by the repeal movement and then went on to play a role in the campaign for the franchise.

The Bristol LNA emphasized the importance of the vote from the beginning and encouraged women who held the municipal franchise to use their influence to prevent the extension of the Acts. At one municipal by-election Mrs Charles Thomas, president of the local group, printed and distributed 30,000 leaflets which made known the candidates' views on repeal and urged women to vote only for the man who would uphold the 'rights of the poorest citizen to just and equal laws'.[59]

Members of the Bristol LNA made persistent efforts to involve working-class women in their campaign. Meetings were held in poorer districts of the city and in the early 1880s a separate branch was formed in Bedminster. Mary Priestman suggested to Josephine Butler that cards should be issued to working-class women as a sign of LNA membership, even if they could not afford the full subscription. The Bristol LNA worked closely with a local trade union group, the Working Women's Association, in collecting 6702 signatures for a repeal petition, the largest from any provincial city.[60]

The Priestman sisters, Dr Eliza Dunbar and Emily Sturge among others, saw working-class women as 'voters, lobbyists and allies', rather than as the subject of rescue schemes, and were more concerned with their wages, employment and education than with their morals.[61] Anna Maria Priestman urged women to take action on their own behalf by forming trade unions and argued that the evils which arose from economic hardship 'can be met neither by friendly counsels nor by almsgiving ... it is not benevolence but justice that can deal with giant evils'.[62] In 1874 she helped to establish the National Union of Working Women, which later changed its name to the Bristol Association of Working Women (BAWW). It aimed to create a fund to assist members in sickness, unemployment and death and to watch for any legislation which might affect the employment of women. It also sought to disabuse the public that trade unions were there for aggressive purposes.[63]

The Bristol Association was one of only seven provincial societies affiliated to the Women's Protective and Provident League (WPPL) which, under the leadership of Emma Paterson, aimed to encourage working women to organize. The officers of the BAWW were drawn largely from middle-class members of the local suffrage group, although a working woman, Mrs Meyrick, was president for six years until 1883.[64] The BAWW never had more than 60 members, but it did provide an avenue through which suffragists could make connections with the labour movement. Eliza Walker Dunbar, medical adviser to the Association, Helen Blackburn and Alice Grenfell, secretary and treasurer of the suffrage society, among others, attended the TUC in the 1870s and 1880s and Eliza Walker Dunbar was a member of the national committee of the WPPL, 1878-9.[65] The Association in turn supported both the repeal movement and the campaign for the vote.

The suffrage and repeal movements were carried on simultaneously, although the extent of activity varied from year to year. A period of intense suffrage campaigning followed the general election of 1880 when a proposal was made to extend the male franchise. Anna Maria Priestman organized a special fund, which raised £1000, to enable the Bristol committee to work systematically over three years in the west country and South Wales.[66] When the Manchester Society, led by Lydia Becker, filled the Free Trade Hall with a women-only meeting in 1880 Bristol was quick to follow. On 4 November over 3000 women from all social classes turned up at the Colston Hall to hear Lydia Becker, Mrs Wolstenholme Elmy, Emily Sturge, Agnes Beddoe, Mrs Meyrick and many other familiar speakers demand votes for women. The hall was so full that an overflow meeting had to be arranged.[67]

This proved to be the highpoint of the local suffrage campaign. In contrast to the success of the repeal campaign, which achieved the suspension of the Contagious Diseases Acts in 1883, women failed to gain inclusion in the 1884 Reform Act. During the late nineteenth century, therefore, the suffrage movement appeared to lose momentum and differences between feminists about what women's emancipation meant, and the best tactics and strategy to achieve it, came increasingly to the surface. Some of these differences could be seen as early as 1881 when Anna Maria Priestman and Emily Sturge established a new, women-only organization, the Bristol Women's Liberal Association, (BWLA), the first of its kind in the country. The BWLA aimed to 'promote Liberal principles and to diffuse knowledge on political questions of general and local interest among the women of Bristol'.[68] Anna Maria Priestman was president of the new organization and Mary Priestman, Margaret Tanner, Helen Sturge, Eva Tribe, Helen Bright Clark and Miss S. J. Tanner, all suffragists, were among the most active supporters.[69]

Sandra Holton suggests that the impetus for the formation of a women-only group came from disillusion with the lukewarm support given by many Liberal men to feminist causes and a growing recognition that the interests of male and female workers were often antagonistic.[70] This was brought into sharp relief by the question of protective legislation. Anna Maria Priestman, for example, claimed that the

> Factory Act of 1874 was originally urged upon the attention of Mr Mundella by working men. They declared it would be a boon to women - it would lessen their fatigue, which was too much for them. Some women remonstrated, for less work and less food struck them as no privilege at all.[71]

Bristol suffragists argued that both sexes should enjoy perfect equality under the law and that women should not be subject to special laws over which they had no say.[72]

The formation of the BWLA also partly stemmed from an impatience with what some women saw as the growing conservatism of the suffrage movement which appeared to have become more narrowly focused and less democratic. Rosamund and Florence Davenport Hill, for example, had always favoured a restricted franchise, while Lilias Ashworth Hallett became more conservative in her approach as the chance of gaining the suffrage receded. During the 1890s she complained that women of property were excluded from the franchise while 'illiterate men' were now included. Women voters would bring 'some balance of intelligence to set against the ignorance that abounded' and would be on the side of 'strong government, law and order and morality'.[73]

The BWLA raised issues about the relationship between feminist and party politics which became more important after the 1884 Reform Act. The Act made it difficult for political parties to employ paid canvassers and they turned to women to provide grassroots support; Conservative women were admitted to the Primrose League in 1884 and a Women's Liberal Federation (WLF) was formed in 1886. The socialist groups which were established in the 1880s invited women to join on the same terms as men.[74]

The BWLA was in an ambivalent position. Fiercely independent and feminist from the start, members saw their aim as 'not to keep our party in office at all hazards, but to keep our party true to its principles at all hazards'.[75] Anna Maria Priestman in particular was adamant that women should not give up their consciences in order to become 'party drudges'.[76]

At a local level, however, the BWLA did work closely with the Liberal Party which contained many men who were sympathetic to women's rights. Two women were appointed members of the Bristol Liberal Thousand at a time when few women in England held that position.[77] Party politics could provide a route for women into local government, in particular as candidates for School Boards. In Bristol the Liberal Party put forward Emily Sturge in 1879 in the hope of winning back a seat lost in the previous election to Helena Richardson, an independent, and in 1883 a second Liberal woman, the suffragist Alice Grenfell, was also elected. When Emily Sturge died following an accident in 1892 she was replaced by Marion Townsend.[78]

Although they had been elected under Liberal auspices, female members of the Bristol School Board managed to maintain a balance between their party politics and their feminism, partly because they had the backing of an independent women's group and partly because the local Liberal men were sympathetic to women's rights. They insisted on working over a 'broad surface' and were responsible for introducing new initiatives. Emily Sturge, for example, brought teachers, Board members and educationalists together in the Bristol Educational Council of 1889 and helped found a training college for women staff long before centres for training pupil teachers were set up in London.[79]

The BWLA, however, found it increasingly difficult to work both for a range of liberal causes and also for the suffrage without incurring criticisms from all sides. Some Liberal Party supporters thought that the group gave too much time to women's suffrage, which brought the retort from Anna Maria Priestman that there could be no security for women's liberty as long as they had no control over laws which they had to obey.[80] Criticisms also came from suffragists, including the national leaders Lydia Becker and Millicent Fawcett, who felt that women should give priority to the vote and not be distracted by a range of party-related questions. This came to a head in 1888 when the suffrage movement split over whether political groups such as the WLF should be able to affiliate to the suffrage societies. Those in favour of such affiliation broke away from the Central Committee for the National Society of Women's Suffrage to form a new group, the Central National Society for Women's Suffrage.[81]

The BWLA affiliated with the latter and Anna Maria Priestman became a member of its executive committee in 1892. Lilias Ashworth Hallett and Agnes Beddoe had spoken very strongly against allowing party politics to intrude into the suffrage movement and they ensured that the Bristol and West Society for Women's Suffrage remained affiliated to the Central Committee.[82] A number of women who stood for election to the Board of Guardians also endorsed this non-party political stance. They had been encouraged to stand by the Bristol and West Society for Women's Suffrage, who were inspired by the work of the Society to Promote the Return of Women as Guardians. Three women were elected in 1883, the best known of whom was Mary Clifford.[83] She had gained experience as a workhouse visitor and emphasized the importance of rescue work among women in workhouses.[84] On the other hand, along with her father, an Anglican clergyman, she was a supporter of women's suffrage and believed that the vote would enable women to have a say in social and moral questions. During the 1890s she took an active role in the National Union of Women Workers which took an interest in employment conditions, health reform and women's role as citizens as well as in rescue work.[85] The Bristol branch was set up by Susan Pease, Mrs Albert Fry and Mrs Edward Goodeve, officers of the Clifton Ladies' Association for the Care of Girls, who all supported the LNA repeal campaign and the suffrage movement.[86] Although women who were primarily interested in social questions took up the demand for the suffrage, their political tactics and approach tended to be different from that of the BWLA. They avoided party politics and adopted a cautious approach; Mary Clifford, for example, 'deprecated pressing women's claims too eagerly'.[87]

In contrast, the BWLA worked energetically throughout the late 1880s and 1890s to persuade other associations and the WLF to take a far firmer stand on women's suffrage by refusing to work for Liberal candidates who failed to support their cause. Anna Maria Priestman wrote to the President of the WLF to make clear that the BWLA had always refused to work for candidates who did not support equal laws for both sexes and claimed that this had gained the respect of the local Liberal Party. She concluded that 'Home Rule would never have reached its present stage if the Irish had worked for Liberal candidates whether they were Home Rulers or not'.[88] Anna Maria Priestman was president of a new group, the Union of Practical Suffragists, which pressurized the WLF to accept the test question. At the Union's request she served on the executive committee of the Federation in the late 1890s.[89]

Members of the BWLA who had been involved with the Association of Working Women continued to try to interest working women in politics. They spoke at meetings in working-class districts on topics such as women's wages and women and the labour movement and in 1886 removed the requirement to pay a subscription of 1s. so that more working-class women could join.[90] They had a close relationship with the local Women's Co-operative Guild which had a thriving branch in Bedminster. Annie Martin held office in both organizations and was an active suffragist. In a paper delivered to the Western Sectional Conference of the Guild she urged married women to see the vote as necessary for the protection of their homes and the well-being of wage-earning women. Members of the Guild spoke to the local branch of the BWLA about their activities and a WLA speaker addressed them in turn on women's suffrage which led to a resolution being passed in favour of the vote.[91]

As already noted, WLA members aimed to encourage independent action among female workers, arguing that 'women should combine among themselves for the good of their common sisterhood', and were concerned to improve wages and employment opportunities for women of all classes.[92] Nonetheless, their liberalism meant that they stopped short of an overall critique of the social and economic system and they remained opposed to protective legislation long after the women's trade union movement came to modify its position on this.[93] They also found themselves on the sidelines when a wave of strikes among less skilled workers in the period 1888-1890 ensured that female trade unionism would be carried forward from within the mainstream labour movement. The unrest was also to prove a turning point in differentiating still further between feminists, when a significant minority of women began to see the socialist movement as the best way forward to achieve women's emancipation.

In Bristol Helena Born and Miriam Daniell, the wife of a Clifton solicitor, both left the BWLA in 1889 when involvement in labour unrest in the city brought them into direct contact with the labour movement.[94] As active members of the newly formed Workers' Organising Committee they helped in disputes among seamstresses and cotton workers and established an Association for the Promotion of Trade Unionism among Women (APTUW).[95] Katherine Conway, a schoolteacher, also claimed that the cotton workers' strike was a turning point in her politics and along with Born and Daniell joined the Bristol Socialist Society (BSS).[96] They gave talks on women's trade union organization and women's rights as well as on more general issues related to independent labour politics. [97]

It was another local schoolteacher, Enid Stacy, who most persistently tried to link feminism and socialism together, as a platform propagandist, an organizer and a writer.[98] She had been brought up in a Christian Socialist household and during the labour unrest joined the Gasworkers' Union. Here she met Born and Daniell and later took over the running of the APTUW. She was responsible for the management of a strike of confectionery workers at Sanders & Son in 1892 and fought against the absorption of the APTUW within the strike organization committee.[99] She was attracted to the BSS 'in the belief that the women's movement was only properly taken up by them' and played an important role in the 1895 Bristol East by-election.[100]

All of these women were influenced by the ideas of the Yorkshire socialist Edward Carpenter. His writings on comradeship, the democratic spirit and the need to develop a different relationship between men and women influenced the new generation of socialists and Bristol women formed part of his friendship circle.[101] By the end of 1895, however, Enid Stacy had left Bristol to become an itinerant lecturer for the Independent Labour Party (ILP); Katherine Conway had already left to marry the ILP leader John Bruce Glasier and Helena Born and Miriam Daniell had emigrated to the United States. Although the BSS retained a nominal commitment to women's rights, feminist issues were no longer given prominence in the city. Socialists had ambivalent attitudes to the 'woman question' which raised awkward issues about the relationship between sex solidarity and class loyalties.[102] Without key female socialists in the city it was unlikely that feminist issues would be pushed to the forefront of local socialist politics.

Questions raised for feminists in the nineteenth century about the relationship between the women's movement and party politics, about the meaning of emancipation and about the extent to which sex solidarity could overcome differences between women remained important after 1900. Nonetheless, they had to be worked out in a new context in which a revived suffrage movement came to dominate feminist politics in the decade before the First World War. In many respects the struggle for the vote could be seen as a high point in attempts to unite women in a common cause on behalf of their sex, but differences between women were never far below the surface.

The Priestman sisters, for example, continued to try to link their suffrage aims with a broad range of causes. They had remained active in the local LNA throughout the 1890s where they joined in the campaign to protest against government attempts to regulate prostitution in India.[103] They played a leading part in the BWLA, but withdrew in 1905, together with their closest supporters, when some members declared that women's suffrage should not be pursued at the expense of everything else. This marked the end of a close relationship between feminists and the local Liberal Party which may reflect the fact that a younger generation of men, who did not have their roots in women's rights, now dominated the local organization.[104] In the early 1900s, showing their usual independence, the Priestmans established their own suffrage group, the Women's Reform Union, which placed suffrage in the context of other social reforms. The WRU drew on former members of the BWLA for support and held a series of meetings. In 1909, however, it amalgamated with the local branch of the National Union of Women's Suffrage Societies (NUWSS).[105]

Bristol women played a full share in the suffrage campaign. In contrast to the nineteenth century, however, they did not take a prominent part at a national level. They were active in the local branches of the two main suffrage groups, the National Union of Women's Suffrage Societies, led by Millicent Fawcett, and the Women's Social and Political Union (WSPU), led by Emmeline and Christabel Pankhurst. The groups shared the same goal of votes for women on the same terms as men, but differed in their methods and political strategies. The WSPU adopted militant methods and, despite its origins from within the ILP, took an increasingly hostile stand to both Labour and Liberal candidates. The NUWSS used more constitutional methods and campaigned for any candidates who supported votes for women.[106] Local women clearly chose which groups to support on the basis of political tactics and methods and it is difficult to distinguish between them on the basis of age, class or political affiliation.

Bristol was targeted by the WSPU to become a centre for militant activity because Augustine Birrell, a Cabinet minister, was one of the city's MPs. Annie Kenney, one of the working-class leaders of the WSPU, was sent to the district as an organiser and inspired a devoted group of followers.[107] They included middle-class women from Clifton with independent means, such as the two James sisters, schoolteachers, nurses and working-class women such as Annie Martin. Colonel Linley Blathwayt, his wife Emily and daughter Mary who lived in nearby Batheaston also gave strong support to Annie Kenney and Mary spent over a year in Bristol between 1908 and 1909 in order to help the cause; she not only organised meetings, sold literature and kept the suffrage shop open, but also dealt with more personal matters such as ensuring that Annie Kenney's clothes were cleaned and mended.[108]

The local NUWSS branch was still largely based on its original Clifton membership, although the Women's Reform Union attempted to interest schoolteachers in the campaign.[109] Members of the different groups attended each other's public meetings and there were occasions on which they met socially. The Priestman sisters, Lilias Ashworth Hallett and Agnes Beddoe all sympathized with the WSPU and gave financial support, although they were also associated with the NUWSS.[110] In many respects the local branches of the NUWSS and the WSPU engaged in similar activities; they held both outdoor and indoor meetings, set up suffrage shops, carried out canvassing and petitioning, sold newspapers and toured the streets in decorated carts at election times.[111]

On the other hand there were real differences between the local branches of the NUWSS and the WSPU which should not be underestimated. Emily Blathwayt claimed that members of the Bristol NUWSS refused to help the militants and noted how 'A K laughs at those Bristol ladies grumbling at her party for coming. They say they have worked so hard for forty years & have never done anything.'[112] Both Emily and Mary Blathwayt were attracted to the WSPU because the members were in real earnest compared to the 'half hearted ones who would not suffer anything for the cause' and encouraged women of all classes to join.[113] WSPU members, whose motto was 'the will to do – the soul to dare,' were altogether more lively than their NUWSS counterparts and engaged in flamboyant direct action.

In the early years their militancy took varied forms and did not involve damage to people or property. They chalked pavements before meetings, went on poster parades to advertise events, which included large rallies with well-known national leaders as speakers, and arranged processions to welcome back suffragettes who had been in prison. They held meetings all over the city, including outside factory gates, and set up a shop in Bristol South, opposite Wills' factory, to attract more working class women.[114] In a famous incident in 1909 WSPU members hid in an organ so that they could disrupt a meeting where Birrell was speaking, while other members shouted through a megaphone from a nearby house.[115] Militancy became more divisive, however, when it began to involve personal violence and the burning of buildings. In 1913-14 buildings were set ablaze in Frenchay, Stoke Bishop and Combe Dingle. This led Mary Blathwayt to resign from the WSPU, although the Blathwayt family remained close friends of Annie Kenney and continued to support imprisoned suffragettes.[116]

Political outlook and tactics also differentiated the two societies. Emily Blathwayt believed that NUWSS members were too sympathetic to the Liberal Party and claimed that the Clifton people 'seem to be what I call Liberal Primrose Leaguers'.[117] The official position of the

NUWSS was a non-party one, although the majority of members had liberal sympathies. Nonetheless, as dissatisfaction grew with the Liberal Government, many women withdrew from Liberal politics at a national level.[118] The NUWSS itself grew closer to the Labour Party and the two organizations formed an alliance for electoral purposes. In Bristol this encouraged more working-class organizations to become involved in the suffrage campaign and a close relationship developed with the NUWSS. In 1913 the East Bristol Women's Suffrage Society, led by Mrs Townley, the wife of a textile worker, and Miss Tothill, both members of the Independent Labour Party, carried out a joint labour and suffrage campaign in support of the prospective Labour candidate. They involved groups such as the Women's Labour League and the Women's Co-operative Guild, held numerous meetings throughout the district and managed to enrol 200 Friends of Women's Suffrage. Walter Ayles, the prospective Labour candidate, an ILP member and committed suffragist, argued that to gain economic freedom the help and experience of women was invaluable, 'but to give this fully they must have political freedom'.[119] Once the vote was won the relationship between suffrage and labour politics became even closer and in the inter-war years many ex-suffragists sought to pursue their feminist policies through the Labour Party.

For many historians the decade before the First World War is viewed as a high point for the women's movement, when women were united behind a single issue, and were able to develop a woman-centred mass movement. After 1918, it is suggested, feminism became more fragmented, as women turned to party politics to achieve specific social welfare reforms.[120] The excitement and sense of sisterhood generated by the pre-war suffrage campaign cannot be denied. Nevertheless, as this study of the Bristol women's movement has demonstrated, the demand for women's emancipation was a complex one from its earliest days. Feminists differed in their analysis of women's social position and in the political strategies they adopted to achieve change, although these differences surfaced more acutely in some periods rather than in others. What feminists agreed upon throughout, however, whether they worked in suffrage groups or in party political organizations, was to 'throw out the notion that politics are unwomanly'.[121] They shared a commitment to the view that women must take a full part as citizens in all areas of public life. This was well expressed by the BWLA in 1890 when it appealed to women to be more active: 'each one has duties as a citizen, as well as private duties, and that it is only when she has fulfilled both that a woman becomes most truly womanly, because her nature is not, until then, fully developed'.[122]

Notes

1   Bristol Women's Liberal Association, *Annual Report*, 1895.

2   The term feminist is used throughout to describe individuals or groups who recognized and challenged in an explicit way women's inequality and oppression.

3   J. Butler, *Personal Reminiscences of a Great Crusade* (1911), 104.

4   P. Hollis, *Ladies Elect: Women in English Local Government, 1865-1914* (Oxford, 1987), 156. See also, J. Walkowitz, *Prostitution and Victorian Society: Women, Class and the State* (Cambridge, 1980).

5   E. Malos, 'Bristol Women in Action, 1839-1919', in I. Bild, ed., *Bristol's Other History* (Bristol, 1983), 97-128.

6   J. Rendall, 'Citizenship, Culture and Civilisation: The Languages of British Suffragists, 1866-1874', in C. Daley & M. Nolan, eds., *Suffrage and Beyond: International Feminist Perspectives* (Auckland, 1994), 127-50.

7   L. Davidoff and C. Hall, *Family Fortunes: Men and Women of the English Middle Class, 1780-1850* (1987); A. Vickery, 'Golden Age to Separate Spheres? A Review of the Categories and Chronology of English Women's History', *HJ*, 36 (1993), 383-414

8   B. Caine, *Victorian Feminists* (Oxford, 1987); J. Rendall, ed., *Equal or Different? Women's Politics, 1800-1914* (Oxford, 1987); S. K. Kent, *Sex and Suffrage in Britain, 1860-1914* (Princeton, N.J., 1987).

9   J. Schwarzkopf, *Women in the Chartist Movement* (1991), 10. For Bristol women's participation in Owenite Socialism, see B. Taylor, *Eve and the New Jerusalem* (1983).

10   D. Thompson, 'Women and Nineteenth-Century Radical Politics: A Lost Dimension', in J. Mitchell and A. Oakley, eds, *The Rights and Wrongs of Women* (1976), 112-38; D. Thompson, 'Women, Work and Politics in Nineteenth-Century England: The Problem of Authority', in Rendall, ed., *Equal or Different?*, 57-81; Schwartzkopf, *Women in the Chartist Movement*.

11   For the importance of family and friendship networks, see P. Levine, *Feminist Lives in Victorian England* (Oxford, 1990).

12   R. and L. Billington, '"A Burning Zeal for Righteousness": Women in the British Anti-Slavery Movement, 1820-1860', in Rendall, ed., *Equal or Different?*, 82-111; C. Midgley, *Women Against Slavery: The British Campaigns, 1780-1870* (1992).

13   Minutes of the Bristol and Clifton Ladies Anti-Slavery Society (hereafter B&CLASS), microfilm of the Estlin Collection in the John Williams Library, held in the BRL.

14   C. Taylor, *British and American Abolitionists: An Episode in Transatlantic Understanding* (Edinburgh, 1974), Introduction.

15   There are numerous obituaries of John Estlin, for example, *BG*, 14 June 1855; *Liberator*, 20 July, 26 Oct., 9 Nov., 16 Nov., 26 Nov., 21 Dec. 1855; *BMirr*, 16 June 1855 in Estlin Papers, BRL.

16   S. Hutton, *Bristol and its Famous Associations* (Bristol, 1907), 394-5; 'Broad Plain Soap Works', *Work in Bristol* (Bristol, 1883), 20-30; Short biography of Charles Thomas, J.P. in *Contemporary Biographies* (Bristol, 1898), 92. Herbert Thomas, aged 41, and his wife Hannah, aged 52, lived next door to the Carpenters in Great George Street. *Census* 1851.

17   J. E. Carpenter, *The Life and Work of Mary Carpenter* (1879); Obituary of Mary Carpenter, *The Times*, 18 June 1877; Obituary of Mary Estlin, *Shield*, (Dec. 1902), 72. Mary Estlin, for example, attended Mary Carpenter's girls' school.

18   B&CLASS Minutes, 27 March 1851. See in particular, Mary Estlin to Miss Weston, 3 Oct. 1851, in Taylor, *British and American Abolitionists*, 382.
19   Midgley, *Women Against Slavery*, 174; See also id., 'Anti-slavery and Feminism in Nineteenth-Century Britain', *Gender and History*, 5 (1993), 343-62.
20   BRL, Letters in the Estlin Collection.
21   For a discussion of women's outlook as philanthropists see J. Lewis, 'Gender, the Family and Women's Agency in the Building of "Welfare States": The British Case', *Social History*, 19, (1994), 37-55.
22   Rendall, 'Citizenship, Culture and Civilisation', 138; one of Mary Carpenter's papers was 'On Voluntary Effort and its True Relation to Institutions Aided or Supported by Government', read at the Annual Congress of the National Association for the Promotion of Social Science, *EWJ*, viii, 43 (1861).
23   R. J. Saywell, *Mary Carpenter of Bristol* (Bristol, 1964); J. Manton, *Mary Carpenter and the Children of the Streets* (1978); J. Parker, *Women and Welfare: Ten Victorian Women in Public Social Service* (1988). For the work of the NAPSS, see K. McCrone, 'The National Association for the Promotion of Social Science and the Advancement of Victorian Women', *Atlantis*, 8, (1982), 44-66.
24   *Women's Suffrage Journal*, 2 April 1877.
25   *EWJ*, 11, 8 (1858). Rosamund Davenport Hill claimed that Mary Carpenter 'conferred a boon on her own sex, by demonstrating that a woman may be as capable of bearing a part in the direction of her country's affairs as her male fellow citizens'. E. Metcalfe, *Memoirs of Rosamund Davenport Hill* (1904), 38.
26   Metcalfe, *Memoirs of Rosamund Davenport Hill*; M. Shaen, *Memorials of Two Sisters: Susannah and Catherine Winkworth* (1908). The Winkworths were daughters of a silk merchant. For Matthew Davenport Hill, see B. Harrison, *Dictionary of British Temperance Biography* (1973), 63.
27   'Interview with Mrs Beddoe', *Women's Penny Paper*, 25 Jan. 1890 and National Union of Women Workers, *Annual Report*, 1892, 51-4. R. Barot, *Bristol and the Indian Independence Movement* (BHA, 70, 1988).
28   F. P. Cobbe, *Life of Frances Power Cobbe: As Told by Herself* (1904), 583.
29   Letters from Cobbe are in the Estlin Collection, BRL.
30   M. Carpenter, 'On Female Education', NAPSS Annual Congress, *Report*, Bristol, 1869, 351-5, 353.
31   *EWJ*, viii, No. 45 (1861); Mary Carpenter, 'Female Education in India', *ER*, v, (Oct. 1868), 316-9; *ER*, xiii, (Jan. 1873). *Journal of Women's Education Union*, ii (1874), 156. Catherine Winkworth ensured that in 1876 the new University College, Bristol, was open to both sexes and provided scholarships for women.
32   *Suffrage Petition of 1866*, Helen Blackburn Collection, Girton College. The Priestmans moved to Durdham Park in Bristol as their permanent address in spring 1869. I am grateful to Sandra Holton for this information from the Clark archives, Street. Margaret Tanner lived in Sidcot, nr Weston-super-Mare, but was a frequent visitor to Bristol.
33   Biographical details in the JB Lett. Coll.; S. A. Tooley, *Ladies of Bristol and Clifton* (1896), 453-4; Obituary of the 'Misses Priestman', *Shield*, (Jan. 1915); Levine, *Feminist Lives*; Walkowitz, *Prostitution*, chap. 6; S. S. Holton, 'From Anti-Slavery to Suffrage Militancy: The Bright Circle, Elizabeth Cady Stanton and the British Women's Movement', in Daley and Nolan, eds, *Suffrage and Beyond*, 213-33. Lilias Ashworth was the daughter of Henry Ashworth, an associate of the free trade campaigner Cobden. *WSJ*, 2 July 1877; *Votes For Women*, 44-5.
34   S. J. Tanner, *How the Women's Suffrage Movement Began in Bristol Fifty Years Ago*

(Bristol, 1918); H. Blackburn, *Women's Suffrage: A Record of the Women's Suffrage Movement in the British Isles* (1902), 66-7; National Society for Women's Suffrage, *Annual Report*, 1872.

35   B&WSWS, *Annual Report*, 1875; A. M. Beddoe, *The Early Years of the Women's Suffrage Movement* (Bradford-on-Avon, 1911), 4-6. Rev. U. R. Thomas acted as one of the secretaries for a short period while the others were on the committee.

36   B&WSWS, *Annual Report*, 1871; Blackburn, *Women's Suffrage*, 116-7.

37   E. Sturge, *Reminiscences of My Life: And some Account of the Children of William and Charlotte Sturge of Bristol* (Bristol, 1928).

38   Blackburn, *Women's Suffrage*, 110, 112.

39   Blackburn, *Women's Suffrage*, 125.

40   *WSJ*, 1 Dec. 1880; Fulford, *Votes for Women*, 147.

41   Rendall, 'Citizenship, Culture and Civilisation'.

42   *WSJ*, 1 Dec. 1880, 210-11; A. M. Priestman, 'The Industrial Position of Women as Affected by their Exclusion from the Suffrage', a paper delivered to the NAPSS Annual Congress, 1875 and reprinted in *WSJ*, 1 Oct. 1875, 138. *Women's Union Journal*, iii, Oct. (1878), 72-3.

43   *WDP*, 10 Mar. 1876.

44   *WSJ*, 1 Dec. 1880.

45   *WSJ*, 1 April 1883.

46   H. Blackburn, ed., *Because* (1888). Views of leading suffragists on why women should have the vote.

47   *WSJ*, 1 Dec. 1880, 210-11.

48   A full account of the operations of the Contagious Diseases Acts and the repeal campaign can be found in Walkowitz, *Prostitution*.

49   The National Association was formed during the Annual Congress of NAPSS which was held in Bristol in 1869. *BTM*, 5 Oct. 1869.

50   *Daily News*, 31 Dec. 1869. The Bristol women were all from nonconformist backgrounds.

51   LNA, *Annual Report*, 1874, 7; LNA, *Annual Report*, 1877. A separate Clifton branch was formed in 1878.

52   'In memoriam: Miss M. A. Estlin', *Shield*, (Dec. 1902), 72. Mary Estlin also gave money to help abolitionists abroad.

53   JB Lett. Coll., Josephine Butler to Anna Maria Priestman, Sept. 1872.

54   JB Lett. Coll., Josephine Butler to Anna Maria Priestman, 13 Oct. 1872; Henry J. Wilson to Margaret Tanner, 24 May 1875.

55   LNA, *Annual Report*, 1877, 17.

56   LNA, *Annual Report*, 1877. List of subscribers.

57   M. Priestman, 'Ladies Branch Associations', *National League Journal*, 1 Dec. 1881, 15; Walkowitz, *Prostitution*, 135.

58   LNA, *Annual Report*, 1877. Subscription list.

59   LNA, *Annual Report*, 1885, 22. There were 2400 women burgesses in Bristol and 1400 of these signed a petition for the Parliamentary vote. *WSJ*, 1 Jan. 1879.

60   LNA, *Annual Report*, 1878, 12.

61   Hollis, *Ladies Elect*, 240. Eliza Walker Dunbar was the daughter of a military doctor in Bombay and graduated from the University of Zurich in 1872. She founded a dispensary for women and girls in Hotwells in 1874 and helped establish a private hospital for women in Bristol in 1895. *Contemporary Biographies - Medical*, 268, BRL.

62   Priestman, 'The Industrial Position of Women', 138.

63   H. Blackburn, *A Handbook for Women in Social and Political Work* (Bristol, 1881).

64   The WPPL is discussed in S. Boston, *Women Workers and the Trade Unions* (1980) and H. Goldman, *Emma Paterson: Her Life and Times* (1974). Reports of the Bristol Union can be found in *WUJ* and *Women's Trade Union Review*, XV, (Feb. 1890). Millicent Fawcett was a trustee of the Bristol NUWW when it was formed.

65   Helen Blackburn (1842-1903) was born in Ireland and from 1880 to 1895 was paid secretary of the B&WSWS as well as secretary of the Central Committee of the NSWS. From 1881-1901 she edited *ER*.

66   *WDP*, 5 Nov. 1880.

67   *BTM*, 5 Nov. 1880.

68   BWLA, *Annual Report*, 1882, 3.

69   In 1882 Mary Priestman was treasurer, and Helen Sturge and Eva Tribe were honorary secretaries.

70   I am grateful to Sandra Holton for allowing me to see her unpublished paper, 'The Strange Death of Liberalism: Anna Maria Priestman, Liberalism and the Women's Movement'.

71   Priestman, 'Industrial Position of Women', 137.

72   For example, see the arguments of representatives of the BAWW at the TUC, *EWJ*, 15 June 1877; also those of Lilias Ashworth Hallett and Emily Sturge at a women's suffrage meeting in the Victoria Rooms, *WDP*, 10 March 1876. Helen Blackburn, the Priestman sisters, Mary Estlin and Mrs Charles Thomas were all members of the Vigilance Association for the Defence of Personal Rights which aimed to 'uphold the principle of the perfect equality of all persons before the law, irrespective of sex and class'. Constitution and Rules, JB Coll., Fawcett Lib.

73   Holton, 'The Strange Death of Liberalism'; Fawcett Lib., National Society for Women's Suffrage, *Occasional Paper*, 1 June 1891, 18-19.

74   For an account of these organizations, see L. Walker, 'Party Political Women: A Comparative Study of Liberal Women and the Primrose League, 1890-1914', in Rendall, ed., *Equal or Different?*, 165-91; C. Hirshfield, 'Fractured Faith: Liberal Party Women and the Suffrage Issue in Britain, 1892-1914', *Gender and History*, 2, (1990), 173-97; J. Hannam, 'Women and the ILP', in D. James et. al., eds, *The Centennial History of the Independent Labour Party* (Halifax, 1992), 205-28.

75   Speech of A. M. Priestman, reported in BWLA, *Annual Report*, 1894.

76   BWLA, *Annual Report*, 1891, 31.

77   BWLA, *Annual Report*, 1884.

78   Hollis, *Ladies Elect*, 156-9; Sturge, *Reminiscences*, 81-3; BWLA, *Annual Report*, 1882.

79   Hollis, *Ladies Elect*, 158-9.

80   BWLA, *Annual Report*, 1892, 17-18.

81   For details of the split, see L.P. Hume, *The National Union of Women's Suffrage Societies, 1897-1914* (New York, 1986). CNSWS, *Annual Report*, 1893.

82   *WSJ*, 1 Jan. 1889, 12-13. B&WESWS, *Annual Report*, 1890, 1899-1900.

83   *WSJ*, 1 March 1883. Lilias Ashworth Hallett claimed that Agnes Beddoe and Helen Blackburn had worked very hard on the candidates' behalf.

84   M. Clifford, 'Women and Poor Law Guardians', NUWW, *Annual Report*, 1894, 127; G. M. Williams, *Mary Clifford* (Bristol, 1920); A. B. Freeman, *Bristol Worthies and Notable Residents* (Bristol, 1907).

85   Blackburn, *Handbook* (1895 ed.); NUWW, *Annual Reports*.

86   NUWW, *Annual Report*, 1892. Dr Goodeve was an *ex officio* Guardian.

87   NUWW, *Annual Report*, 1893.

88 BWLA, *Annual Report,* 1893, 6-7; Women's Liberal Federation, Annual Council Meeting, 1893.

89 BWLA, *Annual Report,* 1896, 9. A. M. Priestman, *Women and Votes,* leaflet no. 11 of Union of Practical Suffragists, 1898. Anna Maria Priestman was a member of the WLF executive committee until 1900.

90 BWLA, *Annual Report,* 1886, 1889.

91 Paper read at the Western Sectional Conference at Gloucester, 25 March 1897, Blackburn Coll. *Summary of Women's Federation News,* 6 Oct. 1893; 6 Nov. 1893.

92 BWLA, *Annual Report,* 1889. This was a statement from the Bristol North branch.

93 The issue of protective legislation was a complex one. Some socialist women as well as liberal women were reluctant to accept restrictions on female labour when women had had no say in the legislation. See discussion in WLF, *Annual Council Report,* June 1893.

94 S. Bryher, *An Account of the Labour and Socialist Movement in Bristol* (Bristol, 1929), 5. Anna Maria Priestman set up a soup kitchen for strikers in 1889.

95 Workers' Organising Committee Minutes, Oct. 1889-July 1892.

96 Bryher, *An Account of the Labour and Socialist Movement,* 29-31.

97 Bristol Socialist Society, Minutes, 1889-90.

98 A. Tuckett, 'Enid Stacy', *North West Labour History Society Bulletin,* 7 (1980/1); K. Bruce Glasier, *Enid Stacy* (1924); H. Pelling, *The Origins of the Labour Party* (Oxford, 1965), 155. E. Stacy, 'A Century of Women's Rights', in E. Carpenter, ed., *Forecasts of the Coming Century* (Manchester, 1896).

99 *WDP,* 19 Oct. 1892.

100 *Rochdale Star,* 18 Aug. 1894, quoted in R. Wright, 'Bristol Socialism and the Local Labour Movement, 1885-1910' (unpublished MA thesis, Bristol Polytechnic, 1986), 54.

101 S. Rowbotham and J. Weeks, *Socialism and the New Life: The Personal and Sexual Politics of Edward Carpenter and Havelock Ellis* (1977).

102 Hannam, 'Women and the ILP'.

103 See LNA, *Annual Reports.*

104 K. Seltorp, 'The Women's Suffrage Movement in Bristol, 1868-1906' (unpublished thesis, Kobenharns University, 1982), Fawcett Lib. Letter written in 1905 from Mary and Anna Maria Priestman, Helen Bright Clark, Rebecca Price and S. J. Tanner to resign from the BWLA, 25 Nov. 1905, in BRL.

105 *Common Cause,* 23 Dec. 1909.

106 For a discussion of the differences between groups, see S. S. Holton, *Feminism and Democracy: Women's Suffrage and Reform Politics in Britain, 1900-18* (Cambridge, 1986); L. Garner, *Stepping Stones to Women's Liberty: Feminist Ideas in the Women's Suffrage Movement, 1900-18* (1984).

107 A. Kenney, *Memoirs of a Militant* (1924).

108 See B. M. Wilmott Dobbie, *A Nest of Suffragettes in Somerset* (Bath, 1879). Mary was in her late 20s when she met Annie Kenney and her home was a meeting place for many of the WSPU leaders. All three members of the family wrote diaries which are held by the National Trust at Dyrham Park. I am very grateful for permission to use these and for the considerable help given to me by the staff.

109 *Common Cause,* 16 Sept. 1909.

110 Kenney, *Memoirs of a Militant;* Emily Blathwayt, Diaries, 6 March 1909, notes how Lilias Ashworth Hallet gave her daughter £5 for self-denial week and donated money so that working-class women could travel to London for a WSPU demonstration.

111 Details of the local campaign have been taken from Mary Blathwayt, Diaries, 1908-

1914; *Votes for Women* and *Common Cause*.

112 Emily Blathwayt, Diaries, 3 April, 1908.

113 Emily Blathwayt, Diaries, 1 & 30 April 1908.

114 *Votes for Women*, 14 June 1909. See also 14 Jan. 1910.

115 Mary Blathwayt, Diaries, 3 May 1909; *Votes for Women*, 7 May 1909; Emily Blathwayt, Diaries, 6 March 1909.

116 Mary Blathwayt, Diaries, 6 June 1913. Emily Blathwayt wrote 'I am glad to say Mary is writing to resign membership with the WSPU. Now they have begun burning houses in the neighbourhood I feel more than ever ashamed to be connected with them,' Diaries, 6 June 1913. Emily left the WSPU much earlier, in 1909, when two local women attacked Asquith.

117 Emily Blathwayt, Diaries, 1908.

118 Hirshfield, 'Fractured Faith'.

119 *Common Cause*, 3 Oct. 1913, 439.

120 See, for example, Holton, *Feminism and Democracy*; J. Alberti, *Beyond Suffrage: Feminists in War and Peace, 1914-28* (1989); H. Smith, ed., *British Feminism in the Twentieth Century* (Aldershot, 1990).

121 Blackburn, *Women's Suffrage*, 172.

122 BWLA, *Annual Report*, 1890, 11.

THE SHAPING OF THE BRISTOL LABOUR MOVEMENT, 1885-1985

Kieran Kelly and Mike Richardson

Our survey covers one hundred years of struggle in Bristol and finishes in a period when, nationally, trade unions had suffered a series of major defeats and electoral support for the Labour Party was in serious decline. The dominant ideology within the labour movement over this period was labourism which saw trade unionism combined with parliamentary politics as the best way to achieve socialism. In effect labourism confined workers' interests to industrial issues. The crisis of labourism in the late 1970s provided the stimulus for debate. In 1978 the historian Eric Hobsbawm presented the first version of his famous thesis entitled 'The Forward March of Labour Halted?' which after Labour's defeat in the General election of 1979 increasingly became the focus of academic discussion as Labour's fortunes declined in the 1980s.[1] After surveying the history of the British working class from the 1880s, Hobsbawm concluded that periods of high union economic militancy did not advance class consciousness. He argued that strike waves, particularly since 1950, were of an economically sectional character that did nothing to promote working-class unity or raise class consciousness, as manual occupations dwindled and growing numbers of women and immigrants entered the workforce. Labour's decline after 1979 was considered by Hobsbawm as testimony to his thesis.

A perceptive critique of this view, put forward by James Cronin, was directed at Hobsbawm's assumptions that the decline of the traditional working class was the reason for the fall in support for Labour after 1951.[2] If Bristol is a reflection of the national picture then this chapter shows that labourism was unable to answer the problems of either the old or the new working class. A focal point of this labour history of Bristol is the impact of strike waves on class consciousness. Of particular significance, and a subject of much debate, is the view that the degree and character of state intervention in managing class conflict, including the option of taking sectors of the economy into state ownership, has a significant bearing on class consciousness.[3] It is not the intention here to engage with that debate but it is presented as an important theme for understanding the shaping of the labour movement. It is whether the State forcefully intervenes on the side of capital or acts ostensibly as a neutral mediator to facilitate industrial and social peace that is most likely to invoke confrontation or conciliation and mould working-class political consciousness.

At the risk of being one-sided it makes sense to focus on periods of industrial strife since the character of demands, and the success or failure of direct action, had a decisive effect on the evolution of the Bristol labour movement. The explosion of strikes, as Hobsbawm suggests, often 'coincided with a clustering of new organisations, and the adoption of new ideas and policies by both new and existing units'.[4] Moreover, given that most commentators including Theo Nichols and Huw Beynon argue that since 1900 evidence of militant union activity in Bristol was rare, a survey of Bristol's labour history that reveals workers' struggle as significant is long overdue.[5] Therefore, an important aim of this chapter is to assess the relationship between workers' militancy and the development of working-class political organizations and see if a common pattern emerges in the development of the Bristol labour movement.

In particular we will look for evidence of two distinct strategies. First, the collective trade union struggle for better wages and conditions. Secondly, the aim to secure labour representation in local and national institutions of capitalist democracy; the intention being to implement a programme of political action to resolve economic and social problems faced by the Bristol working class. Subsequent analysis will show the difficulties the movement faced in reconciling these different forms of struggle. It is for these reasons that we focus on trade union struggles and political organizations, particularly but not exclusively the Labour Party. The Bristol labour movement in this chapter should be taken as including all those who at some point or place were involved to a greater or lesser extent in the struggle of working-class people with questions of employment, social conditions, race and gender.

In Bristol, as elsewhere, the emergence of industrial struggle by unskilled workers and the revival of socialist ideas in the 1880s was a watershed in the history of the labour movement. In the preceding fifty years, that is after the Bristol riots of 1831, Bristol's working class had shown a reluctance to participate in radical movements. Chartism, in the late 1830s and early 1840s, despite drawing some large crowds to its outdoor meetings, failed to attract a following commensurate with the size of Bristol.[6] Moreover, the idea of co-operative production or support for Co-operative societies was lacking before the 1880s.[7]

Some signs of change in the character of Bristol's labour movement began to appear after 1870 as the economy slowed. A number of non-craft unions were formed. Meanwhile some of the older craft unions showed signs of frustration with the laws limiting trade union action. This led a caucus of Bristol trade unionists to launch the Trades Council in 1873 in order to provide a platform to propagate their views. This initiative coincided with the onset of the 'Great Depression' and both the Trades Council and the unions found it increasingly difficult to sustain their respective organizations.[8] In the case of the Trades Council its difficulties were exacerbated by its own actions. In 1874, for instance, it rejected the call to assist in organizing women cotton workers. This provided an opportunity for Emma Paterson, who was averse to mixed unions, to promote the National Union of Working Women which started life in Bristol in 1874. Its impact, however, was limited.[9] The failure by the Trades Council to recognize (or accept) that women, as wage-labourers (or indeed as unpaid domestic labourers) were a vital part of the labour movement not only continued into the 1880s but was institutionalized. Women were excluded from holding representative positions on the political wing of the Council, the Labour League, when it was established in 1885.[10] Nonetheless, despite the attempt to prevent women from fully participating in trade unions and radical politics, the foundations were in place on which organized labour was to build a movement representing skilled and unskilled male and female workers.

The Labour League recorded its first Council election victory in 1887 when its candidate, R. G. Tovey, won St Paul's ward. Given that in practice some workers were disqualified from voting because they did not meet the residence and rate-paying requirements, this was a very creditable achievement.[11] Though Tovey was a 'Labour' candidate he also received significant support from the Bristol Socialist Society (BSS), a diverse group of 'revolutionary' socialists formed in 1885. The BSS played an important part in the emergence of a distinctively worker-oriented political movement, and was a critical development, particularly since it preceded the labour militancy in Bristol in the late 1880s.

Thus by 1889, the year in which the challenge of semi-skilled and unskilled workers to employers' authority was unleashed in a display of militancy, the political and industrial institutions of labour were strong enough to assert their influence. This break from the past, though important, should not be exaggerated as more conciliatory industrial relations resumed in the 1890s following the collapse in militancy as employers re-established their authority.[12] This suggests that the impact of wage militancy in raising class consciousness was weak. It appears that the Bristol labour movement was drawn into trade union economic struggles aimed at winning short-term concessions to satisfy the immediate concerns of the working class. However, the process of working-class struggle in the aftermath of the strike activity of 1889-92 was more profound than this. Before turning to consider the complexities involved, however, a brief exposition of this strike wave in Bristol is necessary.

The strike wave that began in 1889 coincided with a period of relative prosperity. Its participants consisted largely of unorganized non-craft workers, though long-established trade unionists and craft workers were also involved. In Bristol, men employed at the galvanizing ironworks of Lysaght and Tinn were the first to achieve victory in a period of intensive strike activity that was to last three years. While these initial skirmishes were fairly small, success was in no small part due to the Strike Organisation Committee set up by the Trades Council and the BSS to support the strikers, organize them into trade unions and engage in political dialogue.[13] These disputes are marked by their apparent spontaneity and rank-and-file character, characteristics which were a feature of most of the conflicts that followed as the strike wave gained momentum to include

> gas workers, the dockers, stay makers, cotton opera-
> tives, brush makers, hatters, oil and colour workers,
> pipe makers, coal carriers, scavengers, box makers,
> cigar makers, tramway men, hauliers, blue factory
> workers, animal charcoal workers, etc., etc.[14]

Work on identifying the character of these disputes and the impact they had on class consciousness has been done elsewhere, though findings have been inconclusive.[15] What we wish to highlight here are some of the key experiences shaping the thoughts and actions of the Bristol working class at this time.

The rudiments of union organization were in place before the remarkable triumph of the Bristol gasworkers in the strike of October 1889. This is an exceptional example of the impact of 'new unionism' in preparing and organizing direct action to drive on the forward march of labour in circumstances that were far from easy. Gas workers, at this time, were made up of semi-skilled and unskilled labourers. The demand for gas was subject to seasonal fluctuations and the shedding of labour during the summer months was common.[16] The nature of the work, therefore, was casual and as such difficult to organize. However, in the early part of 1889 Bristol gasworkers were unionized in sufficient numbers to form a local branch, following which a demand for wage increases across the board was submitted.[17] Once it became clear that strike action was necessary to achieve their objectives Bristol gasworkers mobilized quickly, organizing a network of support before withdrawing their labour and within a couple of days the dispute was won. These developments demonstrated that the shift in the behaviour of Bristol gasworkers was sudden, substantial and very effective. Significantly, these workers quickly reached a high level of trade union consciousness as is evidenced by subsequent events.

Gasworkers broadened their horizons and invited non-craft workers including women from a diverse range of industries to join their union. This notable development, as Hobsbawm has pointed out, was an attempt 'to create a vast closed shop'[18] and is further evidence of the advancement of class consciousness among this section of workers. The timing was important as a general union open to women workers and an active strike committee were available when over 1000 women cotton workers embarked upon strike action in the last week of October 1889.

To publicize their case for humane conditions of work and better pay these women marched regularly through middle-class areas of the city and on Sundays petitioned church congregations in their places of worship. The strike held fast for a month. The women agreed to return to work only after the employers had conceded to many of the demands concerning working conditions, though no increase in wages was secured.[19] Significantly, however, by March 1890 women cotton workers had increased the ranks of the gasworkers' union by nearly 1400. Other workers who joined the gasworkers union in the strike wave of 1889-92 ranged from building labourers to tanners, and numbered over 1200.[20]

The unionization of Bristol dockworkers developed independently from the gasworkers. A strike in October 1889 by various groups of unorganized waterside workers involving over 2000 men, many of them casual labourers, achieved quick success. One aspect of the unionization of Bristol dockers was that the Corporation employed about one-third of the workforce and was therefore, indirectly, subject to public opinion through the ballot box.[21] The resounding victory of the socialist H. H. Gore, in the local council election for the ward of St Philip's South, during the strikes of 1889 suggests that if political parties ignored the cause of labour then they could well lose popularity. Gore was the first and only avowedly socialist candidate to win a seat on the Bristol City Council that year. This reveals the potential of industrial militancy, in Bristol during 1889, to advance working class consciousness. This point should not be exaggerated, however, as other seats were fought and lost.

The period after 1890 was marked by the employers' counter-offensive and the sponsorship of arbitration and conciliation boards by Bristol Chamber of Commerce and the trade unions. Strikes and lock-outs still occurred but were increasingly concluded in favour of the employers. The best known examples both took place in November 1892. The first involved a stoppage by young women and girls employed at the Redcliff confectionery factory of Saunders & Sons. The second resulted in the deal runners working at the port of Bristol being locked out by their employer. Sally Mullen's detailed account of these disputes, in which the military was used to disperse 20,000 demonstrators on 23 December 1892, does not discuss how concerned demonstration organizers were that a riot would ensue.[22] Tom McCarthy, a dock union official, persuaded many of the demonstrators to repeat after him the following words: 'I promise as a man and a trade unionist – and a non-unionist – to go home after this meeting quietly and orderly.'[23]

The threat of workers confronting troops on Bristol's streets marked a turning point for many of the local trade union, labour and socialist leaders. Revered names in the Bristol labour movement such as Curran, Gore, Watson, Weare, Sharland and Petherick stood on the platform in support of the local trade unionist Harold Brabham who appealed to demonstrators to remove

> the power of the Council from the hands of the people
> who now had it and put themselves in possession of
> it. This could be done very quietly and very peaceably
> by returning Labour candidates and working for
> Labour and Labour politics.[24]

This is the course that the labour movement followed in the 1890s, though it must be said that by then labour politics had adopted a more socialist perspective. In 1890 the radical new programme of the Bristol Labour Emancipation League included:

> Adult Suffrage, Abolition of the House of Lords and
> all Hereditary Authorities, Free Education with one

free meal a day for school children, a legal maximum 48-hour week, Nationalisation of Land, Mines, Docks, Railways, etc.[25]

This move to the left was enough to secure the affiliation of the BSS that now enjoyed the support of the Clifton and Bristol Fabian Society. A Fabian-sponsored enquiry of 1892 highlighted that Bristol was one of the most conservative English municipalities, glaringly illustrated by the fact that water, gas and trams were privately owned and controlled.[26] The Bristol labour movement temporarily overcame its differences and, clearly committed to a reform programme of a socialist character, began an electioneering campaign in an attempt to win seats on the local council. Their attempts, however, coincided with an organized counter-offensive of the employers and the capitulation of the union hierarchy to conciliation and arbitration. As a result strikes increasingly failed to achieve their objectives, as in the case of the defeats suffered by the confectionery workers and deal runners and the setbacks encountered by Malago miners and the boot and shoe workers.[27] Against this backdrop we now turn to examine how the Bristol labour movement fared in local elections.

Local elections not only gave those active in the Bristol labour movement a chance to chip away at the dominance of the old governing elite but more importantly provided the opportunity either to disseminate labourist or more radical socialist views. During the 1890s the BSS, whose political allegiance was heavily weighted towards the Social Democratic Federation (SDF), gained new converts. According to Bryher, however, those workers rejecting the old Lib-Lab politics were more inclined to support an organization espousing a populist socialistic programme rather than the revolutionary scientific socialism of the Marxist variety.[28] Non-Marxists were committed to the gradual reform of the existing social institutions of society, including local government, while many Marxists saw elections as simply opportunities for propaganda. Although relations between scientific socialists and independent labour activists were at times uncomfortable they maintained a united front when it came to fighting elections throughout the 1890s. Even when differences surfaced in 1900 at the founding conference of the Labour Representation Committee (LRC), as the SDF pushed for a sharp break with the Liberals, local labour movement activists in Bristol continued to co-operate.

Nonetheless, the BSS, in line with the SDF, disaffiliated from the LRC in 1901 rejecting the policy of compromise to pick up the mantle of socialism as the only alternative strategy for the working class. However, apart from the victory in 1905 of a socialist candidate in the Bedminster East seat where the vote of local coal miners was decisive, it was those working under a more pragmatic Labour banner who achieved the most political success in Bristol.

TABLE 7: Number of Municipal Seats held by Labour and Socialist Parties in Bristol, 1887-1914.

Year (Nov)	Lab.	Soc.	Year	Lab.	Soc.	Year	Lab.	Soc.
1887	1	-	1897	3	1	1906	6	1
1888	1	-	1898	3	1	1907	7	1
1889	1	-	1899	3	1	1908	6	-
1890	1	1	1900	3	-	1909	5	-
1891	1	1	1901	3	-	1910	3	-
1892	-	1	1902	3	-	1911	4	-
1893	2	1	1903	3	-	1912	5	-
1895	2	-	1904	3	-	1913	7	-
1896	2	-	1905	4	1	1914	7	-

Sources: A. B. Beaven, *Bristol Lists: Municipal and Miscellaneous* (Bristol, 1899), 54; Anon. 'Bristol Municipal Statistics 1898-1944' (unpublished data, University of Bristol).

Table 7 above shows that although Labour candidates could win seats in local elections, gains before 1914 were very modest (e.g. four out of a total of 84 councillors and aldermen in 1897). By 1900 Labour's municipal successes in Bristol had been greater than some west Yorkshire towns like Halifax, Huddersfield and Leeds and were not far short of the Independent Labour Party's (ILP) stronghold of Bradford.[29] After 1900, however, Labour's electoral progress in Bristol was generally rather slow. While Labour municipal representation moved steadily forward in the towns of west Yorkshire, in Bristol the picture was less rosy, despite the creditable performances between 1906-8. By 1910 the number of Labour seats had fallen from a high of seven to just three. Labour's fortunes did not revive until the onset of a new wave of industrial militancy which began with sympathy action taken by Bristol dock workers in support of their Newport comrades in 1910. Bristol dockers responded *en masse* despite the fall in union density among dock workers following the strike wave of 1889-92 and the fact that strikes were normally less frequent in densely populated cities like Bristol.[30] Perhaps the establishment of the Corn Trade Conciliation Board in 1900, which gave dockers' leaders the excuse to oppose strike action, contributed to the decline in union membership and eventually forced dockers to take independent action to protect their interests.

The militant action taken by Bristol dockers in support of their colleagues in Newport was of particular significance. This dispute, as Robert Whitfield's study shows, proved to be the forerunner of a national wave of unrest that lasted from 1911 until the outbreak of war in 1914.[31] As the docks were municipally run, the ability and commitment of the six Labour councillors and one alderman to put the workers' case and persuade the Docks Committee to intervene in the dockers' favour was tested. The Labour councillor for Easton, W. G. Pope, failed to support the dockers' cause and stood as an independent in the 1910 local elections beating Labour into third place, though in 1913 Labour regained its seat and pushed Pope into second place. More importantly the dispute resulted in a strategy being quickly developed to organize all workers engaged in essential dock work occupations into one single union. In Britain, Bristol dock workers stood almost alone in achieving this end.[32]

The outburst of local strike activity in 1911 represented a challenge to the gradualist politics of the Bristol labour movement. Although the more militant workers were largely confined to the dock, transport and mining industries, this wave of militancy did not only take an economic form. The sympathy action taken by Bristol dockers in support of their London comrades, in 1912, and the rush to join trade unions between 1910 and 1914,[33] illustrates that class consciousness amongst certain sections of workers approached the levels attained in 1889. This development coincided with an increase in the militancy of the Bristol suffragettes who had stepped up their campaign with a series of arson attacks.[34] The chance to advance socialist politics presented itself at a time when the local Labour Party had achieved little for almost a decade. However, the Labour Party, ILP and BSS were now almost exclusively bound up with municipal and parliamentary politics where socialist goals were tied to the potential for state intervention rather than through the mobilization of the working class. The leadership of the Bristol labour movement was dominated by full-time trade union officials such as W. Gorman the local dockers' leader, who, in the 1910 dispute, advised his men to return to work, and W. Whitfield the miners' leader, who, in 1911, repudiated strike action taken by local miners. Consequently, the political wing of the movement kept a respectable distance from direct involvement in unofficial militant action, though individual members such as W.

218

Ayles of the IL, (later, in 1923, a Labour MP for Bristol North), gave the strikers active support. Surprisingly, no evidence has emerged of any organized syndicalist influence in Bristol, though Ernest Bevin, who rose to prominence at this time as the carters' union leader in Bristol, toyed with syndicalist ideas.[35]

During the First World War in Bristol, as elsewhere, national and local elections were suspended, women were engaged on 'men's work' for the first time and union membership increased dramatically; thus the focus of working-class discontent was expressed chiefly at the workplace. Laws introduced in 1915 were aimed at preventing strikes but industrial disputes still occurred throughout the UK and Bristol was no exception (see Table 8 below). Many of these disputes were unofficial but a strong rank-and-file leadership in Bristol did not emerge.[36] This perhaps is due to the absence of a syndicalist tradition and the nature of the leadership of Bristol's labour movement which was either preoccupied with supporting the war effort or opposing it on pacifist grounds, thereby missing the chance between 1917-18 to influence a war-weary and dissatisfied workforce.[37]

TABLE 8: Number of stoppages and aggregate number of working days lost, 1915-1918.

Year	All industries and services in the UK		All industries and services in Bristol	
	No. of stoppages	Working Days Lost	No. of stoppages	Working Days Lost
1915	672	2,953,000	8	11,991
1916	582	2,446,000	8	39,846
1917	730	5,647,000	14	14,087
1918	1,165	5,879,000	21	48,997

Source: H. A. Clegg, *A History of British Trade Unionism since 1889, Volume III, 1934-1951* (Oxford 1994), 240; J. Love, 'Some Aspects of Business and Labour in Bristol during the First World War' (unpublished MA thesis, Bristol Polytechnic, 1986), 80.

The end of hostilities in 1918 whipped up a tide of social and industrial unrest. Bristol dockers, seamen, gasworkers, miners and transport workers all took strike action between 1919-20 indicating a move away from parliamentary politics to direct action. A mass meeting of dockers in October 1919 introduced an international dimension to their struggle by demanding a cessation of the government's participation in the blockade against the workers' government in Russia. In 1920 they blacked three ships being used to transport trucks and munitions to the British Forces in Ireland.[38] As John Kelly has argued it is clear that sustained strike activity, especially when directed against the State, could lead to a concern with bigger, more political, issues.[39]

Nonetheless, in the absence of a syndicalist or socialist party with a programme and ideology able to integrate economic and political struggles in Bristol, this action took many forms, some contradictory, some reactionary. Nationalist sentiments were revealed in May 1921 when a ship burning German coal was blacked by Bristol dockers. Perhaps of most significance was the frustration of ex-servicemen at the failure of the government to fulfil its promise of a land fit for heroes. In the absence of serious political or industrial intervention from labour movement activists, ex-servicemen were drawn into a violent campaign demanding that women workers be replaced by unemployed ex-servicemen. Bristol Tramways Company was a particular target and after attacks on its trams and offices gave in to pressure and sacked its women employees. The male tram drivers had threatened to strike if women tramway employees were dismissed but the absence of support among the local union hierarchy stifled this possibility; and by 1923 the anti-union tramway company again boasted a non-union workforce.[40] As a result of the left's failure to act an opportunity was lost to mobilize ex-servicemen.

It was not only ex-servicemen, however, who sought to remove women from their jobs. During 1920, male unionized bookbinders in E. S. & A. Robinson, the printing and packaging firm, forced the management to discontinue the practice of engaging women to work on ruling machines. As more unions, such as National Union of Bookbinders and Machine Rulers, were opening their doors to women workers, many took advantage of the situation to stop women from encroaching on what unions perceived as 'men's work'.[41]

The events of 1918-21 demonstrate that where the left in the trade unions was weakly organized or even non-existent, the right wing of the movement could promote its political ideas, blaming minorities or women for problems of employment and conditions rather than employers or the state.[42]

While working-class struggles in Bristol during 1918-21, particularly among transport workers, were intense, the leadership of the Bristol labour movement seemed intent on keeping its distance, apparently content to see industrial militancy dissipate. Only the Communist Party (CP), formed in 1920, offered an alternative but apart from half a dozen members active in ASLEF it had little local influence at this time. The doubling of Labour seats on the local council in 1919 reassured the political wing of the Bristol labour movement that the parliamentary road provided the best way forward to promote working class interests. It was no accident that on the whole Labour councillors were mainly drawn from unions not engaged in the militant struggles of this period.[43]

Whitfield argued in his thesis 'that in the period 1919-21 workers regarded the trade union struggle and the Labour Party effort at elections as essentially complementary'.[44] Yet, as we have seen, it was those Labour candidates chosen for their moderation and a dislike of extra-parliamentary action that usually won council seats. Though the surge in industrial unrest at the end of the First World War undoubtedly helped to produce greater support for Labour in the municipal elections, it is far from clear that this represented a qualitative increase in class-consciousness. It is more likely that because rank-and-file militancy did not present a political challenge to the local labour bureaucracy the broadening of anti-capitalist feeling among the working class was expressed in support for Labour. The divide between the leadership of the Bristol labour movement and the rank-and-file was largely a conflict between moderation and militancy. There is no evidence to suggest that the overall political direction of the Bristol labour movement was ever in question, though after 1918 the political influence of the Bristol Trades Council was substantially reduced following the changes in the constitution and organization of the Labour Party both nationally and locally.[45] Trade union political objectives were taken out of industrial relations and placed in the hands of the Labour Party to pursue through parliamentary means. Thus the class struggle was confined to economic demands.

As the post-war boom turned to slump in 1921, workers were increasingly subjected to pay cuts, lock-outs and unemployment. Trade union membership fell rapidly. The 1926 General Strike was the last of a succession of defeats experienced by the working class in the industrial sphere. It marked the end of an era of industrial militancy and revealed that without a distinct independent political strategy it was most unlikely that union militancy would secure victory.[46] There is no doubt, however, that on the whole organized workers were prepared to fight. In Bristol some 36,000 workers were eventually involved in the action which was co-ordinated locally by the Trades Council. The news that the TUC had called off the strike was met in Bristol with a mixture of shock, anger and dismay.[47] While many Bristol workers, as elsewhere, demonstrated remarkable loyalty, the class struggle as a method of gaining power had already been rejected by the Labour Party and the trade union hierarchy, and as the CP was too weak to assume the role of leadership, defeat was probably inevitable. The Bristol miners stayed out on their own but they were finally driven back to work, along with the rest of the Miners' Federation, seven months later.

1926 was a turning point for the labour movement in Bristol, just as it was nationally. The end of the strike without any concessions by the government had a demoralizing effect on trade unionists. For example after 1926 the number of strikes in the docks fell dramatically.[48] Whereas workplace organization suffered under the weight of the employers' offensive in the 1920s the Labour Party made significant advances and emerged as a party of government in 1929 but 'found itself incapable of implementing any economic policy other than the palliatives of Treasury and Bank of England orthodoxy' in dealing with the 1929-31 world slump.[49] Workers appear increasingly to have turned to the Labour Party and parliamentary methods to resolve their problems. Those in the labour movement found that the office or factory was no place for the activist. Instead the local Labour Party was a safer place to try and improve the circumstances of their fellow workers. In Bristol this resulted in doubling Labour representation on the local council from 16 councillors and three aldermen it held between 1922-24 to 32 councillors and six aldermen in 1930.[50] At parliamentary elections Bristol gained its first Labour MPs in December 1923 with victories in Bristol East and Bristol North. The Bristol North seat was lost in 1924 but regained in 1929; in addition Bristol South and Bristol Central divisions were won for the first time in 1929 bringing the total of Bristol Labour MPs up to four.[51] The debacle in 1931 when the Labour government split over Prime Minister Ramsay MacDonald's pronouncement of a 20 per cent reduction in unemployment benefit, resulted in the Bristol Labour Party losing public support. This situation, however, proved to be only temporary. By 1937 Labour held a majority on the City Council.

Economic recovery and rearmament prior to the Second World War was to transfer the centre of gravity of the Bristol trade union movement from general workers' unions to skilled engineering workers, particularly in the aircraft industry. The Bristol Aeroplane Company employed 4300 people in 1934, 14,000 at the end of 1938 and reached a peak of 52,000 altogether at the height of aircraft production in the war years.[52] The character of this industry was very different from that unionized by Bevin in the general unions before the First

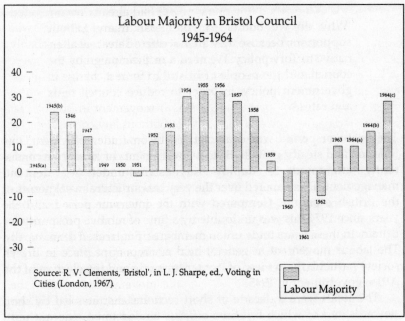

Figure 6.

World War. The new aircraft firms lay within the charmed circle of the defence industry, the Bristol Aeroplane Company receiving some £472,000 in subsidies between 1920 and 1931.[53] Government involvement in production introduced a new 'political' element into Bristol's industrial relations scene as well as boosting local employment and trade union membership. The sacrifices of the war years created an overwhelming desire in British society for a new order. It was expressed in accord with the political traditions of the British working-class movement through the Labour Party and through support for the Beveridge Report. As is well known 1945 saw the return of the Labour government. Bristol's Labour Council increased its majority in the first post-war local elections to 24. The principal aim of the Council was urban regeneration and the provision of housing. The 1951 election was to see the Labour Party nationally sent into opposition for the next thirteen years and Labour lost its majority on the council although it returned to be the majority party for another eight years in 1952. (See Figure 6.) Low turnouts in local elections were a matter of concern to councillors. For Dave Morgan, a teacher and C.P. candidate in the local elections of 1956, it was the difficulty in differentiating the main parties which was at fault:

223

'Why do we bother to vote?' ask many Labour
supporters; because they are not offered any real alternative to Tory policy. We need a real campaign by the
council and the people of Bristol to force a change in
government policy, in order to reduce council rents
and rates.[54]

The post-war period was characterized by low unemployment, low
inflation and steady growth. British governments of either hue consistently attempted to deploy Keynesian models of demand
management. This papered over the very real structural weaknesses of
the British economy. Compared with the inter-war period and the
years since 1974 this was undoubtedly a time of relative prosperity for
Britain. In these years trade union membership increased dramatically.
The labour movement in general held an important place in British
society particularly in view of its war time role and the election of the
Attlee government in 1945.

The 1950s were a decade of short sectional disputes led by shop
stewards and of which full-time officials tended to be ignorant until
after the event. An interesting consequence was that industrial action
tended not to have wider ramifications. Many of these disputes
stemmed from a very real determination amongst ordinary members
to keep a high level of union membership. In one incident at Fry's
factory at Keynsham four non-union women had to be removed from
the shop floor after they were showered with abuse and chocolate by
their fellow women workers. Two thousand women walked off the job
demanding that they be dismissed or join the union.[55] The aircraft
plants experienced a similar problem when 250 engineers stopped
work in protest against the employment of a non-union man in their
shop. In order to reinforce the point the union members insisted that
their new brother pay his arrears of dues or they would walk out
again.[56] Secondary action, after the repeal of the 1927 Trade Disputes
and Trade Union Act in 1946, was unregulated by law until the
Employment Act of 1980 was passed. During this period a walk-out by
one group might stimulate a joint action or support from other groups
in the workplace. When, in 1951, 44 crane men at Avonmouth walked
out on strike in protest at the searching of one of their colleagues they
were joined by engineers and the traffic and grain men.[57] They were
soon back at work but a point had been made. Not all the disputes
were over local matters; in the national railway dispute of that year 875

Bristol railway workers went on strike in support of their national wage claim. However there was no guarantee that local workers would join a national dispute and Bristol dockers failed to support the national unofficial action over the imprisonment of London dockers in 1951 under wartime regulations.[58]

In the 1950s the relationship between the Labour Party and the local trade union movement was a close one but the traditional separation of politics and economics was maintained. It was, however, primarily a relationship between the party and the lower levels of the official union movement. Of 24 candidates for the council nominated by Labour in 1956 there were 14 trade unionists including two full-time officials, one from a building workers' union and the other was Docks Secretary of the Transport and General Workers Union. The Secretary of Bristol Trades Council was also a candidate as was a member of the Union of Shop Distributive and Allied Workers (USDAW) executive. The other six held minor positions in local union branches.[59] Notably no representatives from the defence industry unions were present among this group of candidates who represented the traditional face of Bristol trade unionism, a picture which was to change rapidly over the following years.

In 1963 the Trades Council commissioned a report from the Labour Research Department (LRD).[60] Sponsored by the CP, the LRD was in reality a way in which the CP could disseminate its view of the changing face of British capitalism. The document focused on the current merger wave and the decline of family ownership of local firms as a danger to the interests of working people. The report argued that the most important problem facing Bristol workers was the replacement of local family-owned firms by national and multinational firms. The British Communist Party had long lost its revolutionary enthusiasms and was more a gadfly on Labour in local politics and a campaigner for a more modern and planned British capitalism. Its influence was much more important in terms of its industrial strength than in its electoral fortunes in the city.

In the defence factories at Filton and Patchway the ideas of the CP had very real importance in that they informed the practice of shop stewards throughout the fifties, sixties and seventies. The CP had a small but important presence in the engine plant supplying many stewards and convenors over the years. The craft traditions of the Amalgamated Engineering Union (AEU) meant that even the CP had difficulty in motivating their fellow workers around questions external to the plant or the union. One of the consequences was that the

AEU played little direct role in the local Labour Party. Larry Kedwood, a convenor at Rolls Royce in the seventies and an active Labour Party member himself, was certain that there were never more than two or three AEU branches, out of some 36 branches in the city, affiliated to Labour Party wards.[61] It is conceivable that in a time of consensus politics at a national level political affiliations did not seem so important in securing work, particularly in the aerospace industry.

In the 1960s the local Labour Party seemed to be moving away from its traditional links with the trade unions. There was increasing dissatisfaction among trade union activists with the Labour Party which intensified after the victory of Harold Wilson in 1964. The cancellation of the TSR2 project which led to huge redundancies at Filton and Patchway was met by strikes involving some 12,000 aircraft workers.[62] These tensions made themselves clear inside the local Labour Party. A signed leaflet headed by two councillors was handed out on the day of Wilson's visit to Bristol:

> Yes, Mr Wilson, we are party members who worked for your victory, and are used to serving the Labour Party loyally. But many of us are disillusioned, public enthusiasm has waned, and you are in electoral danger. One way only, stop using Tory policies, and inspire Britain with an immediate initiative towards a new society. Bring into public ownership and control the centres of real power.[63]

According to Tony Benn, MP for Bristol East, the Labour Party at local level was on its knees and Bristol South East Labour Party no longer really existed.[64] This decline, however, was in local organisation not in electoral terms since the 1964 city elections gave the Labour Party a majority of 28 councillors. Benn's response was to focus on a new type of labour member collected together in the New Bristol Group which excited some opposition from more traditional elements. One of the issues of contention was over the question of race. The City Council Labour Group threw out one of the proposals put forward by the New Bristol Group for actively improving race relations in the city.[65] The New Bristol Group's membership was made up of 'councillors, magistrates, engineers, doctors, trade unionists, students, teachers, designers, university professors, and a farmer, many of whom have never been involved in this work before'.[66] For Benn, the trade unions were just one group amongst many others. Nonetheless the trade union connection continued to be of central importance to the Bristol Labour Party. For the six years 1960-65 one person, Leslie Bridges, was secretary of both the Bristol Borough Labour Party and the Trades Council, indicating the close relationship.

All was not well in the more traditional sectors of the local movement. The changing nature of the British working class caused problems for the Bristol trade unions. One of the new factors, alongside the increasing presence of women in the workforce, was New Commonwealth immigration. The Bristol Bus dispute of 1963 drew attention to the existence of a colour bar in employment. Whether it was the case that the trade union, the Transport and General Workers Union (TGWU), and its members in the Bristol Omnibus Company colluded with management in operating racial discrimination is open to question. However, there is little doubt that the TGWU was complacent over this issue as the bus company first introduced a colour bar after union drivers and conductors voted to oppose the employment of coloured workers in 1955.[67] It took a campaign external to the union based in the local black community itself and supported by individuals in the local and national labour movement to bring an end to this formal discrimination. This was an instance of where trade unions and the Labour Party did not adopt progressive policies of their own accord. Notably, it was not until the Race Relations Act of 1968 that the law was extended to cover discrimination in employment, though this proved to be inadequate. And while a new Race Relations Act was passed in 1976 at the behest of a Labour government, enforcement was still difficult and discrimination persisted.[68] It took the St Paul's riots of 1980 to stir Avon County Council into providing extra resources to this deprived multiracial inner-city area. The Bristol Trades Council also responded by sponsoring a public inquiry after the government refused to hold one[69], whilst the Bristol Association of the National Union of Teachers reported on the need for multicultural education in the city.[70]

Another example of the indifference of the TGWU leadership in the city was their role in the 1965 S.S. *Gloucester City* strike. The dockers struck over the piece rate for unloading a new cargo of packaged timber. The long-standing joint negotiating machinery agreed a new rate for the job; however, the rate was unacceptable to the dockers themselves. Allan Flanders was appointed by the Minister of Transport to investigate the three-week strike, an almost unprecedented length of dispute for the times. Flanders reserved his most scathing criticism for the lack of contact between the full-time officers of the union and their members.[71] The strike was said to have cost around £1 million.[72] An interesting aspect of the dispute was the founding of the Bristol and Avonmouth Dockers Liaison Group. Without any particular political direction of its own it was undoubtedly influenced by the example of the London Liaison Group led by the communist dockers' leader Jack Dash. Just a month later Bristol bus workers passed a motion of no-confidence in their full-time TGWU officials as a result of the agreement to the introduction of a new set of schedules.[73]

By the time the new strike wave of 1968-74 was well underway the experience of the stop-go nature of defence projects had stimulated a debate in the plants over the nationalization of the industry. The considerable amount of government investment in the aerospace industry, identified in the Plowden Report, prompted the stewards' committees to question why private interests should be the ones to benefit.[74] As usual the presence of particular individuals played an important role in these debates. Support for nationalization obviously figured amongst the CP members in the engine plant. Stewards financed the publication of a number of pamphlets by Spokesman Books of Nottingham, a publisher associated with the Institute for Workers Control;[75] one of their supporters, Tom James, headed the key industrial committee of the Technical, Administrative and Supervisory Section (TASS) Bristol No. 3 branch based in the aircraft plant from 1963 to 1978.[76] The two plants differed in their political attitudes; the Filton plant which mainly worked on airframes was generally regarded as the less well organised of the two and was seen as a local base for more right-wing elements in the AEU and TASS, the white-collar engineers' union.[77]

The strike wave of 1968-74 evidenced the growth of union confidence and involved a new layer of public sector workers. There was a general increase in the level of trade union activity and for many this was a period when trade unionists had a real feeling of power for however short a time. Paul Chamberlain, an activist in the construction section of the TGWU, described it as a period when a single phone call could deliver blacking or solidarity and stop a job when management proved stubborn.[78] The pattern of short disputes continued but there was a new trend as well. Major disputes such as the 1974 strike at the Imperial Smelting Ltd lasted weeks rather than hours. A dispute at the Rolls Royce plant at the end of 1971, lasted an almost unprecedented eight and a half weeks and involved 6,500.[79] The significance of this stoppage is that Rolls Royce had only just been nationalized to save it from bankruptcy, and workers were thus taking action against the State as an employer. The State was the employer, or held the purse strings, in many of the national stoppages affecting Bristol workers between 1968 and 1972. These disputes ranged from a one day stoppage of university technicians to an all out seven-week strike by refuse workers.[80]

The 1968-74 strike wave was a period when trade union density increased from 44 to 50 per cent and conflict between the unions and the State increased significantly.[81] As indicated above, a high proportion of these strikes involved the State as an employer and resulted in attempts by the State to increase legal control of industrial relations. Labour's restrictive legislative proposals contained in 'In Place of Strife' (1969) never reached the statute book and the Conservative government's 1971 Industrial Relations Act was resisted stoutly by most unions and finally repealed in 1974 by a newly elected Labour government.

The miners' strikes of 1972 and again in 1974 reflected a rapidly changing atmosphere. The '74 miners' strike was posed in very political terms and the Bristol labour movement knew which side it was on. The Bristol Trades Council offered up to a hundred beds for miners so that they could picket local ports.[82] The strike, however, revealed that working for a nationalized industry did not guarantee one's interests.[83] This did not seem to alter the views of leading Labour and trade union activists in Bristol concerning nationalization, for, despite the miners' experience, dock workers in 1974 supported the left-wing City councillor, Ron Thomas, both as councillor and as the city's MP from 1974-79. Thomas was a vigorous advocate of nationalization.[84]

Another aspect of the early 1970s was the spread of militancy to new groups of workers. Glenside Hospital in Bristol was the site of the first ever industrial action by nurses in the west country, and government scientists took a half-day strike action to press a demand for improved wages. Even journalists joined in with a 24 hour strike at HTV, the local ITV franchise, in support of a national claim for parity with the BBC.[85] This new layer of trade unionists, which included substantial numbers of female workers, increasingly resorted to methods usually associated with traditional manual sectors of the movement. There was, however, an indication of the decline in solidarity action when bus workers reversed a branch meeting decision to strike in support of the nurses. Mike Alderson of the Nurses Action Group said that he felt 'let down', a feeling which was to become widespread in the local labour movement.[86] The first 1974 election, government, meant that the separation of political and economic issues which had so characterized the British labour movement since the end of Chartism once again became something of a problem. Straightforward trade unionism no longer seemed to be enough when faced with a Labour government under pressure from the IMF and the World Bank which started to make cuts in public services. It is difficult to trace the local effects of the Social Contract agreed between the TUC and the 1974-79 Labour Government but it appears to have undermined the authority of many of those trade unionists who had only concerned themselves with trade unionism at the level of the office and the plant. According to Chamberlain the 'feeling' in the movement started to become less confident and people were more hesitant about taking industrial action. The distance between the movement and the local Labour Party was also shown up in 1974 in connection with Hill's shipbuilders' decision to close their Albion yard early despite still having orders on their books. Ernest Smith, chair of shop stewards, had known nothing about the closure, expecting the docks to close in 1980 as planned in the 1970 Bristol City Docks Act. Charles Merrett, leader of the Labour Group on the Council, said that the terms of the agreement by which Hills had refrained from objecting to the closure of the City Docks had never been made public and not all the members knew about it. He refused to comment on whether he thought the terms had been hushed up.[87] After so many years in office in local government the Labour Party had other local interests to deal with in addition to those of its supporters in the trade unions.

The 1980s were difficult years for trade unionists. Unemployment, especially in the manufacturing sector, together with major changes in trade union law exerted a powerful disincentive to workers to become involved in disputes. For many trade unionists the alternative was to turn to politics. However simply turning to the Labour Party would have been difficult for left-wing trade unionists. After all, the most bitter battles, characterized as the 'Winter of Discontent', had effectively been a series of strikes against a Labour government and its wage controls involving many local government and health workers. The long established link between trade unionism and the Labour Party made this a particularly disorienting experience. The 1979 'Winter of Discontent' was the very last gasp of a wave of industrial unrest which had started in the late 1960s and included the miners' strike of 1974 which had ended the Heath government. As already mentioned, the feature of this period was that strikes increasingly involved the government as an employer, either directly or indirectly.

involved the government as an employer, either directly or indirectly. To complicate the issue Labour in government once again had proved to be committed, despite its supporters' hopes, to what it saw as the overall needs of British capitalism rather than the needs of trade unionists. Consequently many trade unionists and others who turned to Labour after 1979 first of all wanted to push the party to the left in order to deal with economic as well as social problems facing British workers. The focus of the national campaign was the support for the left-winger and Bristol MP Tony Benn who was seeking the position of Deputy Leader. Not surprisingly Bristol was one of the centres of what became known as the Bennite movement. The consequences for the local Labour movement were twofold. Michael Cocks, the right-wing Labour MP for Bristol South West, was successfully challenged for the redrawn Bristol South seat by Dawn Primarolo, a left-wing activist, well regarded in the local labour movement.[88] In addition a number of local councillors were deselected or transferred themselves to safer seats when it became clear which way the wind was blowing. Some local trade unions particularly the TGWU, National Union of Public Employees and some individual white-collar trade unionists became centrally involved in the movement to deselect Cocks. They were opposed by Cocks' long time supporters in the General and Municipal Workers Union. Tony Benn's supporters achieved important positions on the city council. However, with the defeat of the Labour Party in the 1983 election and Neil Kinnock's attacks on the left in the party between 1983 and 1985 the steam rather ran out of the local Bennite campaign.

Apart from the CP, a number of other left-wing groups were operating outside the Labour Party in the '70s and '80s. They expanded their membership on the basis of supporting working-class struggles, especially strikes. One consequence was an attempt to develop a political response to the actions of the employers. Ron Webb, convenor at the Bristol Commercial Vehicles plant, attempted to counter the decline in trade-union activity and politics via the politics of the extreme left. But despite his efforts, which involved the Socialist Workers Party, this important Bristol plant was closed in 1980 and production transferred to the Leyland bus plant in the north of England with very little real resistance.[89]

It was the question of closures and job losses which underlay the miners' strike of 1984-5; a strike which cut to the core of the local movement. The Bristol labour movement was split, as was the movement nationally, over the issue of support for the miners. Many could not bring themselves to encourage a strike which they felt was disastrously led and had ignored the most basic democratic conventions. For a minority of local trade unionists the niceties of ballots and constitutions were irrelevant. For them the miners were up against a Conservative government dedicated to the destruction of their union and over 100,000 jobs in a time of mass unemployment. The minority bent itself to the question of support for the strikers and their families. Every week saw collections of food and finance, and a number of local factories levied their members. Where there were no official collections individual socialists and trade unionists made their own collections. Miners came to Bristol on speaking tours and visited many local trade-union branches and workplaces. Much of this support was co-ordinated through an office in Transport House.

The miners' strike of 1984-5 demonstrated that the State retained its ability to bring to bear the full force of law and order in industrial disputes. The miners' defeat served to demoralize their supporters in Bristol as elsewhere. The full consequences of the defeat ran deeper than was immediately apparent. In particular it appears that many on the left inside the Bristol Labour Party found it difficult to reconcile their belief in the State as potentially beneficent with the ease with which a Conservative government was able to direct the National Coal Board to rationalize the mining industry in opposition to the interests of mineworkers.

Conclusion

This chapter has surveyed just a few of the highs and lows of a hundred years of trade-union organization in the city. At crucial points and in crucial ways political activity and trade-union militancy have been deeply entwined. In the early years it was a group of socialists and militant trade unionists who were central to giving the movement coherence and tactical clarity. The problem for activists was that the British trade unions in the early years of Labour handed over their political aspirations to that party. While the local economy boomed or even merely bumped along such an approach could deliver reforms in housing, education and health via the local state, and also improved wages and conditions via industrial militancy. In the difficult inter-war years and again in the 1980s it became clear that industrial militancy alone would not be enough. When the very system itself was in difficulty and fighting for survival little was going to be handed over on the basis of limited action, negotiation and democratic representation.

changing situations. These included local strikes across trades in the 1880s, a high level of industrial activity before and after the First World War all alongside the growth of Labour Party organization. The depression and the defeat of the General Strike were followed by eventual Labour control of the city council. The post-1945 boom saw little more than negotiation by strike but as times became tougher from the late 1960s there was a wave of strikes both nationally and locally of increasing bitterness. It was in the 1980s that Bristol played its part in an attempt to bring the Labour Party back to the left, an attempt which with the end of Clause Four may prove to have been the last of its kind. Whatever the continuing relationship between politics and trade unionism, and however they are related, they will continue to be a central part of the social scene. This tends to undermine Eric Hobsbawm's pessimistic view that the onward march of Labour has been halted. What the history of working-class organisation in Bristol demonstrates is that there are high points and low points. Unless Bristol is untypical then it appears that Hobsbawm was commenting on one of the lows rather than the end of the movement itself. The centre of trade unionism has moved from general workers to engineers and thence to white-collar workers and new layers have become active. It is therefore doubly important not to confuse the disappearance of traditional types of employment with the decline of the working class. It is difficult to predict what the future holds in store for the Bristol labour movement. In particular the room to temper the market via local government has become sharply limited. However politics express themselves, the relationship with trade unionism is a continuous and complex one, and one which will continue to change.

Notes

1   Hobsbawm's essay, first published in *Marxism Today* (Sept. 1978), was reprinted with minor amendments in E. Hobsbawm, *The Forward March of Labour Halted?* (1981), 1-19.

2   J. E. Cronin, *Labour and Society in Britain, 1918-1979* (1984), 8.

3   For an examination and assessment of the State, strikes and class-consciousness see J. Kelly, *Trade Unions and Socialist Politics* (1988), chap. 5, 85-127.

4   E. J. Hobsbawm, *Labouring Men* (1968), 127.

5   T. Nichols & H. Beynon, *Living with Capitalism* (1977), 3.

6   Hobsbawm, *Labouring Men*, 14.

7   Attempts to form Co-operative societies in Bristol in 1859, 1860 and 1862 all failed. See E. Jackson, *A Study in Democracy, Industrial Co-Operation in Bristol* (Manchester, 1911), 39-45, 179-86.

8   D. Large and R. Whitfield, *The Bristol Trades Council 1873-1973* (BHA, 8, 1973), 3-6.

9   S. Rowbotham, *Hidden from History* (1977), 60-1.

10   Large and Whitfield, *Bristol Trades Council*, 11, fn. 1.

11   D. Fraser, 'Introduction: Municipal Reform in Historical Perspective', in D. Fraser, ed., *Municipal Reform and the Industrial City* (Leicester, 1982), 3.

12   J. Saville, 'Trade Unions and Free Labour', in A. Briggs and J. Saville, eds, *Essays in Labour History* (1960).

13   B. Atkinson, *Trades Unions in Bristol* (BHA, 51, 1982), 8; S. Bryher, *An Account of the Labour and Socialist Movement in Bristol* (Bristol, 1929), part 11, 19.

14   *British Workman*, March 1890, quoted in Bryher, *Labour and Socialist Movement in Bristol*, 19.

15   Atkinson, *Trades Unions in Bristol*, 25, 26.

16   Hobsbawm, *Labouring Men*, 158-61.

17   Hobsbawm, *Labouring Men*, 164; Atkinson, *Trades Unions in Bristol*, 7.

18   Hobsbawm, *Labouring Men*, 181.

19   Bryher, *Labour and Socialist Movement in Bristol*, 16-18.

20   Atkinson, *Trades Unions in Bristol*, 10.

21   Atkinson, *Trades Unions in Bristol*, 9.

22   S. Mullen, 'Sweet Girls and Deal-Runners', in *Placards and Pin Money* (Bristol, 1986), 112-26.

23   Bryher, *Labour and Socialist Movement in Bristol*, 42.

24   Bryher, *Labour and Socialist Movement in Bristol*, 42.

25   Bryher, *Labour and Socialist Movement in Bristol*, 27. This programme is not dissimilar to that proposed in 1897 by James Bartley of Bradford who went on to become a leading light in the Bradford Independent Labour Party; See K. Laybourn & Jack Reynolds, *Liberalism and the Rise of Labour, 1890-1918* (1984), 32.

26   Bryher, *Labour and Socialist Movement in Bristol*, 28.

27   Atkinson, *Trades Unions in Bristol*, 13-14.

28   Bryher, *Labour and Socialist Movement in Bristol*, 53.

29   Laybourn & Reynolds, *Liberalism and the Rise of Labour 1890-1918*, 109.

30   L. H. Lees 'Strikes and the Urban Hierarchy in English Industrial Towns, 1842-1901', in J. E. Cronin and J. Schneer, eds, *Social Conflict and the Political Order in Modern Britain* (1982), 53-71.

31   R. Whitfield, 'Trade Unionism in Bristol 1910-1926', in I. Bild, ed., *Bristol's Other History* (Bristol, 1983), 73; id., 'The Labour Movement in Bristol 1910-1939' (unpublished MLitt thesis, University of Bristol, 1979), 38-45.

32   Hobsbawm, *Labouring Men*, 210.

33   Whitfield, 'Trade Unionism in Bristol', 77.

34   E. Malos, 'Bristol Women in Action 1839-1919', in Bild, *Bristol's Other History*, 123.

35   Whitfield, 'Labour Movement in Bristol', 58.

36   Whitfield, 'Labour Movement in Bristol', 152.

37   Whitfield, 'Labour Movement in Bristol', 157-8.

38   BRO, Minutes of the Docks Committee of Bristol Town Council, Minute No. 5654, 31 May 1920.

39   Kelly, *Trade Unions and Socialist Politics*, 85-127.

40   D. Backwith and P. Smith, 'Unemployed and ex-soldiers' struggles in Bristol after World War I', in *Somerset Clarion*, June/July 1992; Large & Whitfield, *Bristol Trades Council*, 19.

41   M. J. Richardson, 'Industrial Relations in the British Printing Industry Between the Wars' (unpublished PhD thesis, University of the West of England, 1995), 177.

42   See Kelly *Trade Unions and Socialist Politics*, 104, who highlights the effects of the weakness of revolutionary politics and organization in Britain during this period in

contrast to the rest of Europe.
43 Whitfield, 'Labour Movement in Bristol', 205.
44 Whitfield, 'Labour Movement in Bristol', 206.
45 Large and Whitfield, *Bristol Trades Council*, 17.
46 J. E. Cronin, *Industrial Conflict in Modern Britain* (1979), 129-30; see L. Trotsky, *Trotsky's Writings on Britain* (New York, 1974), 241-46 for a contemporary version of this debate.
47 Large and Whitfield, *Bristol Trades Council*, 27.
48 BRO, Minutes of the Docks Committee of the Bristol Town Council, 1919-1926.
49 R. Eatwell and A. Wright, 'Labour and the Lessons of 1931', *History*, 63 (1978), 38.
50 Bryher, *Labour and Socialist Movement in Bristol*, 8.
51 C. Wells, 'Members of Parliament for Gloucestershire and Bristol, 1900-29, Part II', *TBGAS*, 51 (1929), 321-360.
52 G. Stone, 'Rearmament, War and the Performance of The Bristol Aeroplane Company', in C. Harvey and J. Press, eds, *Studies in the Business History of Bristol* (Bristol, 1988), 191.
53 Stone, 'Rearmament', 189.
54 *BEP*, 8 May 1956.
55 *WDP*, 9 March 1951.
56 *WDP*, 30 June 1951.
57 *WDP*, 21 May 1951.
58 *WDP*, 9 Feb. 1951.
59 *WDP*, April/May 1956.
60 BRL, Labour Research Department, *Who's Who in Bristol 1962*.
61 Interview with the authors.
62 *WDP*, 3 July 1965.
63 *WDP*, 4 Sept. 1965.
64 R. Winstone, ed., *Tony Benn Diaries, Out of The Wilderness 1963-1967* (1987), 213.
65 M. Dresser, *Black and White on the Buses*, (Bristol, 1986).
66 T. Benn, *Speeches by Tony Benn* (Nottingham, 1974), 180.
67 Dresser, 'Black and White on the Buses', 54.
68 J. Gregory, *Sex, Race and the Law* (1987), 2 & 20-1.
69 M. Boddy, J. Lovering and K. Bassett, *Sunbelt City* (Oxford, 1986), 170.
70 Bristol Association of the National Union of Teachers, *After The Fire* (Bristol, 1981).
71 Ministry of Labour, 'Report by Mr Allan Flanders of a Committee of Investigation into the Bristol and Avonmouth Docks Dispute in December 1965' (1966).
72 *WDP*, 21 Oct. 1965, 4.
73 *WDP*, 11 Nov. 1965, 3.
74 C. Smith, *Technical Workers* (1981), 111-12.
75 Bristol Siddeley Engines Shop Stewards Combined Committee *The Aircraft Industry and Workers Control* (Nottingham, 1969); Bristol Aircraft Workers, *A New Approach to Public Ownership* (Nottingham, 1975).
76 Smith, *Technical Workers*, 122.
77 Smith, *Technical Workers*, 121.
78 Interview with the authors.
79 *Department of Employment Gazette*, Dec. 1971, 1185.
80 *Department of Employment Gazette*, Dec. 1969-74.
81 Kelly, *Trades Unions and Socialist Politics*, 105.
82 *WDP*, 13 Feb. 1974, 3.

83   Nichols and Beynon, *Living with Capitalism*, 177.
84   *WDP*, 15 Feb. 1974, 1.
85   *WDP*, 12 Sept. 1974, 3.
86   *WDP*, 19 Aug. 1974, 6.
87   *WDP*, 1 Nov. 1974, 5.
88   R. Winstone, ed., *Tony Benn Diaries, Conflicts of Interest 1977-1980* (1990), 294.
89   Unpublished Typescript.

INDEX

Acts (and Bills):

242